Bombshell

Christmas
1995

Also by David Stenn

CLARA BOW: Runnin' Wild

Bombshell

The
Life and
Death of
Jean Harlow

David
Stenn

Doubleday

New York
London
Toronto
Sydney
Auckland

PUBLISHED BY DOUBLEDAY
a division of
Bantam Doubleday Dell Publishing Group, Inc.
1540 Broadway, New York, New York 10036

DOUBLEDAY and the portrayal of an anchor with a dolphin are
trademarks of Doubleday, a division of Bantam Doubleday Dell
Publishing Group, Inc.

Library of Congress Cataloging-in-Publication Data

Stenn, David.
Bombshell : the life and death of Jean Harlow / David Stenn. —
1st ed.
p.   cm.
Includes bibliographical references (p.   ) and index.
1. Harlow, Jean, 1911–1937.   2. Motion picture actors and
actresses—United States—Biography.   I. Title.
PN2287.H24S74   1993
791.43′028′092—dc20
[B]   93-12399
CIP

ISBN 0-385-42157-5
Copyright © 1993 by David Stenn
Book Design by Gretchen Achilles

1 3 5 7 9 10 8 6 4 2

For my father

Author's Note

Barbara Brown and the late Irene Mayer Selznick endured countless queries with grace and charm. The late George Hurrell shared his memories and shot my portrait. The late Hortense Williams described the summer of 1916 in specific detail.

Millicent Siegel, daughter of Benjamin "Bugsy" Siegel, agreed to an interview for the very first time. So did the families of Charles McGrew, Paul Bern, Dorothy Millette, and Harold Rosson.

Virginia B. Cox provided unrestricted access to previously unseen personal, professional, legal, and medical documents. Dr. Leroy Buckmiller and the descendants of Dr. Harold Barnard, Dr. Sidney Burnap, Dr. Leland Chapman, Dr. Ernest Fishbaugh, Dr. Edward B. Jones, Dr. Saxton Pope, and Dr. Emil Tholen also supplied crucial data.

The private files of Howard Hughes were furnished by Vernon C. Olson of the Summa Corporation. Fellow biographers and film historians Rudy Behlmer, A. Scott Berg, Kevin Brownlow, Gerald Clarke, Ronald L. Davis, Scott Eyman, Neal Gabler, Curt Gentry, Laurie Jacobson, Gavin Lambert, Richard Lamparski, William MacAdams, Patrick McGilligan, Marion Meade, Barry Norman, Barry Paris, and David Thomson contributed information and interviews from their own travails.

Jacqueline Onassis, my editor, and Owen Laster, my agent, offered wisdom and guidance once again. And to all others acknowledged after the text: you made this project possible. I hope you share my pride.

Contents

Prologue

Monday, June 7, 1937

At dawn she was still semiconscious, though her doctors knew she was dying. By 9 A.M. her attempts at conversation, interrupted by cries of pain, grew incoherent as she slipped into a final, fatal coma. Her stoic mother stayed by her bedside, "shaking her lightly" and commanding her to "keep on fighting." Her guilt-stricken lover, who knew she was no fighter, ran crying from the room.

The sight of this sobbing man, a famous star himself, shocked fans and reporters outside Good Samaritan Hospital. Days earlier they had been told that Hollywood's reigning sex symbol had "virtually recovered" from an undisclosed ailment; now, after two blood transfusions and six intravenous injections, doctors summoned the Los Angeles Fire Department as a last resort to resuscitate her.

For the next two hours, a three-man "inhalator squad" pumped four tanks of oxygen into her lungs. Finally, at 11:40 A.M.—two minutes after doctors pronounced her dead—even they lost hope. "I guess we won't need this [oxygen tank] anymore," sighed one. "She's gone." The uproar that followed forced a doctor to step outside and confirm it.

By noon the news had made headlines, though these EXTRA! editions raised more questions than they answered. How could a twenty-six-year-old star with no history of serious illness leave work with "a cold" (her doctor's diagnosis) and die ten days later? Why, if her condition was indeed critical, had she been confined to her home? And why had her mother forbidden visitors, then hospitalized her daughter just a day before she died?

Her death was the final paradox of a life defined by them. This is a tale of two women: the "Platinum Blonde," a dazzling screen queen who iced her nipples and bleached her pubic hair, and "the Baby," a shy, sweet woman-child who wore fuzzy sweaters and flaring slacks, liked to hemstitch on film sets, and shared a house with her mother. It is the saga of a glamorous star who was also, according to screenwriter Anita Loos, "a regular girl" with "no vanity whatsoever—and no feeling about the sensation she created wherever she went."

The contradictions continue. A product of wealth and privilege, she played molls and tramps with empathy and insight. She called herself "the worst actress that was ever in pictures" despite consistent critical raves and director George Cukor's claim that "she played comedy as naturally as a hen lays an egg." She seduced he-men onscreen and married milquetoasts off it, with predictably dire results. She was a liberated woman at the mercy of her mother.

Her screen characters threw objects and tantrums;

"I'm handicapped," she once confessed, "by a very even disposition." So even, in fact, that six decades later she is still mourned as the most beloved star in M-G-M history, a team player who called coworkers "my gang" and whose only sworn enemy was jealous Joan Crawford. "I could be a better hooker than Harlow any day of the year," Crawford would snarl, and no one denied it. Harlow was no harlot. She just knew how to play one.

"Platinum Blonde" and "Baby," glamorous star and regular girl, a no-talent in her own estimation and a natural in everyone else's . . . She truly was two women, yet only one died that Monday morning, leaving a stunned and puzzled public to wonder how it happened. Naturally there was an explanation, though few would have believed it. Time passed. Truth was suppressed. Silence prevailed.

Now that silence has been broken. Now her story can be told. Here is how Jean Harlow died—and how she lived.

Part One

Harlean

Chapter One

The real Jean Harlow differed from her daughter. All they shared was striking beauty, though surviving relatives insist that, when it came to a comparison, no one rivaled the real Jean Harlow. By 1908 she was the belle of Kansas City, a nineteen-year-old, blue-eyed blonde whose buxom figure and regal bearing were widely admired. "She was the prettiest woman I ever saw," states first cousin Hortense Williams. "She was *beautiful*. Her hair was *golden*."

Not only her family thought so. "Strangers would follow her down the street," says second cousin Henrietta Bucker. "She looked like a valentine." The sole offspring of real-estate broker Skip Harlow and the former Ella Williams, Jean Harlow had cash and class. To turn-of-the-century suitors, the combination meant more than looks or brains.

Jean Harlow resented it bitterly. Watching her autocratic father mistreat her helpless mother—a cutting remark or slap in the face were common occurrences—strengthened her resolve to escape the same fate. But where could she go without money, and what could she do with no qualifications besides beauty and breeding? Since childhood she had sought independence, only to see it squelched by a provincial society which groomed women of her station for one occupation: marriage. There was no other option.

Unwilling to wed but too shrewd to show it, Jean Harlow played society's game, hiding her true personality behind a false person. The result: while some thought her charming, others knew better. Jean Harlow's sweetness, they whispered, hid a heart of stone; her vapid conversation masked a conniving mind. Ostensibly meek and gentle like her mother, she was actually forceful and aggressive like her father. She was an iron fist in a velvet glove, a grasping bitch with a gracious manner.

It took a born actress to play the role, and Jean Harlow fit the bill—so fit it, in fact, that her father did not discover her affair with a railroad conductor until it was almost too late. Whether she loved him was beside the point: Skip Harlow did not consider a railroad conductor as suitable son-in-law material, so he selected someone who was.

His choice made sense. Born in Iowa to pioneer stock, thirty-one-year-old Mont Clair Carpenter had come to Kansas City for dental college. He was "handsome and dignified," a solid, stolid Midwesterner whose idea of "daring" was an after-dinner drink and off-color joke. "Mont Carpenter was a gentleman," recalls cousin Hortense, "but he was bland, and Jean Harlow wanted a more exciting existence."

It was too late. "Skip Harlow was the head of the family," explains second cousin Virginia Cox. "He *ran* things. His word was *law*." In this case, the law ruled that

Jean Harlow would marry Mont Carpenter, so on the evening of October 1, 1908, their wedding was held in Skip Harlow's palatial house at 930 Orville Avenue. Sixty guests were present. The service was Presbyterian.

After their honeymoon, the newlyweds moved into Skip Harlow's second home at 3344 Olive Street. When he demanded a grandson to go with it, his daughter balked but complied. By mid-1910 she was pregnant.

Her condition transformed Jean Harlow Carpenter. "From the moment I knew [a child] was coming to me, all other actualities ceased to exist," she confessed. "I had thought I loved other people, but now I know that I never really loved anyone but the Baby." Where most mothers celebrated a life they would bring into the world, Jean Carpenter seized a chance to fill her empty existence. Her baby would not be its own person, but a vicarious vehicle for her failed hopes and dreams. Her baby would not be beloved for who it was, but *whose*: hers.

Basic training began *in utero*. "I *know* how important prenatal days are," Jean Carpenter declared. "And as students cram for examinations, so I tried to fill my life and thoughts with perfection and beauty." She attended concerts, university classes, and museums; she read poetry and "the lives of the poets" aloud. "I wanted perfection," she wrote. "Spiritual, mental, physical *perfection*." Anything less was inconceivable.

It was a tall order for an unborn child, but at least one detail went according to plan: to her grandfather's dismay and her mother's delight, the nine-pound baby born in the Carpenter home at 7:40 P.M. on March 3, 1911, was a girl. Informed that she would be named after her mother, Skip

Harlow laid down the law once again: there was already one "Jean Harlow Carpenter" in the family, and she was enough. His daughter suggested "Shirley Jean." Skip Harlow still objected. Finally a compromise was reached: "Harlean," an amalgam of her mother's maiden name. In case this was lost upon listeners, her middle name would be Harlow.

"Mother Jean" Carpenter, as she now chose to be called, was jubilant. "There is nothing else in my life worth talking about," she announced after the birth of Harlean Harlow Carpenter, "because there *is* nothing else in my life. My life began with her life." Mont Carpenter's reaction remains unrecorded, perhaps because no one bothered to ask. He had served his purpose; Mother Jean had no further use for him. Her world was "the Baby," and that was how she wanted it. "I dedicated my life to her," she asserted. "She was always *all mine*."

No one would feel it as much as Harlean.

Chapter Two

An angelic child with alabaster skin, green eyes, and cotton-white hair which Mother Jean maintained was natural (and neighbors suspected was not), Harlean and her parents occupied a huge home at 4409 Robert Gillham Road with a nurse, nanny, two housemaids, one houseman, and a live-in, liveried chauffeur. Her pet ducks, lambs, kittens, puppies, and pigs roamed the park-sized property, and each summer she rode a Shetland pony at Red Gables, Skip Harlow's twenty-five-room country retreat overlooking the Kaw River.

The horse was a gift from her grandfather, who doted on Harlean. "I have seen him come home, cut out a pattern, sit at a sewing machine, and make her the most beautiful dresses," states cousin Hortense. "He was not nice to his wife, but he *adored* his granddaughter. She was the apple of his eye."

"All through my childhood, my grandfather and I were boon companions," Harlean would recall. "I believe he had more influence in molding my thoughts and ideas than any other person." This was unfortunate, for despite his hand-sewn clothes and spacious houses, Skip Harlow's spartan demeanor turned Harlean into a prototypical "poor little rich girl," showered with material comforts but deprived of emotional support. Sweet, tender, and affectionate, all she sought was unconditional love. She would not find it from Skip Harlow.

Her mother was no help. Equally stoic and desperately unhappy, Mother Jean manipulated "the Baby," as her family referred to Harlean, against Mont Carpenter, who bought his wife a battery-powered automobile to drive through town while he provided free dental care to poor children. His generosity meant nothing to Mother Jean, who confided her hatred to cousin Hortense in the summer of 1916. "Every morning when I wake up," she whispered, "I hope I'll find him lying dead beside me."

Shortly thereafter five-year-old Harlean suffered a sore throat. Taking no chances, Mother Jean consulted Dr. Herbert Lipman, a British osteopath she had met at Excelsior Springs, a tony spa outside Kansas City. According to Mother Jean, Dr. Lipman diagnosed "spinal meningitis," called it "a crisis," and advised her to stay by the Baby. "For eight days and eight nights, Mother never left the side of my little bed," Harlean recounted. With her mother's aid, she recovered.

Seven decades later cousin Hortense disputes this story, citing Mother Jean's penchant for melodrama and noting that an epidemic of influenza, not "spinal meningitis," had struck Kansas City. Whatever her ailment, all Harlean knew—and all Mother Jean told her—was that without her mother, she would not have survived.

Her response exceeded expectations. Always docile, Harlean regarded her mother with slavish devotion, and given her seclusion from other children—her sole playmate was neighbor Virginia Cartlich, whose parents considered Mother Jean "a social climber"—it was not a surprising development. "She was always *all mine*," Mother Jean had said after the Baby's birth. Now both believed it.

In the future, fan magazines would idealize the bond between mother and daughter; in truth, it was less ideal than idolatry. Consider a handwritten note on Harlean's eighth birthday:

Dearest dearest Mother:
    Your gift was the sweetest of all. The little bracelet you gave me is to bind our love still tighter than it is, if that is possible. For I love you better than anything that ever its name was heard of.
    Please know that I love you better than ten lives.
    Yours forever into eternalty [sic],

Your Baby

When isolation led her to invent imaginary playmates, Skip Harlow sent his granddaughter to Miss Barstow's School, a private academy in Kansas City. On her first day there, she finally learned her name was not "the Baby," but Harlean.

Bored and restless, Mother Jean bemoaned her absence, and although Mont Carpenter tried his best, not even an eighteen-room mansion at 1312 East 79th Street could appease her. Instead she disobeyed her father and filed for divorce.

At the time it was no minor matter. Though "the weaker sex" had just won the right to vote, a woman's place was still in her home, not divorce court. Even the subject was shameful, which did not deter Mother Jean: on September 29, 1922, two days before their fourteenth anniversary, she was granted a divorce from Mont Carpenter, who did not contest her suit. Ever the gentleman, he even agreed to give her $200 a month and sole custody of their child.

For the rest of her life Harlean rarely saw her father. "After the divorce, Jean tried to turn her against him," claims cousin Hortense. "But Harlean loved her father, and deep down she resented it." At the time, however, she heeded Mother Jean, who had big plans for them both. They were leaving Kansas City. They were going to Hollywood.

By 1923, the year of their arrival, Hollywood, California, was the hub of a thriving young industry: the motion picture. Fifty-three studios produced four fifths of the world's films, necessitating 150 miles of new streets and pushing Hollywood's population to 100,000, one tenth of all Los Angeles. Lured by rags-to-riches stories in monthly fan magazines, thousands of Americans shared the same aim: to find fame and fortune in the movie business.

Mother Jean was among them. "She went to Hollywood to be a star," confirms cousin Hortense, "and she could have been; she was pretty enough. But she was too old." In an era when leading ladies were teenage girls, thirty-four-year-old Mother Jean was hardly star material. If she did not realize it, there were plenty of producers, directors, and agents to remind her.

At this point a stereotypical "stage mother" would have transferred her dream to her daughter, who was becoming a beauty herself. Mother Jean, however, was different: too fixated on her own aspirations to focus on anyone else, she continued to see herself, not her child, as the center of her existence. And besides a schoolgirl crush on movie cowboy Buck Jones, there was no indication whatsoever that Harlean had an interest in acting. While other girls fantasized about film stardom, she preferred to read books and write stories.

Mother Jean used her alimony to rent a single room in a Sunset Boulevard mansion, and since Skip Harlow had agreed to pay for his granddaughter's education, she enrolled Harlean in the Hollywood School for Girls, located on La Brea Avenue just above Hollywood Boulevard. Its pupils included the daughters of mogul Louis B. Mayer, director Cecil B. De Mille, actor Francis X. Bushman, and actress Irene Rich. To their intense mortification, two boys attended the Hollywood School for Girls: Douglas Fairbanks, Jr., and Joel McCrea.

Two events made 1923 memorable at the Hollywood School for Girls: the introduction of dowdy uniforms and a new seventh-grader who wore them. "Little Miss Harlean Carpenter was unforgettable," wrote Irene Mayer, "even in the school uniform, which was seductive only on her. No middy blouse but hers was cut so low, and, despite admonitions, her hips swayed under the ankle-length pleated skirt. Topping it off was a mop of real tow hair, a color rarely seen beyond the age of three.'' Fellow student Evelyn Flebbe recalled her father's reaction: ''They all just walked, he said, except Harlean—she sashayed.''

''It would have been nice to be her friend,'' Flebbe added, ''but I couldn't figure out how. Girls with a purpose fascinated and alarmed me.'' Actually, Harlean had no purpose; she simply projected one to please others. However her schoolmates saw her was who she would become.

''My first recollection of Harlean was a conversation in the gym,'' says another classmate, Virginia Parsons. ''The subject was sex, and I remember her being very scornful and mocking of our naïveté. She seemed so sophisticated and knowledgeable; she made us feel awkward and gauche. How much was bravado I don't know.'' Apparently it was all bravado, which did not stop her peers from believing it. Cecilia De Mille complained that Harlean made ''so many conquests there aren't enough boys left to go around.'' Irene Mayer dubbed her ''Baby Jeritza'' after Maria Jeritza, an Austrian soprano whose blonde beauty and torrid affairs were as acclaimed as her arias.

Mother Jean was a further source of speculation. ''She was blonde and vivacious in a way that mothers of my closer friends were not,'' noted Flebbe. Virginia Parsons is more candid: ''Mrs. Carpenter was large and blonde, and very theatrical in her speech and appearance. She would arrive unannounced and make a big fuss over her daughter: 'Oh, my Baby, my darling . . .' I don't recall any other parent coming to the school, and I think it embarrassed Harlean.''

Marjorie Kendal, Harlean's best friend at the Hollywood School for Girls, had also moved west when her parents divorced. Sensing the vulnerability beneath her bravado, Marjorie's mother "adored" Harlean, and after Mother Jean became the mistress of "a very handsome Continental gentleman" (of whom no more was known), she would deposit her daughter with the Kendals for weeks. "Harlean sought refuge with us," Marjorie recalled. "She was an unhappy girl, and her mother was a nightmare."

Barbara Brown, a future close friend, never forgot her first glimpse of Harlean. "My father had invited some men over," she reveals, "and while they were playing cards, Mrs. Carpenter stopped by and mentioned that 'the Baby' would be there soon. So I expected this tiny little baby."

Instead she saw Harlean. "The doorbell rang, and there was this *amazing* girl with white-blonde hair and gorgeous green eyes. The men just *stared*." Harlean did not notice.

After two years in Hollywood, a lack of funds forced Mother Jean to move from Sunset Boulevard to 1302 North La Brea Avenue. Apprised of this, Skip Harlow issued an ultimatum: she could remain there alone or come home with Harlean. If she defied him, he would disinherit her.

Harlean would soon claim that she and Mother Jean "were so homesick in Hollywood that we decided to go back to Kansas City." In fact, they returned only for economic reasons, and Harlean's sudden departure from the Hollywood School for Girls in the spring of 1925 did not attract attention. "She dropped out without notice," remembered Irene Mayer, who nonetheless sensed this leave-taking was temporary. "We knew perfectly well we hadn't heard the last of her."

Chapter Three

Compared to Hollywood, Kansas City seemed more stifling than ever, and to Mother Jean's horror, Skip Harlow boarded Harlean at Notre Dame de Sion, a strict convent school. Her grandfather was not Catholic, just determined to separate mother from daughter.

It didn't work. According to Notre Dame de Sion records and Harlean herself, "Mother was so lonely that I left after one semester and became a pupil at Miss Bigelow's School, where I was able to go home every afternoon." Miss Bigelow's was closer but not better: as Harlean admitted, its seven students passed their days "at play."

That summer Skip Harlow sent his granddaughter to Camp Cha-ton-ka in Michigamme, Michigan. "That camp still remains the worst nightmare of my life," Harlean shuddered later. "I don't know how I lived through it." On an overnight hike, she used poison oak as toilet paper and was in agony for days.

Later that summer Harlean caught scarlet fever and was placed in quarantine with another camper. "They put us in a tent away from the main camp, and there they left us," she remembered. "Everyone was afraid to come near us except a country doctor."

Everyone, that is, except Mother Jean. Informed of her Baby's condition, she packed her bags and caught the next train to Cha-ton-ka. Its director met Mother Jean at the station "and told her it would be impossible for her to get to me."

Her daughter knew better. "No director of any camp and no quarantine in the world could have kept my mother from me. She completely ignored that woman and rowed herself across the lake to camp." For the next three weeks Mother Jean stayed at Cha-ton-ka, braving contagion to nurse her Baby. "There's nothing worse than having your mother at summer camp," recalled cabinmate Jean Moore, "especially if you had *her* mother."

Mother Jean's presence delayed Harlean's pursuit of David Thornton Arnold, a sixteen-year-old camper across the lake. Nicknamed "Thor" by smitten Cha-ton-kans, Arnold would wait forty years to divulge what transpired: "One afternoon we went behind the mess hall to a little clearing in the woods. She pulled down my swimsuit and gave me the go-ahead." It was the first sexual experience for both.

"There was no real thrill to it because we were so scared," Arnold added. "We were constantly on the lookout for someone coming." What ensued was scarier. "When we were done, I noticed blood on the leaves and panicked. I thought I'd hurt her, which I wouldn't have done for the world." Arnold "asked if she was OK." Harlean assured him she was.

"She was a sweet girl with nothing pretentious about her," stressed Arnold, and though their rendezvous was not repeated, "we stayed friends for the rest of the summer."

At its end Mother Jean returned to Cha-ton-ka (her second unnecessary trip, since a private railroad car was reserved for campers) to bring Harlean home. Changing trains in Chicago, they stopped at the Sherman Hotel and dined in its posh College Inn. During their meal a tall, dark, and dapper man with a thick Italian accent approached and introduced himself. His name was Marino Bello.

Born illegitimate in 1883, Marino Bello had fended for himself since childhood. What he lacked in brains was offset by style: like a dashing onscreen gigolo, Bello dyed his hair, waxed his mustache, wore white spats, and carried a cane whose tip concealed a sword. He kissed ladies' palms, murmured in their ears, and challenged rivals to duels. However laughable he sounds today, women of his era thought Bello a fantasy come true. "He was a tall, dominating figure," says actress Joan Marsh. "I was in awe of him."

"He was an extremely *exotic* person," agrees actress Madge Bellamy. "You imagined all sorts of mysteries behind him."

Females found Bello irresistible; lacking other prospects, he made them his profession. In 1914 he married Mildred Maas, an American tourist in Italy. The outbreak of World War I forced Bello to bide his time, but after the Armistice he immigrated to Chicago and convinced his wife's cousin, Sherman Hotel owner Ernest Byfield, to employ him at the College Inn. By the time he espied Mother Jean there seven years later, Bello was a naturalized citizen eager to escape his wife and life.

He wasted no time. The first weekend after meeting Mother Jean, Bello traveled to Kansas City—"and that," mourned Harlean, "was the beginning of Mother's romance." From the start she disliked Bello but accepted him anyway. "She didn't take him seriously," shrugs Barbara Brown. "He was someone her mother was in love with, so she had to be nice to him."

Legend contends that Mother Jean and Bello's "romance" was based on sexual enslavement. "She wasn't in love with him, she was *hot* for him," says Marcella Rabwin, who would meet them both in Hollywood. "I guess she'd never had good sex before, and he *was* attractive in a sinister sort of way." Although plausible, this theory remains impossible to prove and beside the point: in Bello, Mother Jean met her male counterpart, a mercenary, "money-grubbing S.O.B." whose sexuality was a commodity. She hid her cunning behind beauty; he masked his with charm. She manipulated men; he exploited women. She replaced his dowdy wife; he succeeded her dull ex-husband and domineering father.

No one loathed Bello as much as Skip Harlow. "He *detested* him," confirms cousin Hortense. "He said Bello was a golddigger, and of course he was right." Enraged and disgusted, her grandfather threatened to seek custody of Harlean.

As a compromise Mother Jean suggested Ferry Hall, an all-girl academy in Lake Forest, Illinois. Though the school had a fine reputation, Mother Jean had an ulterior motive: Ferry Hall was close to Chicago (where Bello worked) and even closer to Highland Park (where Bello lived). The fact that his wife lived with him did not bother

Mother Jean. "Mother took a room at the Highland Park Hotel so I could be with her on weekends," Harlean assumed. She did not know that Bello was three blocks away.

To ease the transition, Ferry Hall paired freshmen students with a "Big Sister" from the senior class. Typical newcomers were awkward adolescents, but as Jada Leland discovered, her "Little Sister" was hardly typical. "Even at that age," she says sixty-five years later, "Harlean Carpenter was the most *gorgeous* creature I ever saw. Flawless skin; so fair she was almost an albino. The blondest hair, and it wasn't dyed. She could comb it from her face, run her fingers through it, and these great big *waves* would set in.

"She was only 5′ 2″, but her figure was beautifully balanced. A great pair of legs, size three and a half feet, and a wonderful smile." Not only her Big Sister thought so. "When we walked down the street, she would literally stop traffic. Men would climb out of their cars and follow her."

A generation earlier Jean Harlow had caused a similar commotion, but unlike her mother, Harlean seemed ambivalent about her beauty. "She knew how gorgeous she was," affirms Jada. "She couldn't help it. But she wasn't conceited; she didn't make you *feel* she knew. She was just a nice person, not like her mother at all."

As usual, Mother Jean made a lasting, unfavorable impression. "Her mother came to see her and it was, 'Oh, my *Baby*, my *darling Baby*!'" mimics Jada. "I thought I would upchuck." Observing them together, she realized what paradoxically united and divided mother and daughter. "Harlean was passive, and Mother Jean was *strong*. She had complete control over that girl. Harlean had no will-power; she did not stand up for *anything*." Nowhere was

this more apparent—and poignant—than her enforced estrangement from Mont Carpenter. "Harlean loved her father, but she never got to see him. Every time she tried, her
mother stopped it."

In the fall of 1926, Jada and her fiancé, Alfred Forrest,
fixed up her Little Sister with his best friend. The foursome
dined in Chicago, and although Jada does not recall it in
detail, she does remember that Harlean and her blind date
"had a wonderful time together."

"That's how it started," she continues. "That's how she
met Chuck McGrew."

Chapter Four

The sole child of a wealthy Chicago couple, Charles McGrew II was born in 1906. At sixteen tragedy struck: while they were sailing to their private island in Wisconsin, his parents' boat capsized. His mother's corpse was recovered. His father was never found.

Chuck McGrew was given to his grandparents, who placed his inheritance in trust and enrolled him at Lake Forest Academy, the male half of Ferry Hall. "Chuck was a terrific guy," says Jada Leland. "Attractive and fun, with a wonderful laugh and a great disposition." On their blind date in Chicago, he "fell completely in love" with Harlean.

She felt the same. Her suitor "was the best-looking boy I'd ever seen," Harlean boasted later. "Every girl had her eye on Chuck, but he had his eye on *me*." Their attraction was not merely physical. "They really related to each other," remarks Chuck's daughter. "They were both only children, and they were both lonely."

Mother Jean had other plans. Informed that Bello's boss had a bachelor brother, Eugene Byfield, she decided

Harlean should "marry him for the millions." What her daughter wanted did not matter. "She would come back from their dates and say, 'He's awful. I don't like him,'" Jada discloses. "But her mother and Bello were trying to make her go through with it." Harlean was saved by Skip Harlow, who sent a friend to spy on Mother Jean and discovered her affair with Bello. Once again he laid down the law: Mother Jean would get married or go home. When she told Bello, he beat her.

He also abused his wife, who fled to her family and filed for divorce. Testifying that Bello had "repeatedly struck and beaten her," she obtained it on December 16, 1926. A month later, on January 18, 1927, Mother Jean married Bello in Waukegan, Illinois. Harlean was not present.

Encouraged to spend more time in Chicago with her mother and new stepfather, Harlean was happy to comply. "She didn't like school, and she and Chuck were getting serious," explains Jada. "They were young, but they were very much in love." As a result, Harlean did not finish her freshman year at Ferry Hall. It was her last formal schooling.

That summer Chuck told Alfred Forrest, Jada's fiancé, that he and Harlean planned to marry in December. The notion so alarmed Forrest, who liked Harlean but felt her mother was a fortune hunter, that he begged Jada to intervene. She wrote a letter to Chuck "telling him what a lovely person Harlean was and how much I liked her, but for God's sake to get her out of her mother's clutches—because if he didn't, he and Harlean wouldn't have a chance."

"So what does Chuck do? Go right to her mother and show her my letter!" Armed with the document, Mother

Jean threatened a "defamation of character" suit unless a hefty settlement was made. "She tried to shake down my father," fumes Jada. "That woman would do *anything* for money."

Amid the controversy, Harlean and Chuck drove to Waukegan and, like Mother Jean and Bello nine months earlier, prevailed upon a justice of the peace to perform a late-night ceremony. As the "St. Louis Blues" blared on a neighbor's radio, Charles McGrew II and Harlean Harlow Carpenter were married. It was September 21, 1927. He was twenty. She was sixteen.

Two months later Chuck turned twenty-one and received $200,000, the initial installment of his inheritance. Suddenly his teenage bride was a wealthy socialite whose life resembled an F. Scott Fitzgerald story, right down to her husband's main diversion: drinking. "He had a problem," admits Chuck's daughter. "He drank heavily, and so did she." Since her sole aim was to please others, Harlean's behavior was hardly surprising. She loved Chuck and wanted to make him happy; if he needed "hooch" to have fun, then she would share it with him. Still, she could not keep his pace: after a Christmas celebration in 1927, Chuck stayed drunk for two days.

In January 1928 the couple sailed from New York to Los Angeles via Havana and the Panama Canal. Taking Jada's advice, Chuck termed the trip a belated honeymoon but secretly hoped to distance Harlean from her mother. To do so, he bought a house at 618 North Linden Drive in Beverly Hills.

Away from Chicago's snowstorms and speakeasies, Chuck and Harlean took all-day hikes in the Hollywood hills. "They loved the outdoors," says his son. "They would picnic in Griffith Park and just sit and talk." Chuck considered Harlean "a very intelligent, deeply sensitive girl" and treated her accordingly.

So did Jetta Belle Chadsey, whom Harlean called "Aunt Jetty" even though she was Ella Harlow's sister and thus Mother Jean's aunt. A bride at sixteen, mother at seventeen, and divorcée at eighteen, Aunt Jetty had lived "in sin" with an Osage Indian, borne twins who died, left her Indian mate, remarried, given birth to a second son, been widowed, remarried again, and moved to California. At the time of Chuck and Harlean's arrival, Aunt Jetty had just divorced her third husband for the second time. She had Mother Jean's strength without her self-absorption, her formidable drive without her inflexible discipline. Harlean adored her.

Besides Aunt Jetty, she befriended Rosalie Roy, a seventeen-year-old Texan who aspired to stardom. Soon after they were introduced at a society "bridge party," Rosalie foresaw Harlean's future. "I can truly say I knew she would be a famous actress," she recalls. "I was ambitious, but she was *stunning*."

In the spring of 1928, Rosalie attended a luncheon in Harlean's home, then excused herself for an appointment at the Fox Studios—"and since she had no car," Harlean said later, "I offered to drive her." Waiting for Rosalie inside the studio, she "was fascinated by the place but didn't feel any urge to be an actress."

What happened next was, in hindsight, historic: as Harlean recalled, Rosalie emerged with three Fox executives, who "noticed me as I stood there and asked if I'd ever thought of trying to break into pictures." Harlean said she had not, which the men mistook for a ploy; why else would a breathtaking blonde be at their studio? Harlean explained that she had accompanied Rosalie; still dubious, the men summoned a secretary and dictated letters of introduction to Fox and the Central Casting Bureau. Harlean thanked them politely, stuffed the letters in her purse, and forgot the entire episode.

At a subsequent luncheon several weeks later, Rosalie related Harlean's "discovery" by Fox. The incident amused her guests, who thought Harlean too shy to act and too timid to try. "They wagered I wouldn't have the nerve to take those letters to the casting directors," she remembered. "In the spirit of fun, I accepted the bet." The following morning she returned to Fox, met its casting director, and continued to Central Casting, a clearinghouse for anonymous extras employed as background atmosphere. Working extra was tedious and unprofitable, yet Central Casting's seventeen thousand registrants shared a single desire: to be plucked from a crowd and turned into a star.

Harlean had no such hope, so her trip to Central Casting was painless and brief. Only one detail was significant: she applied as "Jean Harlow," her mother's maiden name.

After winning her wager, Harlean considered the matter closed until, "a few days later, the phone rang and a strange voice asked for 'Miss Harlow.' At first, in my surprise, I said there was no 'Miss Harlow' in the house. Then I remembered: it was Central Casting, calling for work." Harlean declined. Further offers were also refused.

The interest in her daughter galvanized Mother Jean, who had just relocated to Los Angeles. In the past, she had seen herself as movie-star material; now, with her own prospects dim and her daughter's promising, all her ambition was projected onto Harlean. It was not Mother Jean's first intention, but it seemed like her sole second chance. So whether or not Harlean wished it, she would seek stardom in her mother's maiden name.

Ordered to accept her next offer, Harlean reported to Fox for extra work in *Honor Bound*, a prison drama with George O'Brien. That summer Rosalie Roy introduced her to Paramount casting director Joseph Egli, who put her in *Moran of the Marines* for a box lunch and $7. Arriving at work in her rich husband's roadster, Harlean hardly seemed like a struggling extra. Her wardrobe alone was worth a month's wages.

Her pay rose to $10 a day for *Chasing Husbands*, a two-reel comedy with Charley Chase at the Hal Roach Studios. "She had a perfect figure," proclaims Iris Adrian, who also appeared in the film. "She was marvelous."

Harlean went back to Fox for *Fugitives*, then to First National for *Why Be Good?*. Though she still lacked a screen credit, she did not pass unnoticed. "Look," director William Seiter commanded actress Colleen Moore on the *Why Be Good?* set. "You've never seen anything like it." Following his gaze, Moore saw "this beautiful girl with white hair and a white dress, and she was just sitting there nonchalantly. People were passing by to look at her and asking who she was." It was the sort of attention usually reserved for stars. Already "Jean Harlow" received it.

By December she had graduated to bit parts in Hal Roach Studios two-reelers *The Unkissed Man*, *Why Is a Plumber?*, and *Thundering Toupees*. Billed as "Harlean

Carpenter" in *Liberty*, another Roach Studios two-reeler, she reacted to a rising comedy team: Laurel & Hardy.

Renowned for spotting "star quality," Hal Roach sensed it instantly in Harlean. "She was *different*," he divulged at age ninety-nine. "Her hair was an odd type, and she had a beautiful face and body. There was nobody like her." In this case, talent was irrelevant; after just four bit parts, Roach offered Harlean a five-year contract. "Her mother made the decisions," he discovered. "Not that she was any good at business, but she and Bello were always around."

Chuck McGrew was not. "He said Mother Jean was constantly after Harlean to be an actress," reveals his daughter, "which was *her* ambition, not Harlean's. He resented her terribly." Chuck also blamed Bello, who was still unemployed and expected his stepdaughter to support him.

On December 26, 1928, "Harlean McGrew II, a/k/a Jean Harlow" signed a contract with Hal Roach for $100 a week. Afterward she accompanied Chuck to San Francisco, where he drank, they fought, and she threatened to divorce him. On a rampage, Chuck wrecked their hotel room.

With "talkies" sounding a death knell for silent films, Hal Roach suspended production during January 1929 to construct indoor soundstages. Rather than have Harlean remain idle, her mother took her to Paramount for *Close Harmony*, a primitive musical starring Charles "Buddy" Rogers and Nancy Carroll. Her daughter's temporary demotion to extra work did not faze Mother Jean, who ignored her lowly status and ingratiated herself with the film's leading man. "We talked about Kansas City," recounts Buddy Rogers. "She told me her Baby had gone to Miss Barstow's."

"Did I look at her and think she would be a big star?" Rogers muses of Harlean. "No, I didn't. I didn't look at the daughter, I looked at the *mother*. She was very, *very* attractive."

His costar knew better. "There was something special about the girl," recalled Nancy Carroll. "She was very sweet and seemingly shy, but at the same time she exuded an extreme sexuality. I remember thinking to myself, 'Boy, that's competition!'"

The following month Harlean returned to the Roach Studios for *Double Whoopee*, a silent Laurel & Hardy short. She played a gorgeous hotel guest who steps from a taxi and, unaware that a doorman (Laurel) has slammed her dress in its door, struts through the lobby in a see-through slip. On the film's first take, Harlean played the scene as described.

Chaos ensued. "We weren't told that she was going to come in naked," said actor Rolfe Sedan. "Nobody knew. There was no rehearsal. When she came up to the desk, for a moment I almost didn't say the words." Rushing to the set, Hal Roach ascertained that, prior to the take, Harlean had been asked whether she was "underdressed," a term for the flesh-colored tights worn in so-called "nude" scenes; assuming "underdressed" meant underwear, she said she was. As a result, she had appeared on-camera in a truly transparent slip.

Whisked to a dressing room, Harlean returned to the *Double Whoopee* set in real underdress and reshot the scene. And since she had no inhibitions about nudity, photographer Edwin Bower Hesser posed her in Griffith Park—the site of her picnics with Chuck—wearing only a diaphanous scarf. The results were too racy to publish.

After a bit in *Bacon Grabbers*, her third Laurel & Hardy two-reeler, Harlean visited Hal Roach's office (accompanied, as usual, by her mother and Bello) to request a release from her contract. "She said her husband disliked the motion picture business," he recounts. "She said, 'It's breaking up my marriage; what can I do?' So I told her I'd tear up her contract, which I did."

This was the official version, and Roach believed it. Studio records, however, suggest another story: Harlean broke her contract on March 2, a day before her eighteenth birthday. Since she was no longer a minor, her husband could not impede her career, and freed from her current contract, Mother Jean and Bello could seek a better deal at a bigger studio. This was their game plan, but the only employment Harlean could find was extra work in *Masquerade*, a melodrama at Fox.

That spring another snag arose: Harlean became pregnant. Hoping that motherhood would save her marriage and end her extra work, she was overjoyed.

Mother Jean was miserable. A child could wait, she counseled Harlean; her career could not. Two decades earlier Mother Jean had made a similar mistake with Mont Carpenter; she would not let her Baby follow suit. Bello arranged for an abortion.

The loss broke Harlean's heart. "I wanted the child that was taken from me," she confided later. "My whole life would have been different if I'd been given that baby."

On June 11, 1929, exactly twenty months and twenty days after her wedding, Harlean separated from Chuck McGrew. Whether he learned of her abortion is unknown (Mother Jean called it a miscarriage), but his wife was absolved of all blame. "He said her mother broke up the marriage," states Chuck's daughter. "He said she destroyed his first love."

Mother Jean disagreed. "Chuck went away and Marino and I came to live with the Baby," she contended, "which was the way she wanted it." Perhaps this was true. Without her husband or child, Harlean had no choice.

Chapter Five

After her separation from Chuck McGrew, Harlean worked extra in *This Thing Called Love*, a forgettable farce at Pathé; *City Lights*, a Charles Chaplin masterpiece at United Artists; and *New York Nights*, a Prohibition drama at the same studio. "Did I notice her?" reflects *New York Nights* star Gilbert Roland. "Who *didn't*? But she only worked two or three days, so I didn't know her; I just *looked* at her." So did studio executives, who scheduled a screen test for Harlean and Joel McCrea. "She was lovely," McCrea remembered, "but I couldn't say that I saw she'd be a big star." The test led nowhere for either.

Lonesome and depressed, Harlean had a brief affair with bandleader Roy Fox. Despite his subsequent, fictitious boasts of furthering her career, Fox remained a gentleman regarding Harlean herself. "I can truthfully say," he conceded, "that she was really one of the nicest girls I have ever met."

She was also in debt. Hoping to reconcile with Harlean but aware that any money he gave her would go to Mother

Jean and Bello, Chuck refused to support them. So did Skip Harlow, who saw *Double Whoopee*, despised it, and vowed to disinherit his granddaughter if she continued her career. Bello, of course, was still unemployed.

A year earlier Harlean had gone to Central Casting on a bet; suddenly expected to support herself, her mother, and Bello, she realized her extra work had become a grim necessity. "I turned to motion pictures," she would say without self-pity, "because I had to work or starve." Former schoolmate Evelyn Flebbe saw Harlean at Fox with other struggling extras. "This was not," Flebbe noted, "the glowing way to go."

Harlean would later write about these times. Entitled "Extra Girl Gets Her First Close-Up," her tale, which she admitted was autobiographical, concerns an unnamed nobody chosen for a close-up ("After all, it wasn't *impossible*! It *does* happen to extra girls—well, not regularly, but there is a God, even in Hollywood") only to learn that the shot which will assuredly bring her fame and fortune is not of her face, but her legs. As Harlean knew firsthand, extra work could be cruel and dehumanizing, and though she wrote of it as a star, her story conveys her desperation.

Her luck changed when Joseph Egli, who had hired Harlean for *Moran of the Marines* a year earlier, gave her extra work in *The Love Parade*, a Maurice Chevalier musical at Paramount. Afterward she received a small role in *The Saturday Night Kid*, the studio's latest vehicle for its biggest star, Clara Bow. Known as "The 'It' Girl," Bow was the first Hollywood actress to play sexually aggressive heroines, but her stupendous success was threatened by talkies, which crippled her mobility (in silent films Bow would dart about a set) and left her scared and self-conscious about her Brooklyn accent and lack of training. By the time *The Saturday Night Kid* began shooting, Bow was twenty pounds overweight and frantic about her future.

Harlean hardly helped. "When she walked onto the set, everyone started to whistle," says assistant director Arthur Jacobson, "because she was wearing this black-crocheted dress with *not a stitch* on under it. From where I sat, you couldn't tell whether she had put it on or *painted* it on." It was visibly apparent that she was a natural blonde.

Bow summoned Jacobson to her dressing room. "Tell 'em t'take her off this goddamn set and never bring her back," she ordered. "I don't want her in the picture." Jacobson wondered why. "Are you kiddin'?" shrieked Bow. "If she dresses like that for an interview, how's she gonna dress in a *scene*? Who's gonna see *me* nexta *her*?"

To Jacobson's astonishment, Bow's demand was ignored. "I always wondered who the hell was behind her," he mulls of Harlean, "but I never found out; everybody was very closemouthed. All I know is that *somebody* wanted her in the picture." A possible somebody: *The Saturday Night Kid* hero James Hall, who "made" Harlean during shooting.

By then Bow had warmed to her anyway. "She was simply fascinated by her," stated Edith Head, who designed a bias-cut dress that Bow was too fat to wear. Instead of rejecting Head's costume, the redheaded star not only approved it for her blonde rival, but asked Paramount publicist Teet Carle to have pictures taken of them together. "See if ya can help her out," Bow urged. "She's gonna go places." Harlean was equally enthralled, and for the rest of her life she regarded Bow as "the most vivid and intense person I ever knew."

When her small part in *The Saturday Night Kid* did not lead to larger ones, Harlean resumed extra work in *Weak but Willing*, a two-reel Al Christie comedy at Metropolitan Studios. There she met agent Arthur Landau, who advanced her $500 for unpaid telephone, gas, and grocery bills. In return she signed a management contract.

Landau would later take credit for what befell his new client, though in truth he had nothing to do with it: while working extra in *Weak but Willing*, Harlean encountered ex-lover James Hall, who was at Metropolitan Studios for *Hell's Angels*, a World War I aerial saga produced, directed, and financed by a tall and lanky, twenty-three-year-old Texan. Heir to a fortune from an oil-drilling bit developed by his father, his unearned income exceeded $5,000 a day. Hollywood considered him "a country hick" and "the sucker with the money." His name was Howard Hughes.

In October 1927 Hughes had started a silent version of *Hell's Angels* with James Hall and Ben Lyon as brother aviators betrayed by the same woman. Seventeen months, one marriage (Hughes' wife left him during shooting), two directors, three lives (two stunt pilots and a mechanic), and $2 million later, Hughes' obsession had become an anachronism: a silent movie in a talkie market. Undaunted, he added sound effects to *Hell's Angels'* aerial sequences and decided to reshoot its dramatic ones, which posed a new problem: the accent of Norwegian actress Greta Nissen, the film's original temptress, did not befit a British lady.

A replacement was needed, and since Hughes "feared embarrassment in directing an established favorite"—i.e., no reputable actress wanted the part—he sought an unknown.

The search had lasted six months when James Hall spotted Harlean at Metropolitan Studios. "Gee, kid," Hall told her, "I think I can sell you." He promised to introduce her to Hughes that day.

True to his word, Hall returned to the *Hell's Angels* set where, according to crew member David Marx, "Jimmy told Hughes he knew a perfect girl for the part. Hughes said he'd like to see her but couldn't break because we were shooting. So I had to wait until noon to get her, which I did."

Marx found Harlean on the *Weak but Willing* set. "She dropped everything," he divulges. "Right in the middle of shooting, she grabbed my hand and we ran to see Hughes. 'Make a test of her,' he told [cameraman] Tony Gaudio." Harlean was given a gown to wear, a scene to memorize, and a request to return after work.

Her test was shot that night. While Tony Gaudio prepared two cameras, *Hell's Angels* screenwriter Joseph Moncure March studied Harlean. "She had almost albino blonde hair," he noted, "a puffy, somewhat sulky little face, and she was dressed in what appeared to be an evening gown that fitted her tightly in the bodice and hips."

"My God," said March. "She's got a shape like a dustpan."

The next morning Mother Jean drove her daughter to Hughes' office on the Metropolitan lot. Harlean approached his bungalow, halted outside a screen door, and spoke through it for several minutes. Then she walked back to the car and sat down in silence. "Well?" demanded Mother Jean. "What happened?"

Harlean seemed dazed. "He hired me, Mommie," she murmured in amazement. "He hired me."

Part Two

Platinum Blonde

Chapter Six

On October 24, 1929, while "Black Thursday" devastated Wall Street, Howard Hughes' Caddo Company (named for a Louisiana field where his father struck oil) signed Jean Harlow to a five-year contract. Her $100-a-week salary was no raise from the Roach Studios, but this opportunity was unique: unlike fellow film companies, Caddo had no other actress under contract. Both the company's time and Hughes' money would be invested in Harlow, and as even she knew, the starmaking process depended on promotion.

The buildup began with a Caddo press release describing Harlow as "a nineteen-year-old Chicago society girl" chosen to appear in *Hell's Angels*. That she was actually eighteen, and that her sole connection to Chicago society was Chuck McGrew, did not matter. Both Harlow and her image belonged to Caddo.

Naturally she was grateful, as a handwritten letter on "Harlean McGrew II" stationery attests:

Dear Mr. Hughes,

Your faith in me has been a great influence in my life. To have a man like you believe in me—and with that faith, create a place for me in the industry is something I shall never cease to be grateful to you for.

It is something also for which I shall never let you regret. I want only to have the opportunity to prove to you that your faith was not misplaced.

I am so happy to be with you and am wishing you all the happiness and success you so richly deserve.

Devotedly,
Jean

As genuine as such sentiments may seem, their gushy style hardly sounds like Harlow, nor does the handwriting resemble hers. Indeed, the letter's actual author was Mother Jean, who signed documents and autographs in her daughter's stead. Misidentified by fans and collectors, many are still sold today.

The following month Harlow went to work on *Hell's Angels*. Too "insecure" to supervise its dialogue sequences, Hughes had hired British director James Whale, a decision which delighted Harlow until she asked for advice about "Helen," her character. Whale called Helen "a pig" and refused to discuss her.

To a teenage girl with no experience except extra work, his comment was crushing. Harlow needed all the help she could get; lacking sympathy or support from her director, she grew "nervous and tense."

The strain showed. "Harlow was quite aware of her

deficiencies," confirmed *Hell's Angels* screenwriter Joseph Moncure March, "and a lot of the time it must have seemed like a nightmare to her. Even her ability to be seductive was questioned, and in one scene which demanded considerable allure, she could not seem to please Mr. Whale.

" 'Tell me,' she said with desperate earnestness. 'Tell me exactly how you want me to do it.'

"Whale, his patience sorely tried, said, 'My dear girl, I can tell you how to be an actress, but I cannot tell you how to be a woman.' "

Given her role, it was hard to be either. As Whale had realized, Helen was less a character than a caricature, a one-dimensional vamp who smokes, drinks, wears low-cut dresses, and seduces any man at hand. Even her style was hokey: upon meeting "Monty" (Ben Lyon), her latest suitor's brother, Helen lures him to her London flat, downs a stiff drink, removes her wrap, and says, "Would you be shocked if I put on something more comfortable?" Though her proposition would become a catchphrase, Harlow thought it "the corniest line in movie history."

Appalled by dailies of his discovery, Hughes tried directing Harlow himself. The results were equally unimpressive. "It was impossible to get *any* sort of scene out of Jean Harlow," said assistant director Reggie Callow. "She was one of the world's worst actresses." At least she looked striking, so Hughes ordered a two-color Technicolor sequence to showcase her green eyes, provocative figure, porcelain skin, and white-blonde hair.

The process turned shooting into torture. "It was practically unbearable to stand under those lights," remembered Callow. Forced to do so for sixteen hours a day,

Harlow suffered from "Klieg eyes" (burnt eyeballs) and was in anguish for weeks.

Hell's Angels finished shooting in late 1929. For the next six months, while Hughes and his editors fought to reduce 2.5 million feet of film to a 15,000-foot movie, Harlow collected her salary without working for it. Certain that *Hell's Angels* would end her career before it began and struggling to support herself, her mother, and Bello (unable to afford the Linden Drive house, the three had rented a bungalow at 300 North Maple Drive in Beverly Hills), she found a sympathetic ear in M-G-M executive Paul Bern. Unlike most powerful men in Hollywood, Bern was not "on the make"; instead he comforted Harlow and encouraged her career. At a time when everyone else deemed her hopeless, Bern provided Harlow with a small degree of self-confidence. She could only hope he was right.

The Hollywood premiere of *Hell's Angels* resembled a Nathanael West novel. Still the largest event of its kind in history, its May 27, 1930, opening at Grauman's Chinese Theatre drew a mob of 50,000 (Caddo claimed 500,000) to Hollywood Boulevard, which was illuminated at dusk by 185 arc lights rented by Hughes for $14,000. Scalpers sold $11 tickets for $50. Fans gasped at the sight of an actual fighter squadron flying overhead.

By 8 P.M., when *Hell's Angels* was scheduled to start, traffic had slowed to a standstill. Celebrity guests Charles Chaplin, Buster Keaton, and Gloria Swanson cowered in terror as the mob swarmed their cars. Unable to control the crowd, the Los Angeles police department called the National Guard.

Harlow made her entrance almost two hours later.

Surviving newsreel footage shows her in solid white from hair to toe, with an enormous orchid corsage. Her escort is Paul Bern, with Bello and Mother Jean behind them. Asked to address a nationwide radio audience, Harlow approaches the microphone. "Thank you," she tells cheering fans. "I would like to use this occasion to publicly thank Mr. Hughes for the opportunity he gave me." Her words were forgettable. Her appearance was not.

Though she was poised and assured in public, her first Hollywood premiere filled Harlow with terror. "How I got through that night and talked in the microphone I'll never know," she said later. "I don't remember seeing the picture at all, and what's more I never intend to. If I had to look at myself in it, I'd lose all confidence in my ability. I'd feel there was no hope."

Critics agreed. "While she is the center attraction, the picture is a most mediocre piece of work," noted the *New York Times*. "Jean Harlow," jeered *The New Yorker*, "is plain awful." Only *Variety*, the "show-biz Bible," appraised her appeal. "It doesn't make much difference what degree of talent she possesses," its reviewer noted, "for this girl is the most sensuous figure to get in front of a camera in some time. She'll probably always have to play these kind of roles, but nobody ever starved possessing what she's got."

Despite high grosses in the United States and abroad, *Hell's Angels* could not possibly recoup its $3.8 million cost. It did, however, make Harlow an overnight, international star. No one claimed she could act yet everyone clamored to see her, and sixty years later the cause seems clear: as American culture shifted from boom '20s to bust '30s, a new symbol of female sexuality was needed to embody the era. In the previous decade, Clara Bow had possessed the appropriate abandon, but by 1930 her appeal had dated. As sexually liberated as she may have seemed, "The 'It' Girl" saved herself for marriage; the antiheroine of *Hell's Angels*, by contrast, sought sex without love and mocked men who equate them. "You and your high ideals," she sneers at a lover. "You're just a stupid prig. I *hate* you." It was a far cry from Bow, whose "It" girls were aggressive but good. Harlow was bad through and through.

Needless to say, she had nothing in common with her screen persona. Helen's allure hid a predatory nature; Harlow's protected a soft and vulnerable core intensely affected by controversy and criticism. Suddenly subjected to overwhelming amounts of each and then treated, in her words, "like a bitch in heat," she felt ashamed of her fame. "Harlow hated herself," Arthur Landau admitted. "She wanted to quit and go work in a store."

"She was disgusted with the sort of success she was having," discovered an interviewer at the time. "She wanted to be famous, but not that way."

Chuck McGrew knew it and vowed to win her back. Determined to stop him, Mother Jean intercepted his calls, then changed Harlow's telephone number. Meanwhile Chuck drove to Caddo and told Hughes to "lay off." He was ejected from the studio.

Chuck appealed to Aunt Jetty, who "spent an hour with Harlean *alone* and told her how it was." Harlow listened, then burst into tears. "Chuck isn't bad," she cried. "I don't hate him. I don't hate my father. I don't hate *anyone*." Since her stardom, Mother Jean had demanded that she divorce Chuck, but for once Harlow had balked. She wanted a husband, not a career. If Aunt Jetty said as much to Mother Jean, maybe she would understand.

Aunt Jetty tried. "Her eyes shot *fire* at me," she wrote of Mother Jean's reaction. "I saw Skip Harlow all over again." Ignoring all evidence to the contrary, Mother Jean claimed that "Chuck did not love her Baby."

"He does so," insisted Aunt Jetty. "But he's not going to give you and Marino money without even seeing her."

Mother Jean was unmoved. "If she goes back to him," she warned, "her career is *ruined*." Hearing this, her daughter ran from the room.

"All your talk about Chuck makes her crazy," Mother Jean complained. "I can't handle her."

"Why *should* you handle her?" countered Aunt Jetty. "She *needs* Chuck; she needs love besides yours. You're wrong, Jean, and someday you'll be sorry."

Someday was not soon enough: though Chuck called her daily, Harlow "gave up" and Mother Jean had her way. "Nothing on earth," Harlow sighed to Aunt Jetty, "is worth what I go through when I don't let her dominate."

At 4 A.M. on June 28, a drunken, desperate Chuck burst into Harlow's bedroom and informed her that in two hours he would fly to Chicago. "I know interstate service of divorce papers is no good," he vowed, "so you'll never serve any on me." His wife had a choice: she could remain in California without him and his money, or return to Chicago with both.

Overhearing this, Mother Jean telephoned her attorney, who rushed to Maple Drive and served papers on Chuck. Afterward he slapped Harlow's face, called her "a vile name," and burst into tears. He did not blame their breakup on his drinking or her career. He knew who had caused it.

Chuck walked down Maple Drive, leaving his car behind. And though their divorce did not become final for another six months, he never saw Harlow again.

Having disposed of her daughter's husband, Mother Jean decided to dispose of her own. Not only was Bello still jobless, but his newfound status as a movie star's stepfather had increased his infidelities. Enraged and disgusted, Mother Jean consulted her lawyer in secret until Bello discovered her scheme, contacted Chuck, and offered to sell "objectionable photographic poses" of Harlow for display in divorce court. Though the pictures in question had been taken by esteemed photographer Edwin Bower Hesser, titillating references to them in the press caused Harlow (who denied their existence entirely) considerable embarrassment. It was a sample of the trouble her stepfather could cause, and Mother Jean knew it. Her plan to divorce Bello was quietly dropped.

Except for the New York and Seattle premieres of *Hell's Angels*, Hughes had no further plans for Harlow and no future productions in sight. Nonetheless he picked up her option and raised her salary to $150 a week, a paltry sum for a star who already received so much fan mail that Mother Jean hired family friend Barbara Brown to help answer it. To Brown's surprise, Harlow "got letters from all over the world. And not just from men; women wrote her, too."

"I get about fifty letters from women to every one from

a man," marveled Harlow, "and they all seem for me." When their eastbound train stopped at various stations en route to New York, passengers Maurice Chevalier, Hughes, and his mistress, actress Billie Dove, all went unnoticed. Harlow was mobbed.

To further her popularity and promote his film, Hughes sent Harlow to Kansas City in November. In two days she gave a dozen interviews, participated in a local radio program, and appeared onstage before each showing of *Hell's Angels*. Her presence at the four-thousand seat Midland Theater broke house records.

Harlow's homecoming was a professional success and personal strain. Seeing her father felt awkward and painful; so did meeting Maude Carpenter, his new wife. Uncomfortable with a daughter he hardly knew, the gentle dentist fixed Harlow's teeth. He did not discuss his disapproval of her public image.

Harlow could not understand how people confused her with her screen character. "He should be ashamed of himself," she fumed of a childhood friend's adult proposition. "This is my hometown, and that dope made mud pies with me."

Reporters found such candor refreshing. Expecting a woman of experience, they encountered "a beautiful young girl with an unaware, babyish quality. It was almost as if she had played the torrid scenes in *Hell's Angels* without realizing their import."

Harlow did realize her reputation. "I know I'm the worst actress that was ever in pictures," she acknowledged, "but I can learn, and I will."

The question was whether Hughes would give her a

chance. By late 1930 Harlow had not acted in a year and Caddo had no future projects planned. Instead she returned to New York for more promotion of *Hell's Angels*. "She was very unhappy about it," recalled Arthur Landau. "She had constant quarrels with Hughes, whom she disliked very much." It was a frustrating and unfair dilemma, yet her agent did nothing to help. So Mother Jean, with her daughter's career stalled and spending money scant, reduced Landau to a nominal figurehead. Henceforth she would manage Harlow herself.

This was not as absurd as it sounds. At a time when agents were pawns of omnipotent studios, no one would fight Harlow's battles more fiercely than her mother. She may have seemed vain and silly, but those who knew Mother Jean knew better. "She wasn't foolish, she was *calculating*," says Landau's son. "She had everything under control." She also had enough sense to know that a male would make a better front and thus appointed Bello as Harlow's "business manager." It was his first work since his wedding.

Bello's first move (at Mother Jean's behest) was to accuse Hughes of "persecuting" Harlow by not permitting her to work, which (in Mother Jean's mind) put Caddo in breach of contract. Because of this, Bello demanded its immediate termination.

Hughes was livid. MISS HARLOW GENEROUSLY TREATED AND SPLENDIDLY HANDLED BY CADDO, he wired. REFUSE TO CANCEL CONTRACT AND RESENT HER IN-GRATITUDE IN REQUESTING IT. MISS HARLOW HEREBY INSTRUCTED TO COMPLY OR WE WILL NO LONGER BE RE-SPONSIBLE FOR HER HOTEL BILLS WHICH BY THE WAY HAVE BEEN EXTREMELY LARGE. WILL EXPECT MISS HARLOW TO

JUSTIFY THEM. It was a direct dig at the Bellos, who accompanied Harlow everywhere at Caddo's expense.

Since their actual relations were hostile and unhappy, rumors of an affair between her and Hughes angered Harlow. "I haven't seen him more than a half-dozen times [since *Hell's Angels*], and then in his office," she maintained. "As a matter of fact, I haven't gone out with anyone except Paul Bern.

"I am not," Harlow added, "a party hound." She only wished that people would believe it.

Chapter Seven

In November 1930 Paul Bern persuaded Hughes to loan Harlow to M-G-M for *The Secret Six*, an underworld drama with Wallace Beery. Though she played Beery's mistress in the movie, most of Harlow's scenes were with fellow newcomer Clark Gable. "Neither of us knew much about the business," he said later. "At the end of every scene she would ask me, 'How'm I doing?' And I would ask her the same."

"She was quite an amateur," agrees assistant director Joseph Newman, "but she was bright, astute, and observant. You could see it right away." Newman also noticed that Mother Jean bleached her hair to match her daughter's. It did not, he felt, befit a forty-one-year-old woman.

After *The Secret Six* Hughes loaned Harlow to Universal for *The Iron Man*, a trite boxing tale starring Lew Ayres and Robert Armstrong. Her role as a prizefighter's wife was her least sympathetic yet, and so were her reviews. "It is unfortunate that Jean Harlow, whose virtues as an actress are limited to her blonde beauty, has to carry a good share of the picture," lamented the New York *Times*. *Variety* concurred: "Woefully lacking in several spots, Harlow can by no means be classed as an actress."

Instead she was classed as something else. "You oughta go over to stage 20," a studio makeup man advised actor William Bakewell. "Boy, oh boy!" Hurrying to *The Iron Man* set, Bakewell watched in astonishment as Harlow played a party scene in a see-through sheath. "She made her entrance down some steps," he remembers, "and as she did, everything under that dress kept coming out and going in! People were swarming from all over to see it." Seated in a director's chair off-camera, Mother Jean beamed with pride. "My Baby," she whispered to Bakewell, "gives everything to her work."

Bakewell got Harlow's home telephone number from Lew Ayres, who thought her "a sexy-looking gal who was actually a very nice one." After Bello had hung up on him four times, Bakewell finally reached Harlow, asked her to dinner, and discovered that appearances were deceiving. "Despite her provocative style," he said later, "I found her to be an ordinary, average kid." Hoping nonetheless that her "warm and friendly" demeanor would develop further after dinner, Bakewell invited her to go dancing. Harlow shook her head. "I have a better idea," she exclaimed. "Let's go to my secretary's house and see my new scrapbook." Bakewell brought Harlow to Barbara Brown's, "and that's where we spent the whole evening.

"Not at *all*," he admitted, "what I had in mind."

Amid production on *The Iron Man*, Harlow returned to M-G-M for retakes of *The Secret Six* and went to Warner Brothers for *The Public Enemy*. Making three films at once was arduous and distracting, but Hughes did not care.

Warners was paying $1,000 a week for Harlow, from which she got $200 and he kept the rest.

Developed as a routine gangster story, *The Public Enemy* shifted radically when, after several days of shooting, director William Wellman switched leading man Edward Woods and supporting actor James Cagney. Short, tough, and cocky, Cagney was a new breed of Hollywood hero: the ruthless punk who assassinates all rivals and feeds his moll (Mae Clarke) a grapefruit face-first. *The Public Enemy* made Cagney a star and defined the genre. It was Harlow's best film to date.

It was also her worst performance. "Her mother was making her take speech lessons, so her voice was self-conscious and phony," remembers Edward Woods' widow. "Eddie thought she was terrible." In spite of this, Harlow endeared herself to her costars. "They considered her a beginner but a sweet kid. They liked her because she wanted to learn."

"She was an original," explains Cagney's screen mistress, Mae Clarke. "She had personality and presence, and that came through whether she could act or not." What also came through was Harlow's cleavage, which fascinated Cagney. "How," he finally asked her, "do you hold those things up?"

"I ice 'em," said Harlow, then returned to her dressing room to do so.

Actually, this was Mother Jean's job, as cousin Mary Williams saw for herself. "Come on, Baby," coaxed Harlow's mother, then applied chunks of ice to her daughter's breasts. Too appalled to look and too polite to leave, Mary Williams remained in the room, mortified by the ritual.

After three movies in six weeks, Harlow and the Bellos left Hollywood for New York. During their stay she met showman Harry Richman, the self-proclaimed "King of Broadway" and former lover of Clara Bow. A blowhard and braggart, Richman had used Bow for publicity, and now he announced that Harlow had accepted his proposal of marriage. "Harry Richman would do anything to get his name in the paper," scorns actress Lina Basquette. "He announced his engagement to me, and I was already married."

As Richman knew, Harlow was news. By May 1931 *The Secret Six* was a moderate success, *The Iron Man* a marginal one, and *The Public Enemy* a genuine sensation. More important, all were in wide release, making Harlow the only actress in America with three movies playing simultaneously. Critics still mocked her, but no star had as much exposure, or set as many trends. Women wanted hair like Harlow, her bell-bottom pajamas in *The Public Enemy* created a fashion craze, and "I Surrender, Dear," the song heard during her onscreen seduction of Cagney, became an anthem of sexual conquest. In a tribute to their former foil, Laurel & Hardy used Harlow's photograph in *Brats*, a two-reeler that pictured her as their sons' putative mother, and *Beau Hunks*, a four-reel parody of *Beau Geste* that portrayed her as "Jeanie-Weenie," the faithless hussy who drove an entire regiment to join the Foreign Legion. Harlow also made an unbilled cameo appearance in *Scarface*, a gripping gangster saga and Hughes' latest production.

What she needed was a strong part in a substantial production; what she got was *Goldie*, a quickie sex comedy for Fox. The first film in which the word "tramp" was used to describe a woman, *Goldie* featured, among other indignities, costar Spencer Tracy branding and beating Harlow, whose character was meant to deserve it.

By now her mishandling was well known in Hollywood. Interested in Harlow for *The Greeks Had a Word for Them*, producer Samuel Goldwyn found Hughes' price so prohibitive that he offered to buy her contract outright. Hughes refused. Goldwyn asked United Artists studio chairman Joseph Schenck to intercede. Schenck tried but failed. His letter to Hughes summarized the situation:

My dear Howard:

On many occasions I have advised you to transfer the Jean Harlow contract to [Goldwyn's] Art Cinema Corporation. You have had her under contract for quite a period of time and have done absolutely nothing with her and I understand that you do not intend to do anything with her. You have no plans for her.

There is a possibility of developing Jean if she is properly handled. She is wasted talent under your management as you have neither the time nor the inclination to handle her.

You come to me frequently for advice and assistance which I readily extend; the former you never take but the latter you are willing to accept. I am writing you because I am probably the best friend you have in the picture business and the one friend you have who is not looking to get something from you.

Sincerely,
Joe

Unfortunately for Harlow, Hughes did not respond, and Goldwyn dropped the idea after Warner Brothers executive Darryl Zanuck advised against it. SHE PROBABLY WORST ACTRESS THEY HAVE EVER KNOWN, Goldwyn wired Schenck. ZANUCK SAYS IT TOOK DAYS TO DO ONE SCENE WITH HER. SAYS THEY HAD TO CUT HER ROLE [in *The Public Enemy*] DOWN TO HALF AND EVEN THEN DIFFICULT GETTING HER TO HANDLE IT. UNDER CIRCUMSTANCES I CANNOT AFFORD TO TAKE CHANCE USING HER IN *GREEKS* WHERE ROLE REQUIRES QUICK REPARTEE AND MARVELOUS ACTING . . .

Because she had already made four movies in five months, Hughes sent Harlow to Chicago for a week of personal appearances at the 3,200-seat Oriental Theater; and because her contract contained no provision freeing her from such duties, she was forced to comply. Hughes charged the theater $3,500 a week. Harlow got $200.

A personal appearance presented a film star in a brief skit or song, two prospects that terrified Harlow. "She dreaded personal appearances," Mother Jean admitted, and under the circumstances, it was easy to see why. Harlow had no "act." Instead she would walk onstage, "trembling like a leaf" while the master of ceremonies dropped his handkerchief and ordered her to pick it up. "That's all he had to do," explained actor Reginald Owen, "because those wonderful breasts almost fell out, and that was worth any kind of admission."

Others were less impressed. "Jean Harlow can't dance, sing, or talk above a whisper," sneered a Chicago critic. Harlow was humiliated, yet Hughes sent her directly to Detroit's 2,300-seat Fisher Theater. It was also a disaster.

Harlow returned to Hollywood depressed and disillusioned. She had sacrificed her marriage for a career she neither controlled nor enjoyed, and her personal life seemed equally empty. During *Goldie* she had dated Ernest Torgler, a thirty-year-old stockbroker from the wealthy Wilshire district. A "terrific drinker" and "constant partyer" who eventually died of liver disease, Torgler was hardly the stable influence she needed, but Lina Basquette, who had also appeared in *Goldie*, says Harlow wanted him anyway. "She would borrow my car so she could go out with Ernie and not be followed by her mother," reveals Basquette. "She used me to hide her affair with him."

Torgler was tame compared to the suitor who succeeded him: Abner Zwillman, the most notorious mobster in New Jersey. Nicknamed "Longy" from *der langer*, a Yiddish term meaning "tall one," he had been born and raised in Newark's poorest Jewish neighborhood, where his immigrant father peddled live chickens. After his father's death, ten-year-old Longy Zwillman left grammar school to support his mother and six siblings, at first selling fruit but soon turning to crime, and when Prohibition made Newark the bootleg capital of the country, the enterprising teenager bought a fast boat for rum-running. In 1925 he was hauling fifty truckloads of liquor a night; by 1930 his organization imported 40 percent of all contraband crossing the Canadian border. Newspapers labeled Newark's thug-filled Third Ward "the Longy Mob," while Zwillman himself, along with Louis "Lepke" Buchalter, Meyer Lansky, Charles "Lucky" Luciano, Jake Shapiro, and Benjamin "Bugsy" Siegel, became one of the "Big Six," an informal cartel which controlled bootlegging across the country. Internal Revenue Service agents estimated his tax-free income at $40 million.

Eschewing the stereotype, Zwillman dressed conservatively, spoke softly, and had no hubris. "He was very charming," remembers Barbara Brown. "A regular guy." So Zwillman seemed, though by the time he met Harlow, he had already been convicted of "atrocious assault and battery" for the savage beating of a black pimp named Preston Buzzard (whose life was spared, bragged Zwillman, only because he felt sorry for him), done time in a New Jersey prison, and seized control of every racket in the state.

During a trip to Chicago, host Al Capone took Zwillman to see Harlow at the Oriental Theater. Afterward both men were invited backstage by Bello, who admired gangsters and used his glamorous stepdaughter to attract them. "He wanted to be a sport, so he'd throw cash around to impress us," says Zwillman crony Vince Barbie, "but it was *her* cash! Bello was a zero."

In this case Harlow did not care. Despite her screen image, she was still an immature and impressionable twenty-year-old who, like most Americans at the time, regarded a private encounter with a public enemy as dangerous and exciting. "She *loved* to hang out with guys in the mob," recalls Lina Basquette. "She wanted to be a rebel herself, but she didn't have the guts to go against her mother."

Zwillman did, and Mother Jean knew it. She also knew he could help her daughter's career, which he proved by securing a two-picture deal for Harlow with Harry Cohn of Columbia Pictures. Eager to curry favor with Zwillman, Cohn offered Hughes $5,000—twice the asking price—for

Harlow, and when Hughes still refused to raise her $250-a-week salary, Zwillman upped it to $1,000 and covered the difference. He also loaned Cohn $500,000 in cash.

By all accounts Zwillman was "obsessed" with Harlow, who was less in love than in awe. Her part in *The Public Enemy* had become a real-life role, and at first she relished it. Zwillman's stipend allowed her, Mother Jean, and Bello to move from their present apartment at 152 Peck Drive in Beverly Hills to a two-story house at 1353 Club View Drive in West Los Angeles, and according to Blanche Williams, Harlow's personal maid since *Hell's Angels*, her mobster lover also bought her a jeweled charm bracelet and a red Cadillac. Chuck McGrew was a callow youth by comparison, which was just what worried Mother Jean. In the past Harlow had been helpless against her mother's iron will, but now she had a powerful ally to protect her. Mother Jean risked losing Harlow. Her Baby would become an adult.

This, of course, was unthinkable. Mother Jean could deal with her husband's infidelity, but not her daughter's independence. Confronted by both, she sought comfort elsewhere.

She found it in Christian Science.

Chapter Eight

ounded in 1879 by Mary Baker Eddy, the First Church of Christ, Scientist applies "spiritual healing" to physical and mental problems. Christian Scientists believe that only "Spirit" (God) is real, while its opposite, physical matter, is merely an illusion. In this religion God is the sole power, and since God is completely good, evil and disease do not exist. This renders medical care unnecessary. Where others call doctors, a Christian Scientist turns to God.

Christian Scientists with a physical or mental problem may consult "practitioners," certified members of the "Mother Church" who join a patient in prayer until a "healing" has transpired. And while nonbelievers regard such healings as miraculous, a Christian Scientist accepts them as the logical, natural reward of a faith which attributes no power to man and all power to God.

Viewed with skepticism since its inception, Christian Science is especially controversial today, when modern technology has brought progress to medicine undreamed of a century ago. But in the days before antibiotics and health insurance, and at a time when man was considered more a metaphysical entity than a biochemical one, the concept of spiritual healing was widely accepted as a legitimate form of treatment. During the Depression there were approximately 250,000 practicing Christian Scientists across America, and despite her claim "not to accept the God of any creed or sect or person," Mother Jean was among them.

What she practiced, however, was not at all what her religion preached. Mother Jean called herself a Christian Scientist yet never joined the Mother Church. She disregarded its teachings by summoning practitioners and doctors simultaneously. And though Mary Baker Eddy emphasized that "human willpower is not Science . . . and its use is to be condemned," Mother Jean took pride in her willpower and used her newfound faith as divine justification for it. Given this definition, her support of Christian Science made sense. Mother Jean had always sought control. Now she embraced a religion which, in her misinterpretation, espoused a belief system based upon it.

She also used Christian Science for social climbing and selected her first practitioner, May Joy Zeidler, for that purpose. The mother of actress Leatrice Joy, Zeidler preferred to dwell on the "spiritual perfection," not the specific personality of her patients, though she saw through Mother Jean anyway. "Grandmother didn't like her at all," recalls Leatrice Gilbert. "She and my mother were serious about Christian Science, while Mother Jean was a dilettante. She did it because it was fashionable, and she dragged her daughter along."

Mother Jean admitted as much. "To the Baby all churches were alike," she stated. "They represented the reaching out for something higher than us." Nonetheless Harlow enjoyed her healings and basked in Zeidler's affection. "Grandmother adored her," adds Leatrice Gilbert. "She said Jean Harlow was a lovely girl."

She yearned to play one. "I'll either be a good girl with breeding or I'll step out of pictures," announced Harlow, and with Longy Zwillman backing her, Harry Cohn listened. Her first film for Columbia would be *Gallagher*, a conventional comedy about a streetwise reporter (Robert Williams) who weds a snooty blonde socialite but returns to his true love, "Gallagher" (Loretta Young), in the final reel. In the summer of 1931, Cohn assigned the project to Columbia's most promising director: Frank Capra.

The thought terrified Harlow. "The first day she came on the set we were all conscious of her strained aloofness," cameraman Joseph Walker recounted. "I soon learned, however, that her reserved demeanor came from outright awe and fright at being in the company of such seasoned performers and an important director like Capra." It also came from Capra's dismay with her enforced casting and awkward performance. "She didn't know what a society girl was like," he assumed. In fact, Ferry Hall had been full of society girls; Harlow simply did not have the skills to play one. Told to ask Williams, "Would you step into the library?" she pronounced it as "liberry" for fourteen straight takes. Finally, on her fifteenth try, she said it correctly.

Capra liked Harlow for trying. "She wanted to learn all the time," he said later. "I remember telling her to go home when her scenes were finished, [but] she'd always stick around the set [and] watch the others, trying to learn how to become an actress." As her director knew and the New York

Times noted, Harlow was "spectacular rather than competent." She had never been better, but she was still not good.

In search of a promotional gimmick, Hughes had ordered Caddo publicity director Lincoln Quarberg to devise a tag for Harlow as lasting and effective as "America's Sweetheart" had been for Mary Pickford and "The 'It' Girl" for Clara Bow. Quarberg devised, then dismissed "The Joy Girl" and "The Passion Girl" as derivative, while "Darling Cyclone" and "Contagious Desire" were neither clever nor catchy. "Blonde Fury," "Blonde Landslide," and "Blonde Sunshine" highlighted Harlow's most famous attribute but did not do it justice. Finally he coined a phrase which did: "Platinum Blonde."

A publicity blitz began. Although its plot had nothing to do with her hair, Hughes convinced Harry Cohn to change the name of Harlow's new film from *Gallagher* to *Platinum Blonde*, and in conjunction with its release, Caddo organized over three hundred "Platinum Blonde" clubs across America, offering $10,000 to any beautician who could chemically match Harlow's mane. None won, but the craze boosted peroxide sales by 35 percent despite the Depression and widespread warnings against "going platinum" without a professional hairdresser's help. Women who did faced disastrous results: according to one report, three would-be platinum blondes botched the job, ruined their hair, and had to shave their heads.

The fascination with Harlow's hair was exceeded only by how it got that way. In *Hell's Angels* she had been an ash blonde, while by *Platinum Blonde* she was just that. Obviously she dyed it, yet Harlow denied it. "I shampoo it every four or five days," she proclaimed, "and put a few drops of liquid bluing in the shampoo soap, not in the rinse water." This made the process sound easy and natural, but her hairdresser knew better. "I used to bleach her hair," reveals Alfred Pagano, "and to make it 'platinum blonde,' we used peroxide, ammonia, Clorox, and Lux flakes! Can you *believe* that?" The formula forced Harlow to spend every Sunday at Jim's Beauty Studio on Sunset Boulevard, where "bleach and dye specialist" Pearl Porterfield applied touch-ups to her ash blonde roots.

Harlow's reaction to her "Platinum Blonde" tag was characteristically ambivalent. Admitting that "if it hadn't been for the color of my hair, Hollywood wouldn't know I was alive," she nonetheless loathed her new label and resented Hughes for exploiting it. "She wasn't too keen on being the 'Platinum Blonde,' " recalls *Hell's Angels* camera operator Osmond Borradaile. "Everybody used to kid her, and she didn't like it."

On October 1, Harlow began *Blonde Baby*, her second film for Columbia and first "wholesome part." Her enthusiasm for the role did not enhance her performance. "She does her best to suggest the innocent young thing," conceded *Variety*, "but she fails to be convincing, and Mae Clarke takes the acting honors from her."

Clarke herself concurs. "She was embarrassing in *The Public Enemy*," concedes Harlow's costar, "and she was embarrassing in this movie, too." To avoid confusion with *Platinum Blonde*, the title *Blonde Baby* was changed to *Three Wise Girls*.

With no further offers forthcoming, Harlow turned once again to Paul Bern, her friend and ally at M-G-M. Bern arranged to borrow her for *Freaks*, but instead of feeling grateful, Harlow was horrified. She had played "wretches" in the past, but her proposed role in *Freaks* outdid them all: an amoral trapeze artist who marries a midget for money, poisons him, then receives retribution from a band of legless men, armless women, hermaphrodites, dwarves, and "pinheads" who turn her into a monstrous hybrid with a human head and chicken's body. Shocked and appalled (as were audiences; after its initial release, *Freaks* was withdrawn for forty years), Harlow begged Bern for a different assignment. He obliged with *The Beast of the City*, an anti-gangster drama with Walter Huston. Harlow's part was not sympathetic, but at least she would play a character much like herself: a mobster's mistress. It was her seventh film in a single year.

As soon as *The Beast of the City* finished shooting, Bello booked his stepdaughter on a ten-week personal appearance tour of East Coast movie palaces. The prospect petrified Harlow but would provide $3,500 a week, more than ten times her present $300 salary. Aware of this discrepancy, Hughes awarded Harlow a belated $8,500 "bonus" and demanded a cut of her upcoming tour revenues. She returned his check and left Hollywood.

Accompanied by Mother Jean, Bello, and Blanche Williams, Harlow arrived in Kansas City two days later. Rushing past fans and reporters, the "Platinum Blonde" hugged Ella Harlow. "Baby, I wish you didn't have to play such bad girls," sighed her grandmother.

"So do I," said Harlow, "but they've typed me as a menace in Hollywood." She shrugged. "Well, anyway, it's something for Kansas City to produce a menace." A reporter inquired about the trend her trademark hair had started. "It can't be good to bleach hair with chemicals," mused Harlow even though she did so every Sunday. "As for mine, it's never touched with anything but soap and water."

Since Bello had not hired a writer for her tour, Harlow faced humiliation six shows a day, six days a week. Even the support of a friendly MC in Pittsburgh, future film star Dick Powell, could not assuage her fears. Finally, two days after Christmas, she collapsed backstage at the city's 3,000-seat Stanley Theater. "Her body just went to pieces," Mother Jean told reporters. "This tour is too much for her." Ignoring her professed faith in Christian Science, she summoned a local doctor, who diagnosed "intestinal influenza" and ordered bed rest. Instead her mother persuaded Harlow to keep touring. On their next stop, Philadelphia's 4,300-seat Mastbaum Theater, she was so weak that Bello had to carry her onstage.

Still lacking an act, looking ill, trembling visibly, and mumbling inaudibly, Harlow was so hopeless that a call was placed to veteran MC Nils Thor Granlund in New York. "See if you can do anything for her," he was entreated. "She's playing the Mastbaum and laying an egg."

Granlund arrived in Philadelphia, saw the show, then went backstage. At the sight of him, Harlow "threw herself on a cot" and wept hysterically. "I can't make up words," she sobbed. "I have to study them, I have to have a script."

It was the least of her problems. "In addition to her ordinary and understandable stage fright, I discovered she was suffering from another complex," wrote Granlund. "Jean Harlow, who played the wanton on the screen, was afraid the public hated her for those roles and thought she was the same in real life. Nothing was further from the truth, but she really felt the customers might voice their disapproval of her in actual physical violence." To his astonishment, the hardboiled "Platinum Blonde" was actually "as naive and guileless as a child."

Agreeing to salvage Harlow's "act" for $600 a week, Granlund hired veteran gagmen Al Boasberg and Edgar Allan Woolf and staged her showstopping entrance. "The curtains parted on a darkened stage," Arthur Landau remembered, "and gradually a spotlight came up—and there she stood, atop a staircase in a white satin gown. The shining blonde hair, the gorgeous figure, and most of all, her smiling, beautiful face . . . The public didn't give a damn about an act; they wanted to see *her*." As spectators gasped, Granlund rushed onstage. "Take my word for it, she doesn't steal husbands like they make out in the movies," he shouted. "And just between us, she is scared to death, because her whole future depends on what you think of her. Here she is, the adorable lady herself, Miss Jean Harlow!"

"The scene was pure corn, of course," confessed Granlund, "but with Harlow it was a sensation." The first time they tried it, in a sold-out show at Brooklyn's 3,500-seat Metropolitan Theater, she received two curtain calls; by her next stop, a police escort was necessary. Impressed by her stage presence, Broadway showman Florenz Ziegfeld offered Harlow a role in his *Follies*; instead she traveled to Newark, where Granlund credited himself for the huge turnout at its 2,800-seat State Theater. Actually, it was due to Longy Zwillman, who stayed with Harlow at the Riviera Hotel.

Her tour continued in triumph. Cleveland's crowds roared with delight when ex-heavyweight champion of the world Jack Dempsey paid a surprise visit, then toppled to the ground after Harlow's knockout kiss. "I don't remember her act," admits Harry Friedenberg of Harlow's next stop in Columbus, "but I'll never forget the sight of her in white satin against a black velvet curtain." Afterward the smitten Ohio State freshman sneaked backstage, knocked on Harlow's dressing room door, and found her *"darling;* just as charming and nice as could be."* He asked Harlow to dine at his fraternity house, and to his amazement, she accepted. "So I took her," says Friedenberg, "and when I walked in with Jean Harlow, there was a long, hard silence—and then, pandemonium! I was a big man on campus for weeks."

By February 1932 Harlow was in such demand that her tour was extended an additional six weeks. That same month *The Beast of the City* was released, and for the first time ever, critics praised her performance. "The platinum baby really acts in this one," declared the New York *Daily News,* while *Time* pronounced Harlow "a shiny refinement of Clara Bow" and devoted the bulk of its review to her. In the month between *Three Wise Girls* and *The Beast of the City,* she had improved dramatically, due in part to Paul Bern's support. Now Harlow wrote him daily, expressing her gratitude and detailing her progress.

Bern interpreted their correspondence differently. "On his way home from M-G-M, he would stop by and read her letters to me," recalled Irene Mayer Selznick, the daughter of Louis B. Mayer, wife of David O. Selznick, and Bern's best friend. "One day he asked me, 'What would you think if I married her?' "

The question stunned Irene Mayer Selznick. Prior to it,

there was no sign whatsoever that Bern and Harlow were intimately involved; indeed, the Hollywood community presumed the "Platinum Blonde" was simply his latest "protégée," as good a word as any to describe Bern's platonic relationships with doomed beauties like drug-addicted Barbara La Marr, schizophrenic Clara Bow, and alcoholic Lila Lee, as well as current M-G-M stars Joan Crawford, Greta Garbo, and Norma Shearer. Befriending such women was Bern's forte, but the prospect of this balding, potbellied, perennial bachelor marrying Jean Harlow was preposterous. Few knew it more than Irene Mayer Selznick, who, as both the wife and daughter of moguls and a Hollywood School for Girls classmate of Harlean Carpenter, was an authority on the subject. As such, her response to Bern's query was blunt. What would she think if he married Harlow? "I think," said Irene Mayer Selznick, "you'd blow your brains out."

Most of the theaters in which Harlow appeared were owned by Loew's, Inc., the parent company of M-G-M. Since the studio's films were shown in Loew's theaters, Harlow and *The Beast of the City* were often on the same bill, and their success led Loew's president Nick Schenck (whose brother Joe had asked Hughes to sell Harlow's contract to Samuel Goldwyn a year earlier) to suggest that M-G-M sign Harlow to a long-term contract.

Louis B. Mayer balked. Despite aberrations like *Freaks*, M-G-M produced "clean" fare featuring ambitious shopgirls like Joan Crawford, remote exotics like Greta Garbo, or refined sophisticates like Norma Shearer. Whatever their differences, all three actresses played ladies with morals; Harlow, however, played floozies and tramps, a type Mayer found vulgar and distasteful. If his studio needed her, as it had for *The Secret Six* and *The Beast of the City*, it could always borrow Harlow from Hughes.

His attitude overlooked her potential. As her current tour made clear, Harlow had a wide following despite bad films and worse parts, while her personal style was already so prevalent that even Crawford and Garbo had "gone platinum" in recent movies. In addition, M-G-M's female stars were approaching age thirty; at only twenty, Harlow had a long and potentially lucrative future. And though Mayer took pride in his studio's ability to cultivate stars, in Harlow's case it would already have one. She was the wisest investment M-G-M could make.

When Mayer could not be convinced, Paul Bern launched a campaign with his close friend and associate, M-G-M production head Irving Thalberg. A legend in his own time, Thalberg had run Universal at twenty-one, then transformed M-G-M into the most efficient and profitable movie studio in history. A frail, driven perfectionist with an incurable heart condition (at thirty-one, he had already exceeded his life expectancy), Thalberg revered Bern, entrusting him with M-G-M's most prestigious productions. Bern had developed projects for Thalberg's wife, Norma Shearer, with tremendous success; if he now backed Harlow, then Thalberg was willing to try her. Nick Schenck agreed, so over Mayer's objections, M-G-M opened negotiations with Hughes to buy Harlow's contract.

At that moment she and *The Beast of the City* were playing the 3,200-seat Century Theater in Baltimore. Harlow was still there on March 3, her twenty-first birthday, when Bern called from Hollywood with the news: Hughes had agreed to sell her contract to M-G-M for $30,000. Harlow would report immediately to the studio's New York office and make a screen test for *Red-Headed Woman*.

A bestselling novel of a shameless stenographer who, in *Time*'s words, "cooed and screwed her way to the top and got away with it," *Red-Headed Woman* had become the most notorious unmade movie in Hollywood. Mayer himself had disowned the project, which already had plenty of problems: F. Scott Fitzgerald's script was unusable, French director Marcel De Sano was fired, and censorship czar Will Hays forbid its antiheroine from misbehaving on-screen as she had in the book. A warning letter explained why:

Dear Mr. Thalberg:

We have read [M-G-M's adaptation of] *Red-Headed Woman* and are convinced that the possibility of its production presents a very grave problem.

Briefly, the story is of a girl who virtually forces a married man to have an affair with her; who pursues the man with the promise of further sex relations in spite of his efforts to avoid her; who creates a scene in his house which leads to his separation from his wife; who takes the man's beating only to force him to end his attack by sleeping with her; who marries him after his divorce; who then sleeps with another, older man in order to break into society; who creates another scene in the street in her underclothes; who goes to New York and continues her affair with the older man until, through detectives, the latter discovers that she meanwhile is having an affair with his chauffeur; who plans to "keep" the chauffeur after her second divorce and remarriage to the older man; who tries to rebuild her fences when she is found out; and who, after shooting her husband, goes to Paris and is shown at the end living in luxury provided by a Marquis, and receiving the Grand Prix award from the President of France while still carrying on with her chauffeur.

The girl is a common little tart, using her body to gain her ends. We cannot see how it is possible to use such an out-and-out harlot in such questionable scenes . . .

Thalberg was more concerned with casting. Despite studio publicity claiming all its female stars sought the part, no M-G-M actress wished to play a "common little tart" and "out-and-out harlot." Offers to Clara Bow and Colleen Moore, both in search of a comeback vehicle, were also rejected. Paramount refused to loan Nancy Carroll.

Unable to sign a famous name, Thalberg began testing second leads and starlets like Wynne Gibson, Harriette Lake (the future Ann Sothern), Dixie Lee, Margaret Perry, Lillian Roth, and Alice White. GETTING TERRIBLY DESPER-ATE, he wired Nick Schenck in New York. WOULD LIKE ETHEL MERMAN TEST AIRMAILED. The auburn-haired stage star did not win the role.

That he would even consider casting the "Platinum Blonde" as a *Red-Headed Woman* shows how "terribly des-perate" Thalberg was. Harlow's hair was her major asset; to change its color seemed foolish and risky. Perhaps her screen test, shot in New York on March 19, persuaded

Thalberg otherwise, though his reaction to it renders this unlikely. "Well, you know, that girl's so bad she might just be good," concluded Thalberg with uncharacteristic bewilderment. Apparently, in this instance, he valued Bern's opinion above his own.

So did Harlow, who disliked *Red-Headed Woman* but trusted Bern enough to fight for it. Her battle was waged onstage, where she ended each appearance with an appeal for the part. JEAN'S SPEECHES ASKING AUDIENCES TO ANSWER BY APPLAUSE [its] OPINION OF JEAN PLAYING *RED-HEADED WOMAN* DELIVERED EVERY SHOW, Bello wired Thalberg. EVERY HOUSE BROUGHT THE MOST ENTHUSIASTIC UNANIMOUS APPLAUSE. Still dubious, Thalberg ordered a test of Dorothy Mackaill.

Ten days later another telegram arrived. REFERRING TO *RED-HEADED WOMAN*, AUDIENCE ANSWERED WITH SAME APPROVING ENTHUSIASTIC APPLAUSE AS IN OTHER CITIES, Bello persisted. PRESENTLY PLAYING [LOEW'S] ORPHEUM. ALTHOUGH RAINING HARD EVERY HOUSE PACKED. It was enough for M-G-M. Harlow was hired.

"The public makes the stars," said Louis B. Mayer, and Harlow was proof. Five months earlier she had been at a professional standstill; now, after a triumphant East Coast tour, she returned to Hollywood with a seven-year contract starting at $1,250 a week. It was well below Crawford's $3,000 a week, Garbo's $6,000 a week, or Shearer's $110,000 per picture, but Harlow was a beginner by comparison. Besides, M-G-M handled its stars with calculation and care, and Bern considered her career a personal priority. He even planned to oversee *Red-Headed Woman* himself.

Becoming a property of the world's foremost dream factory made Harlow feel like two separate entities: a person, and a product. But unlike others in her position who sought to integrate the two, she reacted as if what was happening in her life was not happening to herself. "I never quite believe," she told a jubilant Mother Jean, "that I am *me*." To prove it, the "Platinum Blonde" signed her letters "me." Without her own identity, she did not require a name.

Chapter Nine

ean Harlow joined M-G-M on April 20, 1932. Arriving at its fifty-three-acre, twenty-two-soundstage, four-thousand-employee plant in Culver City, she was taken to the makeup department, where several red wigs were glued to her scalp with spirit gum, then tested by cameraman Harold Rosson to determine which looked best on black-and-white film. An industry veteran with a sly sense of humor, "Hal" Rosson sensed Harlow's fear and resolved to relax her. "He refused to act serious and joked and laughed," she said later. "That relieved the strain and tension." Besides his humor, Rosson's technical expertise earned Harlow's trust. "You can't understand the feeling an actress has about the man who is photographing her," she explained. "He's sort of like the family physician: if she has confidence in him, everything is all right." On her first day at her new studio, Rosson provided such comfort.

After her wig tests, Harlow met author Anita Loos, another future coworker and friend. In 1912 Loos had sold a scenario to director D. W. Griffith while still in her teens;

thirteen years later she wrote *Gentlemen Prefer Blondes*, an international bestseller whose dumb-blonde heroine, gold-digger Lorelei Lee, considers diamonds a girl's best friend and manipulates men to obtain them. The novel's synthesis of sex and comedy was just what *Red-Headed Woman* needed, and Paul Bern knew it. Junking the original story and F. Scott Fitzgerald's failed screenplay ("Scott tried to turn the silly book into a tone poem!" said Thalberg), Bern asked Loos to adapt *Red-Headed Woman* and "make fun of its sex element just as you did in *Gentlemen Prefer Blondes*." It was the only way to appease censors and amuse audiences.

Summoned by Thalberg to meet *Red-Headed Woman*'s star, Loos expected a femme fatale; instead she discovered a girl next door. "She looked about sixteen," observed Loos of Harlow, "and her baby face seemed utterly incongruous against the flaming wig."

Thalberg got to the point. "Do you think you can make an audience laugh?" he asked Harlow.

She hesitated. "*With* me or *at* me?"

"*At* you."

"Why not?" shrugged Harlow. "People have been laughing at me all my life." And with "a quick, bright little nod," she left Thalberg's office.

"I don't think," he told Loos, "we need to worry about Miss Harlow's sense of humor."

Loos agreed but saw more beneath the surface. "Underlying Jean's raffish sense of humor was a resignation unusual for one so young," she wrote. "Nothing would ever surprise Jean. She knew exactly how people were going to react to her." Loos' own reaction was an outrageously sexy

Red-Headed Woman script which showcased Harlow's unique personality and habits; even her "quick, bright little nod" was incorporated into several scenes. "We made it over completely for her," Loos commented. "It was, to all intents and purposes, a Jean Harlow story."

Harlow worried anyway. "She really didn't want to make *Red-Headed Woman*," recalls Virginia Conway, the widow of director Jack Conway, "because she didn't like the part. She was terribly sweet, and she had absolutely nothing in common with the character." Harlow herself explained her predicament: "The problem," she told reporters, "is to play her so that the audience likes her in spite of herself." It was a daunting task for a twenty-one-year-old, though there was an upside as well. "It's the first chance I ever had," admitted Harlow, "to do something in pictures other than rotate my hips."

Red-Headed Woman began shooting a week later. To a cast and crew accustomed to Joan Crawford's insincerity, Greta Garbo's eccentricity, and Norma Shearer's superiority, Harlow was a godsend. "Everybody loved her," states sound mixer Bill Edmondson. "So sweet and thoughtful, and always on time. She was a doll." In what would become a custom on all Harlow's movies, each morning her maid Blanche Williams would serve coffee and doughnuts to the entire crew, a gesture which annoyed cost-conscious executives but endeared Harlow to technicians working twenty hours a day, six days a week without overtime or benefits.

M-G-M spent time and money concealing its stars' physical flaws, so after Crawford's freckled skin, Garbo's flat feet, and Shearer's lazy eye, Harlow's natural beauty was both welcome and awesome. "She had the most *unbe-*

lievable complexion I ever saw in my life," asserts Bill Edmondson. "Like milk and honey. 'My God,' we all said. 'It's a shame to put makeup on a face like that.' " It was also a hazard: during shooting, Harlow had an allergic reaction to her heavy makeup. As usual, Mother Jean relied on a mixture of religion and medicine, calling both Genevieve Smith, her new Christian Science practitioner, and Dr. Harold Barnard, who treated Harlow and became her close friend.

Most astounding to M-G-M crews was Harlow's attitude toward her body. Told by Jack Conway to remove her jacket in a *Red-Headed Woman* scene, she obeyed—and wore nothing underneath. "Nudity was rarely seen in those days," reminisced Anita Loos, "and Harlow's had the startling quality of an alabaster statue. Visitors on the set scarcely believed their eyes. The lighting crew almost fell out of the flies in shock."

The commotion puzzled Harlow. "I'm sorry," she said innocently, "but nobody gave the order to cut." To most people this was beside the point, but what others attributed to exhibitionism, Loos understood as detachment. Harlow, she realized, "was rather like a boy; she had no vanity whatsoever. Things which she did [that] seemed outrageous, she did because she had no feeling of any kind herself, so she didn't think they affected other people. Also, she had this extraordinary beauty which she'd been born with and had for her whole life, so she wasn't conscious of it. But utterly no vanity. None at all." An unwitting beauty was ideal comic material; if Harlow could convey this innate quality on-screen, her latest film seemed bound for success.

On June 2 a rough cut of *Red-Headed Woman* received

a sneak preview in Glendale, a suburb of Los Angeles. Too apprehensive to attend, Harlow sent Barbara Brown, who thought it "a knockout." Thalberg felt otherwise because of its beginning, in which redheaded "Lil Andrews" (Harlow) decides to seduce her boss. "Bill Legendre's crazy about his wife," scoffs a skeptical girlfriend. "Well, he's a *man*, isn't he?" snaps Lil, who struts braless down Main Street, preparing to stalk her prey. The scene was so startling, and its star so brazen, that the film's preview audience did not know whether to laugh or leave.

To ensure the former, Thalberg asked Loos to create an introductory sequence which would capture Lil's character in swift comic strokes. Loos obliged, and a week later the *Red-Headed Woman* company reassembled for three new scenes: first, a close-up of Lil lying in a barber's chair, her breasts draped by silk, her red hair on her bare shoulders. "So gentlemen prefer blondes, do they?" she muses, then studies herself in a mirror. "Yes, they do," says Lil sarcastically.

The next scene brought an even bigger laugh. "Can you see through this?" Lil asks of her skintight dress.

"I'm afraid you can, miss," replies an offscreen salesgirl.

"I'll wear it," says Lil as she beams with delight.

The third scene featured only Lil's shapely leg. "The boss' picture," she announces off-camera, then places his photograph in a garter around her thigh. "Well, it'll get me more there than it will hanging on the wall," Lil explains. Evidently she speaks from experience.

Thalberg's use of sneak previews and reshoots had saved prior films from failure, and *Red-Headed Woman* proved no exception. The movie's new opening made its main point up front: *Red-Headed Woman* poked fun at sex, with Harlow as its comic embodiment. It was her best work to date.

Even she knew it. "For the first time since I've appeared in pictures, I really enjoyed looking at myself," Harlow admitted, "and I didn't have any particular feeling it was me." Her reaction was hardly surprising. Harlow had no idea who "me" was.

The same week that *Red-Headed Woman* began shooting, Paul Bern escorted Harlow (in a red wig to promote her new role) to the Hollywood premiere of *Grand Hotel*, an all-star production he had supervised. Its enormous success was Bern's greatest triumph, and his wish to bring Harlow indicated his feelings for her. Nonetheless their appearance in public together—the first since *Hell's Angels'* premiere two years earlier—caused neither curiosity nor comment. Bern always squired beauties. The notion of him and Harlow as an actual couple was too absurd to contemplate.

Six weeks later Bern and Harlow attended a dinner party in David O. and Irene Mayer Selznick's home. After the meal its hostess, who was seven months pregnant, excused herself and headed upstairs to her dressing room. Harlow followed. "Would you mind terribly," she wondered, "if I put a hand on your stomach?"

The question startled Irene Mayer Selznick. "I tried to refuse politely, but she said, 'Please. It would mean so much to me.'" Seeing her sincerity, Selznick let Harlow place a palm on her belly. "Oh," sighed Harlow, "how I *long* to have a baby."

Returning downstairs to the party, Harlow made a bee-line for Bern. "You know, I may really marry you," she informed him. "I want a home and family like Irene." The following morning Bern phoned Irene Mayer Selznick to say that she was "partly responsible for his incredible good fortune": the previous evening, after her party, Harlow had accepted his proposal.

It was a strange start, and it soon grew stranger. That night the couple dined with Douglas Fairbanks, Jr., whose troubled marriage to Joan Crawford had led him, like so many others, to seek Bern's advice. Unaware that Bern and Harlow were a couple, Fairbanks was thrilled when the "Platinum Blonde" began "playing very active 'footsie' with me under the table." At first he responded timidly, "but then, to my surprise, I felt her hand on my knee! There was no misunderstanding this and only with effort did I suppress a shiver." While Fairbanks fought for composure, an unwitting Bern announced his engagement to Harlow. "Shocked" and "angry" by her behavior, Fairbanks congratulated the couple, ordered champagne, and "kept a long distance" from the bride-to-be that night and thereafter.

Irene Mayer Selznick witnessed a more ominous incident at actor Fredric March's party in Bern and Harlow's honor. "Paul was adamant about my coming, even though I didn't want to go out during the last weeks before the baby," she recalls. "He said I only had to do it twice—to that party and to his wedding."

At the party, Selznick felt her effort "pointless, because I saw Paul only to greet him. When I went to take an early leave, I learned he was tired and had gone upstairs for a brief nap, a strange thing for the guest of honor to do." Selznick searched for her escort, East Coast socialite Cornelius Vanderbilt Whitney, and found him playing the piano for a satin-clad Harlow, who was "singing to him and moving her body in a most provocative way." Embarrassed by the sight, Selznick turned to leave and found herself facing Bern, who "gripped me roughly by the arms, spun me around, shook me, and said, 'Look at her, look at her! She is an angel from heaven. I want you to remember and never forget it. No matter what happens, you are to remember that she is an angel from heaven!' " Selznick departed as soon as possible.

On June 21 Bern and Harlow made their plans public by applying for a marriage license. Though blessed by the press—"Congratulations, Paul! And worlds of happiness for you, Jeanie!" gushed *Motion Picture*—the Hollywood community snickered at the impending union of M-G-M's "palace eunuch" to its "Platinum Blonde." It was, wags whispered, a toss-up as to who was less lucky: Bern, whose future bride was dismissed by Thalberg as "nothing more than a booby trap for male stupidity," or Harlow, whose devoted crew mourned the match of "a middle-aged mama's boy with the most gorgeous creature in Hollywood."

"Everybody wondered why she'd marry him," sighs Bill Edmondson. "We never knew; we couldn't even *guess*."

Others could. Since her future at M-G-M still hung in the balance, Harlow's marriage was viewed as a canny career move. Norma Shearer had already snared Thalberg, so the next-best catch was Bern.

Another theory had Harlow enticing Bern at the behest

of her mother, who was more concerned with Harlow's career than her happiness. Actually, Mother Jean had grave misgivings about the marriage. "She worried about it," remembers Marcella Rabwin, an executive assistant to David O. Selznick. "She was a shrewd dame, and she knew this man was a phony." Mother Jean also knew that, if expressed aloud, her opposition to Bern could backfire and drive Harlow closer to him, just as Skip Harlow had done with his daughter and Bello. So she kept quiet and hoped for the best, and to ensure her constant presence in the couple's new home, Mother Jean gave Harlow a photograph of herself as a wedding present. BABY MINE, she inscribed with a bold, looping scrawl, YOU HAVE FILLED MY LIFE WITH SUCH BEAUTY AND SUCH GREAT HAPPINESS. NO MOTHER EVER HAD DEVOTION, FRIENDSHIP, OR EXQUISITE LOVE SUCH AS I HAVE HAD FROM YOU—MY BABY—MY LIFE—MY EVERYTHING. MOMMIE.

Contrary to such rumors, Harlow's reason for marrying Bern was basic and touching: burdened by a public image which bore no resemblance to her private self, this naive and trusting twenty-one-year-old felt she had found someone who could distinguish between the two. She also relished the fact that, thus far, the relationship was not physical. "She was pawed and chased so much," said director Howard Hawks, "that anyone who was gentle and nice she liked."

Harlow acknowledged as much. "He explains things and lets me know I've got a brain," she allegedly told Jack Conway. "He's different and doesn't talk fuck, fuck, fuck all the time." Like all who knew her, Virginia Conway insists that Harlow never used such language; although her words here are false, their meaning rings true. Bern *was* "different." If his fiancée had been older or more practical, she might have paused to wonder why.

Instead she ignored all signs. Notified that his erstwhile mistress would marry another man, Longy Zwillman had Bern investigated by local gangster Johnny Rosselli, who reported that "Bern was a pansy who liked pretty girls around him."

Zwillman confronted Harlow. "Have you laid him?" he demanded.

"No, I haven't," she said proudly. "He's a *gentleman*." Realizing she was "angry and resentful," Zwillman explained why he asked. Harlow listened, then said she would marry Bern anyway.

Adela Rogers St. Johns possessed equally disturbing information. A tough, smart, and independent "sob sister" for the Hearst newspaper syndicate, St. Johns had known Bern since his infatuation with Barbara La Marr, whose refusal to marry him had led Bern to attempt suicide in his toilet; instead of succeeding, a plumber was summoned to separate his head from its seat. Not surprisingly, St. Johns thought Bern "a neurotic, pretentious little man," and though she later embellished events to discredit him, daughter Elaine St. Johns confirms her mother's account of Bern's botched suicide and recalls her advising Harlow that, based on La Marr's account, Bern "had no right to marry *any* woman." Despite her delicate phrasing, the implication was clear.

According to St. Johns, Harlow heard this and burst into tears. "Then it's true," she cried. "Paul loves me for . . . *me*. He's paid me the highest compliment I've ever had."

Whether or not Bern was homosexual or dysfunctional, Harlow intended to marry him. Their wedding would take place as planned.

Until now Harlow's claim to fame was her hair, not her talent. *Red-Headed Woman* changed that forever. "Jean Harlow, hitherto not highly esteemed as an actress, gives an electric performance," *Variety* proclaimed. "This shapely beauty will amaze you," raved the New York *Daily Mirror*, "out-Bowing the famed Bow as an exponent of elemental lure and crude man-baiting technique." Sixty years later critic Leonard Maltin called Harlow's portrayal "the sexiest performance in screen history."

Despite a restricted audience—the film was banned in Britain, though King George kept a print at Buckingham Palace—*Red-Headed Woman* grossed $761,000, almost double its $401,000 cost. Meanwhile its star busied herself with prenuptial preparations. "Dearest Pal," she wrote fan Lenore Heidorn on Saturday, July 2, "it is the morning of the day I walk down the aisle . . ." Another fan was promised a piece of wedding cake, which Harlow would mail herself.

At 8:30 P.M. that evening, in an informal ceremony at Club View Drive, Paul Bern and Harlean Carpenter McGrew were married. Besides the Bellos, guests included Aunt Jetty and son Donald Roberson; Barbara Brown and her parents; Irving Thalberg and Norma Shearer; David O. and Irene Mayer Selznick, who was the wedding's official witness, "admittedly with mixed feelings"; Arthur Landau; actor/best man John Gilbert and his fiancée, actress Virginia Bruce; Bern's brother and sister-in-law, Henry and Miriam Bern; his sister, Friederike Bern Marcus; and his lawyer, Oscar Cummins. On their license, Harlow listed the marriage as her second, Bern as his first.

After toasting the couple with champagne, the guests took their leave and the newlyweds traveled to a hillside home at 9820 Easton Drive in Beverly Hills, Bern's wedding gift to his bride. If Harlow had not yet learned the truth about her husband, she would surely uncover it now.

Chapter Ten

*P*aul Bern was born Paul Levy in 1889, one of eighteen children of Julius Levy, a German-Jewish candy maker, and Henrietta Hirsch Levy, his emotionally unstable wife. Nine years later, with nine of their children already dead, the Levys immigrated to America and rented a tenement flat on East 114th Street in Manhattan.

His family's poverty did not prevent Paul Levy from befriending Edward L. Bernays, a fellow German-Jew from more distinguished stock: his mother was Sigmund Freud's sister, and his aunt married Freud himself. "A brother and sister married a sister and brother," explains Bernays ninety years later. "Paul was fascinated." Invited to dine at the Bernays' three-story brownstone, Paul Levy learned about abnormal psychology and Freudian analysis, and given his mother's neuroses, his interest in such subjects made sense. While other boys dreamed of becoming President or policemen, Paul Levy planned to study psychiatry.

His hopes were dashed by his father's death in 1908. To support his siblings and mother, eighteen-year-old Paul

Levy became a commercial stenographer, then enrolled at the American Academy of Dramatic Arts. Advised to take a more theatrical, less Semitic name, he paid tribute to his favorite family by abbreviating "Bernays" to "Bern" and making it his own.

Paul Bern graduated from the American Academy of Dramatic Arts in 1911 and began his show-business career. He acted on Broadway, toured with an East Coast stock company, wrote scripts for a Toronto film studio, and managed a Manhattan theater owned by Joe and Nick Schenck before they ran United Artists and Loew's. The positions were not prestigious, but they did acquaint Bern with every aspect of the movie business. By 1920 he was ready for Hollywood.

A family tragedy delayed his departure: on the morning of September 15, 1920, seventy-two-year-old Henrietta Levy hurled herself from an embankment and drowned. Though her son persuaded authorities to rule her death "accidental," in private he called it a suicide.

After his mother's death, Bern went to Hollywood and became a prominent writer, director, and producer at Goldwyn, Paramount, and Pathé, then an executive at M-G-M. He also made a hobby of the human psyche, consulting "alienists" and specialists about mental and emotional maladies. "I heard Bern hold forth on many subjects, not all taboo, but close to the borderline," recalled screenwriter Frances Marion. "He always seemed to be exploring the dark tunnels of the human mind." It was Bern who classified a movie character's motivation as "sadistic or masochistic," developed Eugene O'Neill's psychoanalytic drama *Strange Interlude* for Norma Shearer, and urged

Irving Thalberg to read Freud. Most people in Hollywood viewed his interests as intellectual, but Anita Loos knew better. Paul Bern, she wrote, was "a German psycho."

Adela Rogers St. Johns agreed. Beneath Bern's gentlemanly exterior, she wrote later, lurked a "morbid, pessimistic side. He was interested in abnormality and complexes, in inhibitions, perversions, suicide, and death." Had she known more about him, St. Johns would have understood why: in an era when mental illness was believed to run in families, Bern had seen it in his mother and, as he readily admitted, himself. "Mother said he had *enormous* swings of mood; according to her, he was either on top of the world or had hit rock bottom," recalls Leatrice Gilbert, the daughter of actress Leatrice Joy. "Being a Christian Scientist, she wouldn't have known what the term 'manic-depressive' was, but that's what she meant."

Bern's psychosexual split also caused comment. Despite "his courtly manner, there was in him a lascivious torrent under suave control," noted journalist Jim Tully. "He was the essence of the emotionally disembodied." His profound detachment led Bern to declare himself "a student of the psychology of sex" without ever partaking of it; regardless of rumors, absolutely no evidence of physical intimacy between Paul Bern and *anyone*, either male or female, exists. In a community in which sex was commerce, its psychology seemed to be Bern's limit. That he would marry a sexual icon says more about his emotional torment than any "alienist" could.

Bern's disturbed psyche was not his sole problem. As Adela Rogers St. Johns had noted, he "had no right to marry *any* woman" due to a deformity described by Barbara

La Marr in "graphic, technical, and explicit" detail. La Marr's words are lost, but Leatrice Joy saw Bern's shortcomings with her own eyes. On a visit to ex-husband John Gilbert, who was sharing a house with Bern and screenwriter Carey Wilson at the time, Joy accidentally saw Bern nude. His penis, she confided, "was the size of my pinkie."

Apparently Harlow did not know this before she married Bern, and her wedding night proved no more enlightening. After the couple's arrival at Easton Drive, Blanche Williams turned back the sheets on Bern's double bed, then left for the night. When she returned the next morning, Bern met her outside his bedroom. "The Baby's still a virgin," he said. Aware of Harlow's previous marriage and prior lovers, Williams wondered what he meant.

Harlow herself told M-G-M publicity department head Howard Strickling what happened. "Sex is not the most important thing in our lives," Bern had assured her. "We'll have a long life together and a long marriage."

To Strickling's amazement, Harlow believed it. "There was no distress on her part," he remembered. "Paul had completely sold her on this 'respect' business."

"As far as I could tell, she was happy," agrees Barbara Brown. "I think she was touched by the way he treated her."

The day after their wedding, Harlow and Bern held a reception on the grounds of their home. Arriving early, Colleen Moore noticed nothing amiss: "if she was anything other than her usual self, she was happier." Harlow's carefree manner seemed to confirm this. "Oh, Anita," she told actress Anita Page, "if I ever have a little girl, I want her to be just like you."

However content she appeared, Harlow's mismatch

with Bern was as obvious as ever. At the reception, actress Maureen O'Sullivan overheard "everyone wondering why she would marry him" and wagering how long it would last.

Bern's brother and sister-in-law, Henry and Miriam Bern, stayed in Beverly Hills for two weeks after the wedding and observed only "genuine affection" between the couple. "She idolized Paul," says Miriam Bern, who thought Harlow "a lovely person, both inside and out." Evidently she had told Howard Strickling the truth: in her marriage to Bern, sex was secondary. Friendship came first.

So did work. Buoyed by the success of *Red-Headed Woman*, Bern had convinced Thalberg to cast Harlow in *Red Dust*, a 1927 play originally purchased for Greta Garbo and John Gilbert. "Harlow was supposed to help Gilbert's waning popularity—make a bull out of him," recalled *Red Dust* screenwriter John Lee Mahin. True to form, Bern not only tried to save Gilbert's career, but intended to show Harlow in "a seething pit of lust, jealousy, and hate." He even encouraged producer Hunt Stromberg, director Jacques Feyder, and Mahin to emphasize such elements.

Mahin had other ideas. "I saw Clark Gable in a picture, and I went to Stromberg and said, 'This guy's got eyes like a child and a build like a bull. This is a perfect team.'" Sensing that Harlow and Gable did indeed share the same combination of childlike innocence and adult sexuality, Stromberg bypassed Bern and pitched their teaming to Thalberg, who approved the idea, raised *Red Dust*'s budget, replaced Jacques Feyder with veteran director Victor Fleming, and ordered the film's sets rebuilt and its script rewritten.

With production on *Red Dust* delayed, M-G-M

assigned photographer Clarence Sinclair Bull to soften Harlow's hard-boiled image. Bull posed her swimming at home, golfing with Bello, confiding in Mother Jean, and nuzzling Oscar, her pet Pomeranian. Unlike her suggestive screen wardrobe, Harlow wore her own favorite outfit: a loose blouse, bell-bottom trousers, tennis shoes, and no make-up or brassiere. The results revealed her youth and vitality, but Bull was not satisfied. "The prints showed her hair as a burned-up snow-white blob," he recalled. "I felt like the hero of *The Light That Failed*." Shooting at the studio near a hospital set, Bull noticed a small surgeon's lamp and aimed it at Harlow's hair. The effect "worked like a charm; it easily adjusted to any amount of light." Bull called the lighting "Harlow's halo" and never used it on anyone else, and although she rewarded him with a kiss "smack on the lips," his feelings for Harlow were fatherly. "I wanted to protect her, which sounds corny as hell," he wrote later. "But that was my love for the little girl" who was also "the most considerate and thoughtful star I ever worked with."

"All I want is to be able to sit at Paul's feet and have him educate me," confided Harlow to Colleen Moore at a party that summer. She also wanted to deed her Easton Drive home to Mother Jean and invest in a Mexican gold mine, Bello's latest business venture. Bern resented this bitterly, and his attempts to wrest his docile wife from her domineering mother strained relations not only between Bern and the Bellos, but him and Harlow as well.

The first public sign of their marital problems occurred at Moore's party. "A German stickler for protocol," Bern had instructed Harlow to address honored guest Prince Ferdinand von Liechtenstein as "Your Serene Highness." She did so throughout dinner, then during a poker game with the Prince. Eager to please her exacting husband, Harlow seemed more concerned with her manners than her cards.

Her opponent noticed and held up a hand. "Please, Jean," Prince Ferdinand chided. "No formalities. We're friends, aren't we?" Confident of victory, he showed his hand—a full house—without waiting to see hers. "Now, what do you have?" he asked politely.

Harlow grinned and laid down her cards. "Four queens, tootsie-boy Prince!" she whooped in triumph. Her behavior delighted "His Serene Highness" but outraged Bern, who grabbed Harlow and dragged her out the door. Fetching his coat, Moore felt a gun in its pocket.

Like most incidents involving Bern, this would later be embellished to include him hitting Harlow. Those present deny it. "His abuse was verbal," specifies Elaine St. Johns. "He belittled her intellect and character." By constantly trying to educate her, Bern made Harlow feel intellectually inferior and, both alone and in public, would remind her repeatedly of it. It was the sort of treatment "that she could least stand," says St. Johns. "For someone like Jean, even a black eye would have been better."

Unconsciously or not, Harlow tormented him, too. Attending the summer Olympic Games with the newlyweds in Los Angeles, Anita Loos watched Bern make "a great issue of his bride's comfort; supplying her with a cushion, a lap robe, a hot dog, a bottle of soda. Finally, he asked if he could get her anything more." Harlow indicated a muscular athlete. "Yes, Daddy," she giggled. "Get me that one!" Unaware of the couple's unconsummated marriage, Loos laughed aloud. Later she considered the taunt "thoughtlessly cruel."

By now Bern had entered a severe depressive stage. He bought another gun, wrote a new will, drank brandy heavily, and consulted two physicians, Dr. Herman Sugarman and Dr. Edward B. Jones, about his condition. Both prescribed sedatives but could not cure Bern's impotence. Despite his fixation with Freud, he did not seek psychotherapy.

On August 4, 1932, Irene Mayer Selznick gave birth to a son. Bern's refusal to visit the hospital hurt her deeply, though Harlow appeared alone and confided that she planned to adopt a baby. She also promised Skip and Ella Harlow that they would meet her new husband in October, when Bern stopped in Kansas City en route to New York on business. Meanwhile he prepared a future project, *China Seas*, for her.

On August 17, with *Red Dust* still not ready, Harlow and the Bellos went to San Francisco. An hour after their arrival, Hunt Stromberg called the Mark Hopkins Hotel and ordered Harlow to return immediately. She obeyed and discovered that, during her one-day absence, Bern's spirits had suddenly lifted. Reiterating his undying devotion, he filled her M-G-M dressing room with flowers and gifts. *Red Dust* actress Mary Astor envied the hand-embroidered handkerchiefs that Bern sent Harlow on the set.

Such gestures provided a brief relief from *Red Dust*'s production. "It was a difficult picture to do," recalls actor Gene Raymond, "because it was set in Indochina, but the whole thing was done at M-G-M. Stage 6 was now a jungle with a hut in it, and it stank to high heaven. The rain would seep in and all of a sudden you had mud. Then they put the hot lights on and it steamed up. So it was not a pleasant picture; it was hard for everybody, especially the crew." During a scene in a rainstorm, Mary Astor noticed steam "rising in waves" and realized the lights had literally "vaporized the water on our clothes and skin." Prop man Harry Edwards solved the problem by heating water in a teapot, then pouring it atop the actors before each take.

Harlow endured such conditions without complaint, earning the respect of Stromberg, Fleming, Rosson, and *Red Dust* technicians. "Garbo and Shearer would go straight to their dressing room between scenes, but Harlow would hang around with the crew like she was one of 'em," says Harry Edwards. "She was a regular gal, and we loved her for it." Unlike her haughty counterparts, Harlow listened to their dirty jokes, loaned them cash, and protected them from exploitation and mistreatment. When production manager J. J. Cohn abolished the crew's coffee break, Harlow summoned him to the set. "If they don't get a break," she warned, "then I don't come to work." The coffee breaks continued.

Red Dust provided additional perks. While shooting a scene in a rain barrel, Harlow suddenly stood up, bared her breasts, and shouted, "Something for the boys in the lab!" Before they could see it, Fleming yanked the film from the camera. "He knew it would've been all over the country instead of the lab," laughs Bill Edmondson. "Guys would've paid *anything* to see her like that."

Twenty months earlier Harlow and Gable had helped

each other through *The Secret Six*; though no longer neo-phytes, their mutual admiration remained. "Clark was *nuts* about the Baby," continues Edmondson. "He just thought the world of her." Asked about Harlow by actress Ida Lupino, Gable spoke from the heart. "She isn't full of shit," he stated. "She's the real thing." The result was an on-screen rapport which all assumed was real. "I've never seen two actors make love so convincingly," claimed Clarence Sinclair Bull, "without being in love."

Even during shooting, *Red Dust* was notorious. Visiting the steamy jungle set, newspaper columnist Sidney Skolsky was stunned to find the "Platinum Blonde" playing a pros-titute who bathes nude in a rain barrel, beds Gable *gratis*, and delivers wisecracks which, Skolsky wrote, "will never get past the censors." Even Gable admitted to "shock" at its script.

On August 31, Skolsky, his wife, Harlow, and Bern attended a dinner party in the apartment of M-G-M story editor Samuel Marx. "My first impression," remarks Es-telle Skolsky, "was that Jean Harlow was *gorgeous*—and she wasn't wearing underwear." By the evening's end, Es-telle Skolsky noted another, more troubling detail: beneath her obvious "sweetness," Harlow seemed "deeply inse-cure." Why? "Paul Bern *made* her insecure. He made her feel stupid, and she was not a stupid girl."

After dinner Sidney Skolsky mistook Bern's jacket for his own and, like Colleen Moore a month earlier, discov-ered a pistol in its pocket. "Oh, that's a new gun I got," said Bern. "I intend to use it someday." Believing him "too effeminate" to do so, Skolsky discounted Bern's "weird comment."

The following day, September 1, Dr. Harry Brandel of the Prudential Insurance Company came to M-G-M to examine Bern, who had purchased an $85,000 life insurance policy. The next day, September 2, Bern developed a story for *China Seas*, then dined at home with Harlow and *Freaks* co-writer Willis Goldbeck. When she went to bed at 9 P.M., the two men were still talking.

On Saturday, September 3, Harlow worked on *Red Dust* and Bern submitted a nine-page plot of *China Seas*. In its climax, the hero (Gable) forsakes his American fiancée (Harlow) for his Oriental mistress, "Yu Lan," and her criminal clan. "Stoically he goes back to the inner chamber where the others are gathered," Bern wrote. "He bares his arm, and in the presence of Yu Lan submits to the torture— finally dying in Yu Lan's arms." It was hardly appropriate for an M-G-M movie.

That night Bern and Harlow were expected at Fredric March's thirty-fifth birthday party but *Red Dust* delayed her. "I won't go without my darling wife," Bern told studio bootblack Harold "Slickem" Garrison, so instead he dined in an Ambassador Hotel bungalow with M-G-M producer Bernie Hyman and actress Barbara Barondess. "We talked about the theater," says Barondess. "He did not seem hilariously happy, but I had no idea of what was about to happen." Afterward Bern left Hyman and Barondess and returned home.

Harlow did not. Expected at the studio early Sunday, September 4, she decided to save time and sleep at Club View Drive, which was halfway between M-G-M and Easton Drive. Bern read scripts until sunrise, awoke on Sunday afternoon, and lay in bed with three books he had just bought. Their titles: *Discourse on the Worship of Priapus*, a 1786 treatise on the little god with a large phallus distributed by "The Dilettanti Society"; *The Glands Regulating Personality*, a classification of human character into glandular cases like "the Eunuchoid Personality," defined as "a flabby freak" with "the reproductive organs of a little boy"; and *The Biological Tragedy of Woman*, which cited German philosopher Arthur Schopenhauer's belief that "sexual love . . . exacts sacrificial offerings, sometimes of life."

While Bern was immersed in such subjects, Harlow worked on *Red Dust* and awaited Labor Day, which she would spend at home with her husband. Mother Jean objected, and since her own spouse planned to go marlin fishing before sunrise, she convinced her daughter to spend the night at Club View Drive. So that evening after shooting, Bello drove Harlow from M-G-M to Easton Drive, where she could get her own car and invite Bern to dinner. Blanche Williams accompanied them.

What occurred next will never, despite six decades of intense speculation, be fully known. For the rest of her life Harlow denied a rift with Bern although butler John Carmichael overheard "a big fight" between them about the Bellos, who were still pressuring Harlow to deed them her home and invest in a Mexican gold mine. Infuriated by their greed and manipulation, Bern refused to dine with his in-laws. Harlow offered to stay home. Bern ordered her to leave.

Harlow emerged in tears. "He wants me out of here," she told Blanche Williams, who did not inquire further.

Bern had always been strange. Nothing he did surprised her.

Nothing, that is, until now: the following morning, on September 5, 1932, Paul Bern stripped naked, stood before a full-length mirror, put a gun to his temple, and pulled the trigger.

Or did he?

Part Three

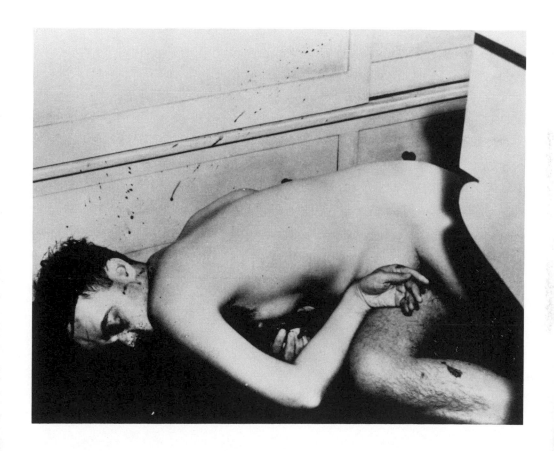

Who Killed Paul Bern?

Chapter Eleven

*S*chedule for a scandal:

Monday, September 5 (Labor Day)

3 A.M. Long before sunrise, M-G-M wardrobe man Ted Tetrick awakens Clark Gable and Marino Bello at their homes. The three men drive to Long Beach, then sail to Catalina Island, where they will spend the holiday fishing for marlin. None are aware of anything amiss.

11:30 A.M. John and Winifred Carmichael, butler and cook, arrive at Easton Drive. She makes coffee in the kitchen; he finds Bern's corpse on the dressing room floor. "It was quite pitiful," says Carmichael later. "He was lying in a puddle of blood." Bern's butler faints at the sight.

"You know, I was quite nervous and have been ever since," Carmichael will soon testify. At the time, he regains consciousness and runs from the house to get gardener

Clifton Davis. Meanwhile Winifred Carmichael calls Club View Drive. Mother Jean answers, learns of Bern's death, and calls Louis B. Mayer at his Santa Monica beach house. She does not tell her daughter.

Mayer calls M-G-M security chief Whitey Hendry and publicity department head Howard Strickling. While Hendry hurries to the studio, Strickling calls still photographer Virgil Apger and orders him to report to M-G-M immediately. Apger obeys without asking why.

Apger and Hendry meet at M-G-M, then leave for Easton Drive. Their driver is studio bootblack Harold "Slickem" Garrison. As the world will soon learn, Garrison also drove Bern to the Ambassador Hotel the previous Saturday night.

Back at the beach, Mayer leaves for Beverly Hills, instructing his wife to notify Irving Thalberg and Norma Shearer at their own home nearby. The news of Bern's death affects Thalberg so deeply that Shearer fears for his health.

Thalberg calls fellow beach-dweller David O. Selznick, whose wife overhears his side of the conversation. "Irving? My God! No! When? Oh, God, no!"

Irene Mayer Selznick senses the truth. "It's Paul, he's killed himself!" she cries. "I will kill her!" she vows, already blaming Harlow for Bern's suicide. Within hours all Hollywood will agree.

Recently recovered from childbirth, Irene Mayer Selznick takes to bed once again. Her husband departs with Thalberg and Shearer for Easton Drive.

12:15 P.M. Whitey Hendry and Virgil Apger arrive at the death scene. "Nobody was around but us," states Apger sixty years later. "The only other people there were the servants."

Apger photographs Bern's nude body. "It was gruesome," he says. "He was lying there all doubled up . . . It was a very sad thing."

It is also suspicious. "Why did they want *me* to take pictures?" Apger wonders. "Why not a *police* photographer?" Apger gives his film to Howard Strickling. He never sees it again.

12:30 P.M. Strickling arrives and combs the house for clues. On a table near Bern's body, he finds a morocco-bound guest book containing signatures from, among others, actor Gary Cooper (who drew a caricature of himself as a caballero); actress Lupe Velez; producer Ben Fineman; and Fineman's wife, the former Margaret de Mille.

On page thirteen of Bern's guest book, Strickling discovers a mysterious message:

> Dearest dear,
>   Unfortunately this is the only way to make good the frightful wrong I have done you and to wipe out my abject humiliation. I love you.
>
>   Paul
> You understand last night was only a comedy

12:45 P.M. Mayer arrives. Strickling shows him Bern's body and guest book, which Mayer decides to destroy. Strickling objects. Without it, Bern's suicide has no motive. Without it, Harlow might be suspected of murder.

Mayer agrees. Strickling puts back the guest book and leaves it open to page thirteen.

1 P.M. After an hour-long drive from the beach, Irving Thalberg, Norma Shearer, and David O. Selznick arrive. Reporters surround Easton Drive. No police are present.

Another hour passes. What transpires inside Bern's home remains unknown. Word of a studio cover-up spreads.

2:15 P.M. Two hours and forty-five minutes after John Carmichael found Bern's corpse, Thalberg reports his death to a police detective. "I told him where I was and what had happened and asked him to please send someone and do it as quickly and quietly as possible," he testifies later. Since newspapers are already running EXTRA! editions, his request is irrelevant.

2:30 P.M. Lieutenant detectives Joseph Whitehead and Thomas Sketchley arrive at Easton Drive. Because at least a dozen people have preceded them to the scene, it is impossible to tell whether evidence tampering has occurred.

Bern's body lies untouched. Hidden from sight beneath it, Whitehead finds a .38 revolver in Bern's right hand with its forefinger on the trigger. Since rigor mortis has already set in, he must pry the gun from Bern's grip.

Whitehead inspects the weapon, whose chamber holds six bullets. He finds five still inside and one embedded in a nearby wall. Its calibrations match the others.

On a nearby table, a second .38 sits beside Bern's open guest book. Whitehead and Sketchley examine each. The gun has not been fired. Bern's note seems suicidal.

Whitehead calls the coroner and, unaware of Virgil Apger's prior pictures, summons a police photographer. The investigation proceeds as normal, albeit three hours late.

3:15 P.M. Thalberg, Shearer, and Selznick arrive at Club View Drive. Sharing his prostrate wife's fury, Selznick stays in the car. So does Shearer.

Thalberg enters and informs Harlow of her husband's death. She collapses.

4 P.M. After a full day's fishing off Catalina Island, Ted Tetrick leaves Clark Gable and Marino Bello to buy more supplies. While ashore he sees a newspaper headline announcing Bern's death.

Tetrick rejoins his buddies and breaks the news. Gable is stunned; Bello barely reacts. "He wasn't upset at all," says Tetrick. "There was no love lost between him and Bern."

Tetrick and Gable prepare to return. Bello balks but is overruled. The three men leave for Los Angeles.

6 P.M. Harlow is hysterical. "Isn't this too horrible, isn't this too terrible," she moans repeatedly. Unable to calm her, Mother Jean calls Dr. Harold Barnard, who puts Harlow under sedation.

From his home in New Rochelle, New York, Henry Bern admits that his brother lived "under almost unbearable tension" but refuses to accept his suicide. "I read the 'Dearest dear' note in the newspapers and can't make head or tail of it," he tells reporters. "I'm going out there to find out what's behind it all."

Back in Hollywood, butler John Carmichael calls Bern and Harlow's marriage "blissful." He is contradicted by gardener Clifton Davis, who recounts the couple's fight the previous night and divulges that, after Harlow left Easton Drive on Sunday evening, a "big limousine" appeared. "I saw a woman in the car," claims Davis, "but I didn't know who she was." Bern's neighbor, montage editor Slavko Vorkapich, reports "a powerful car" roaring down Easton Drive early Monday morning.

Tuesday, September 6

"You're talking too much. Move your wife and children to the garage and keep your damned mouth shut," Marino Bello commands Clifton Davis, who follows orders and refuses to discuss Bern's death. Without his assistance, no clues are forthcoming.

Confronted by reporters, Bello "vigorously denies" seeking the deed to Easton Drive or funds for a Mexican gold mine. "I have more money than Bern ever had," he brags. "There was no occasion for any financial dealings between us."

Bello calls Harlow "ideally married" and claims he

learned of Bern's suicide upon his arrival home last night. Tetrick and Gable know better but say nothing. Neither wants any part of a potential scandal.

Describing her daughter as "delirious," Mother Jean prevents police detectives from questioning Harlow. Meanwhile Bello attends an emergency conference in the office of M-G-M's attorney, Mendel Silberberg. The studio has a serious problem: its most beloved executive is dead, and many hold his widow responsible. "If Jean Harlow doesn't make Paul Bern happy, there are hordes of women who will wring her shapely neck," a fan magazine had announced after their marriage; now, in the aftermath of her husband's mysterious death, "the press pilloried Jean; she became a villainess, not a victim," asserts Irene Mayer Selznick. "The community's hostility ran high. There was conjecture and hysteria." With a suicide motive missing and his widow incommunicado, District Attorney Buron Fitts decides to exploit public sentiment and indict Harlow for murder.

M-G-M takes charge. After an all-day delay, four detectives are suddenly admitted to Club View Drive. There, in the presence of Louis B. Mayer, Howard Strickling, Mendel Silberberg, and Dr. Barnard, a barely coherent Harlow discusses Bern's death. "I can't understand why this terrible thing should have happened," she sobs. Bern's so-called "suicide note" also bewilders her. "I have no idea what it means," Harlow wails. "This 'frightful wrong' Paul apparently thought he'd done me is a mystery." She recalls Bern's references to his mother's suicide but "never once" his own. "There was nothing between us," insists Harlow, "that would have caused him to do this."

The detectives depart. Mayer follows Harlow to an upstairs bedroom, shuts its door, and says he has just received word from Dr. Edward B. Jones, whom Bern had consulted after his wedding, that the deceased man suffered from "a terrific mental depression" due to his lack of "domestic relations." Harlow maintains that her marriage was happy. Mayer wants her to admit it was not consummated. Doing so will explain Bern's death and save her career.

Rather than consent, Harlow runs to the bedroom's balcony. Mayer restrains her. Later he boasts of saving her life.

His daughter believes it. "My father told me she tried to throw herself off the balcony," states Irene Mayer Selznick, "which hung over a rocky chasm. Only by catching hold of her robe was he able to stop her." Actually, the bedroom's balcony overlooks a flagstone terrace fifteen feet below, making Club View Drive's "rocky chasm" a figment of Mayer's imagination.

It does not matter: with melodramatic flourish, Mayer recounts Harlow's "attempt to follow her husband into eternity" to reporters, then claims Bern's demeanor "had entirely changed" during the last days of his life. "I had never seen him act so strangely before," says Mayer. "He had the queerest look in his eyes and appeared to have something preying on his mind." Besides Dr. Edward B. Jones, two other physicians confirm Bern's "acute melancholia" due to "a physical condition" which made him "unfit for matrimony." An autopsy report labels his genitals "underdeveloped."

A new rumor rages through Hollywood: Harlow's husband was a hermaphrodite.

Wednesday, September 7

Red Dust resumes shooting. Victor Fleming directs Gable, Mary Astor, and Gene Raymond in scenes without Harlow, whose fate on the film remains undetermined. Aware of this, Bello promises to deliver his stepdaughter to the studio soon. The fact that she is still semihysterical does not faze him.

Meanwhile, in his M-G-M office, an "oily and patronizing" Mayer asks actress Tallulah Bankhead to replace Harlow in *Red Dust*. She terms his offer "one of the shabbiest acts of all time." Mayer proceeds "to act out the circumstances of Bern's death." Bankhead departs in disgust.

After a two-day transcontinental flight, Henry Bern arrives in Los Angeles. "I want no secrecy veiling the matter of my brother's death," he declares. Stories of Bern's shrunken sex organ have reached him en route, and Henry Bern intends to refute them. As proof, he mentions a woman to whom Bern was once "morally married."

"She is alive," Henry Bern assures reporters. "I will reveal her identity later."

Howard Strickling takes Henry Bern directly to Club View Drive, where Mayer and Mendel Silberberg await him. He also talks to Harlow, and though the nature of their conversation is unknown, both seem shaken by it: Harlow sobs hysterically and Henry Bern leaves the house. "Certain complications make it impossible for me to give a statement," he tells newsmen tersely. "Please don't ask me what they are."

Back in his hotel room, Henry Bern places a call to "Miss D. Millette" at the Plaza Hotel in San Francisco. He is told that she checked out the previous day.

Thursday, September 8

10 A.M. The Los Angeles County coroner's inquest into the death of Paul Bern begins. Though served with a subpoena, his widow is not present. "Miss Jean Harlow has been under my care [for] a severe nervous collapse," reads a letter from Dr. Robert Kennicott. "Her appearance before the jury would gravely endanger her life." Henry Bern is also absent.

Bello is the first witness questioned. Listing his occupation as "mining," he lies under oath about when he learned of Bern's death. Bello also calls Bern "melancholy" and "extremely nervous" but insists that his marriage to Harlow was happy.

Asked whether or not Bern shot himself, Bello shrugs. "All I know is what I heard," he tells the jury.

The next witnesses, John and Winifred Carmichael, repeat M-G-M's official version of events. Naturally this excludes Bern and Harlow's fight on the night before his death, as well as Whitey Hendry and Virgil Apger's presence at Easton Drive the next morning. John Carmichael also swears that Irving Thalberg called the police at 1 P.M. even though detectives did not speak to him until 2:15.

Thalberg himself takes the stand. He describes Bern's mood swings, admits that Bern spoke of suicide, and identifies the "Dearest dear" note as Bern's handwriting. By now Bern's morocco-bound guest book has become a "diary" and is sensationalized as such.

The next witness, M-G-M business manager Martin Greenwood, offers no new details. Neither does gardener Clifton Davis, who now denies any "domestic inharmony" between Harlow and Bern and does not mention the mysterious woman in the large limousine. Fellow eyewitness Slavko Vorkapich, who could confirm her appearance at Easton Drive, is not called to testify.

The seventh witness, Harold "Slickem" Garrison, provides the first fresh information. According to Garrison, Bern always carried a gun and spoke "quite often" of suicide. "He said his mother had and it ran in his family, but he hoped he never would," Garrison testifies. He also admits driving Bern to the Ambassador Hotel on Saturday night but has no idea why he went there.

The subject is dropped during the testimony of Blanche Williams and detectives Joseph Whitehead and Frank Condaffer, who believe that Bern died by suicide. All the case lacks is a compelling motive.

The inquest's final witness, Dr. Frank Webb, provides one. Dr. Webb performed Bern's autopsy, so the coroner asks him what the world waits to hear:

Q. Did you examine all the organs?
A. I did.

Q. Find any diseased?

A. No disease of the organs.

Q. Find any deformities?

A. Only as stated, slightly underdeveloped.

Q. What was that?

A. Sexual organs showed slight underdevelop-
    ment—I would correct that. I would not
    say "underdevelopment," I would say *under-
    sized*. They were developed normally but
    undersized.

Q. Were they of such a character to indicate
    impotence?

A. No, sir.

All this means, of course, is that Bern's penis was physically capable of sexual intercourse. Whether he was emotionally equipped for it remains unresolved.

The jury reaches a verdict: suicide, "motive undetermined." The case is officially closed.

Unofficially, it is still wide open.

2 P.M. Barbara Barondess is beside herself. Through bad
luck and worse timing, Barondess and her married lover,
producer Bernie Hyman, had used Bern as their "beard" on
the last Saturday night of his life; now, after Harold
"Slickem" Garrison's inquest testimony, newsmen seek
Bern's "secret date" in the mistaken assumption that she
caused his suicide. "I needed this notoriety like a hole in the
head," recalls Barondess today. "Bernie avoided me and
smiled sickly when we did see each other on the M-G-M
lot." Desperate to disassociate herself from Bern's sordid

death, Barondess calls columnist Sidney Skolsky, who once loaned her $300 for an abortion. Returning the favor, she tells him the truth.

Skolsky gives M-G-M a choice: either he receives exclusive access to the studio, which has been off-limits to reporters since Bern's death, or he runs the Barondess-Hyman item in his column. M-G-M is so anxious to avoid further scandal that it accepts Skolsky's terms. No other newsmen uncover his "scoop."

Barondess asks no more. "Howard Strickling was amazed that I didn't demand stardom, but I didn't want it that way," she states. "I didn't want to be one of those girls who gets under a good producer and works her way up."

5 P.M. A second "mystery woman" surfaces, and unlike Barbara Barondess, her connection is not coincidental: according to initial reports, the lady in question lived at the Algonquin Hotel in New York as "Mrs. Paul Bern." Front-page stories surmise that she is the "phantom mate" to whom Bern was once "morally married."

Henry Bern confirms it. More defensive than ever about his brother's sexual behavior, he describes Bern's "tragic affair" with a woman who was once his common-law wife. Her name, he divulges, is Dorothy Millette.

Actually, she was born Dorothy Roddy on March 15, 1884, in Columbus, Ohio. Orphaned as a child, she had moved to Indianapolis, Indiana, and married journalist Lowell Mellett in 1907. When Mellett migrated west, his wife went to New York and enrolled at the American Academy of Dramatic Arts. Registering as "Mrs. L. Mellett," she took "Dorothy Millette" as her stage name and met a student in the senior class: Paul Levy, a/k/a Paul Bern.

Whether their relationship was physical or platonic is not known, but for the next nine years Bern and Millette cohabited in Toronto, Canada; Woonsocket, Rhode Island; Wilmington, Delaware; and Manhattan. Charging his wife with "continual abandonment," Lowell Mellett obtained a divorce, and although Bern never married Millette, he called her "my wife" and listed her as such on his 1917 naturalization petition and 1920 last will and testament. Nonetheless he hid her from friends and family, and with good reason: like his mother, Millette was mentally ill, and both women were obsessed with him. "Our mother told Paul she would die if he ever lived with a woman," said Bern's sister, Friederike Bern Marcus. Apparently she kept her word: informed of her son's secret life with a common-law, Gentile wife, Henrietta Levy jumped from an embankment. Bern blamed himself for her suicide and became preoccupied with the subject.

Millette's reaction was even more morbid. Convinced that she had caused his mother's death because of their different faiths, Millette developed "a religious complex," ranting to God and promising to join Him like Henrietta Levy. Bern sent her to the Blythewood Sanitarium, a posh "mental hygiene clinic" in Greenwich, Connecticut. She registered as "Mrs. Paul Bern." He went to Hollywood.

Several months later "Mrs. Paul Bern" returned to Manhattan and settled at the Algonquin Hotel. During the ensuing decade, while America's foremost wits held court at its "Round Table" (writer Dorothy Parker was also an Algonquin resident), Dorothy Millette remained in her room, a virtual recluse dependent on funds from her "husband," which she honestly thought Bern to be.

So did he. "Paul talked about her a great deal," says Irene Mayer Selznick. "He would say, 'I'm as good as married. There was no ceremony, but I was married to Dorothy.' And he supported her; Irene Harrison, his secretary at the studio, sent her money each month." Though he rarely corresponded himself, Bern saw Millette during business trips to New York but "came away sick" from the experience.

In May 1932, after a dozen years at the Algonquin, Millette moved to San Francisco to be near her sister, Violet Roddy Hessler. Irene Harrison rented a room at the Plaza Hotel, where for the next four months "Miss D. Millette" lived in anonymity, "avoiding all guests and repulsing all attempts at conversation."

The sudden revelation that she is Bern's "other woman" renders Millette's privacy impossible. Now her name makes headlines. The world awaits her story.

There is no one to tell it. Dorothy Millette has disappeared.

Friday, September 9

7 *A.M.* BERN RIDDLE INCREASES; 'OTHER WOMAN' SUICIDE FEARED, claims the Los Angeles *Times*. Contributing to "the huge question mark" hovering over Bern's death is the discovery that, a day later, Dorothy Millette boarded the *Delta King*, a riverboat bound for Sacramento. She has not been seen since.

Henry Bern admits that upon his arrival in Hollywood, he had tried to call Millette at her hotel. "I wanted to tell her to keep calm and not worry about anything," he explains, "[but] they told me she had checked out."

Bern's brother knows better. "I'm afraid poor Dorothy is dead," he sighs. Others speculate that Millette has staged a "hoax suicide" to elude San Francisco police, who search every hotel and rooming house in the city. Meanwhile the muddy Sacramento River is dragged for her body.

2 P.M. Paul Bern's funeral service begins in the Grace Chapel of Inglewood Park Cemetery. While fifty invited guests assemble inside, thousands jam the streets, gaping at celebrities and jostling for position. "The place was *swarming*," recalls M-G-M publicist Dean Dorn. "The crowd, the press, the cameras . . . We could barely cope with it."

Howard Strickling orders Dorn to guard Bern's body. "With all the stories going around, he wanted to make sure it wasn't desecrated," Dorn continues. "The studio had enough on its hands already."

A "wan and haggard" Harlow makes a dramatic entrance with Marino Bello and Willis Goldbeck, who had dined with her and Bern on the Friday before his death. Clad in widow's weeds with a black veil hiding her face, she "leans heavily" on Bello and Goldbeck as they approach a side entrance reserved for family members.

Although other mourners cannot see her, Harlow's sobs are audible throughout the service. Irving Thalberg also weeps openly, as do Irene Harrison and Friederike Bern Marcus. "In shock" over Dorothy Millette's disappearance, Henry Bern does not attend.

By M-G-M standards, the service is "simple and unpretentious." Actor Conrad Nagel delivers a brief eulogy denying Bern's "self-destruction" (a devout Christian Scientist, Nagel refuses to accept his suicide), then Rabbi Edgar Magnin recites the Kaddish, a Hebrew prayer for the dead. Afterward Mayer himself leads Harlow to the open casket. She bursts into tears at the sight, "crying openly and staggering." Bello and Goldbeck escort her outside.

A mob scene ensues. "When I left the chapel after Paul's funeral, people broke through the police lines and surged around me," Harlow would shudder later. "There were ghastly words and demands for autographs.

"I was shocked. They seemed heartless. To them I was not a person, I was an institution. I had no more personality than a corporation." Hurt and dehumanized, she secludes herself at Club View Drive.

Back at the cemetery, M-G-M prop man Ray O'Brien accepts a grisly assignment: to witness Bern's cremation. "They asked other people, but no one would do it," recalls Harry Edwards. "The body was covered, but the head was visible so he could identify it." This guards against a stolen or substitute corpse.

O'Brien oversees Bern's cremation. His ashes remain at the cemetery.

Saturday, September 10

With a "motive undetermined" for her brother's suicide and his "ex-mistress" still missing, Friederike Bern Marcus holds a press conference. "Why did he do it?" she demands.

"What drove him to it? Aren't we entitled to know? Why don't the ones who *do* know tell us?" It is a direct hint to Harlow, who does not respond. Word spreads that she will flee Hollywood forever. The fate of *Red Dust* is still undetermined.

According to tabloids, Harlow traveled to San Francisco in August for "a secret meeting" with Millette. Bello denies it. "We knew nothing of Bern's past life," he proclaims. "If we had, the wedding would have taken place over my dead body."

A Sacramento judge issues a search warrant for Millette's belongings. Police find polite letters from Bern and Irene Harrison but no incriminating information. A bathing cap that matches an empty container on the *Delta King* is also discovered. The swimsuit is missing.

Though men still drag the Sacramento River and motorboats search its still waters, experts believe that a body would have surfaced already. Since it hasn't, a new hypothesis replaces the "suicide hoax": Millette has been kidnapped and murdered.

Sunday, September 11

Instead of sympathy or compassion, Mother Jean reads Rudyard Kipling's poem "If" to her daughter. Afterward she "made it applicable to the situation, pointing out to the Baby how poor, defeated Paul might not have been defeated had he met the challenge in that great poem."

Harlow telephones Irving Thalberg. "Staying around here is driving me crazy," she says. "I've got to get busy."

Thalberg confers with Mayer, who senses a shift in public opinion. Stories of Bern's secret past have won sympathy for his widow, and letters of support deluge the studio. "She was truly a heroine," realizes Irene Mayer Selznick. "When I learned of her gallantry, I was ashamed of my violent feelings."

Mayer makes a decision: *Red Dust* will finish shooting with its original star. She will report to its set tomorrow.

Monday, September 12

Without fanfare or publicity, Harlow slips into a side entrance at M-G-M and resumes work on *Red Dust*. Bello and private nurse Adah Wilson accompany her. "Jean is going on," approves a fan magazine. "And that's the best tribute she could pay to Paul's memory."

"The day she came back, she was really subdued, and for the Baby to be subdued was *something*," recalls Bill Edmondson. To ease the tension, Victor Fleming approaches and puts his arm around Harlow, "which wasn't his style at all." Privately he is appalled. "How," he murmurs to Mary Astor, "are we going to get a sexy performance with *that* look in her eyes?" For the rest of the day Fleming uses Harlow in long shots, which hide her haunted expression.

"There was a lot of deference to her, but she didn't seem to want it," adds Edmondson, "not even at a time like that. She was a trouper." Harlow's sole request occurs the next day, during retakes of the film's raciest scene. "Don't you know?" she must boast while bathing nude in a rain barrel. "I'm La Flamme, the gal that drives men mad."

Harlow looks to writer John Lee Mahin. "I don't have to say that, do I?" she asks quietly. "I'm sure you don't," he assures her. The retake is unusable anyway.

Wednesday, September 14

Seven days after her disappearance, two fishermen find Dorothy Millette's "terribly decomposed" body in a slough off the Sacramento River. Evidently she had jumped from the *Delta King* and been washed away by its paddle wheel. An autopsy determines "asphyxiation by drowning." The coroner calls it "suicide."

Held in the county morgue three days later, Millette's funeral draws neither friends nor relations. Now the editor of the Washington, D.C., *Daily News*, ex-husband Lowell Mellett wants no part of her notoriety, while the $38 found in her purse will barely buy a pauper's grave in a potter's field. Apprised of this, Harlow arranges "a decent burial" for Millette at her own expense. A granite gravestone bears the heading:

DOROTHY MILLETTE BERN
1886 [*sic*]–1932

Whether this name confirms her common-law marriage is a matter of speculation, then litigation: located by lawyers, Millette's two sisters, Mary Roddy Hartranft and Violet Roddy Hessler, sue Harlow for half of Bern's estate. Estimates of it exceed $100,000.

His legal wife learns otherwise. Despite his $1,500 per

week salary, Bern's bank account contains exactly $360.86. He owes $19,000 on a Beverly Hills property worth half that, $16,000 to assorted creditors (including M-G-M, which bills Bern's estate for studio police posted at Easton Drive after his death), and $12,000 in back taxes. Purchased four days before his death, his $85,000 life insurance policy contains a "suicide clause" and is automatically canceled.

Bern's estate is insolvent, and Harlow is held accountable. She pays his debts without complaint.

Six decades later, one question persists: who killed Paul Bern? Longy Zwillman liked to take credit for the crime, while Henry Bern blamed a paid assassin acting on Bello's orders. Only District Attorney Buron Fitts considered Harlow a suspect, though her absence from the coroner's inquest caused such conjecture that five months later Fitts personally questioned her in, of all places, a suite at the Ambassador Hotel. Recorded in shorthand, her statement was never transcribed.

At the Ambassador, the corrupt DA also conferred with gardener Clifton Davis, bootblack Harold "Slickem" Garrison, and cook Winifred Carmichael, all of whom contradicted their sworn testimony at the coroner's inquest. Asked again about the last night of Bern's life, Davis described Bern's row with Harlow over the deed to Easton Drive; Garrison confirmed it; and Carmichael recalled hearing Bern shout, "Get out of my life!" to a fleeing female figure. The next morning Carmichael found a woman's swimsuit by the pool. It was not Harlow's size, and it was still wet.

Fitts showed Carmichael a photograph of Dorothy

Millette. "This is the woman I saw," she said. "I'm sure of it." Her statement was also suppressed.

It did not matter. After abundant circumstantial evidence—Clifton Davis saw a woman arrive in a limousine, Slavko Vorkapich heard her depart, and the mysterious swimsuit found by Winifred Carmichael matched both a bathing cap in Millette's hotel room and an empty container on the *Delta King*—an eyewitness had placed Dorothy Millette at Easton Drive on the night of Paul Bern's death. This did not necessarily make her a murderess, yet Bern's friends believed she was. In an unpublished interview fifty years later, director Henry Hathaway still insisted that Bern had "scored with women all the time" until his prowess proved fatal:

> Paul had lived with a woman in New York who considered herself his wife. When he married Harlow, she went berserk. She was living at the Algonquin Hotel and the owner, Frank Case, wrote Paul a letter suggesting he do something. Well, Paul was in no position to do *anything*. "I can't go back there," he told me. "You know Dorothy." That was her name: Dorothy Millette.
>
> The day Paul died, I went to the house and talked to John Carmichael, the butler. He told me Dorothy Millette had come to the house and Harlow had walked in and found out what was going on. They had an argument, and finally Harlow said, "Well, when you find out who you're married to, let me know." And she went to her mother's.
>
> Paul finally got rid of Dorothy Millette and sat down

to write Harlow a note. The "comedy" and his "abject humiliation" were about the accidental meeting between his two wives! He was going to send it to Harlow with flowers the next day, which is what he usually did—but before he could, Dorothy Millette came back and shot him. Then she went to San Francisco and committed suicide.

The studio covered the whole thing up. Better to impugn Paul's masculinity and make Harlow an innocent dupe than have her party to bigamy.

Minor errors aside (Millette "went berserk" in 1920, not 1932, and was in San Francisco, not New York, when Bern and Harlow married), Hathaway's allegation ignores the case's single piece of solid evidence: Bern's gun, which police detective Joseph Whitehead found beneath his body and pried from his grip. Until then it had been hidden from sight, leading Hathaway, who saw the body *before* Whitehead's arrival, to a false conclusion: observing Bern's corpse but not the gun beneath it, the director noticed a .38 on a nearby table—Bern's *other, unused* gun—and mistook it for the death weapon. And since "a suicide does not usually throw a gun six feet away after killing himself," Hathaway viewed the coroner's verdict as an M-G-M cover-up. Actually, it was accurate. Bern committed suicide. Had the police been called promptly, no confusion would have occurred.

His "motive undetermined" remained a mystery. Besides the standard theory of sexual impotence, stories circulated about a masochistic "mistress" whom Bern liked to watch naked or, in another version, abuse with a whip. When he married Harlow, this jealous mistress supposedly summoned Millette from New York. Faced with scandal and disgrace, Bern shot himself. His mistress was supposedly his secretary, Irene Harrison.

Harrison had refused to discuss Bern's death, "I don't know anything," she told newsmen at the time, "and if I did, I wouldn't tell you." Sixty years later, at age ninety-one, Bern's secretary finally breaks her silence. "Dorothy Millette did not murder Paul Bern," she states today. "She was a gentle person. But she *did* get upset about his wedding to Miss Harlow—who, by the way, knew all about her." And the rumor that Harrison was Bern's masochistic mistress? "I was his *secretary*. I took care of the files and kept my mouth shut." Hounded by the press and her "emotions running haphazard," Harrison left M-G-M to work for fan dancer Sally Rand.

Bern's sexuality was still insoluble. Always a friend but never a lover, his asexual image was widely assumed to hide homosexual instincts, resulting in a textbook case of sexual repression and suicide. Sidney Skolsky, who thought Bern "too gentle, too effeminate," heard that Howard Strickling had destroyed a second suicide note "addressed to one of Bern's superiors at the studio [that] implied a relationship between the two men that would have been extremely embarrassing to the executive." Since only Mayer and Thalberg occupied such positions, Skolsky's unnamed source was mistaken—unless, of course, this purported piece of evidence concerned a third party.

According to Ted Tetrick, it did. "Bern was a homosexual," he states. "That's the reason for his suicide." Tetrick was told of "a boyfriend" named "Jack" who did bit parts at the studio. "He was a good young actor, but not a famous one. He's dead now." At the time, however, Bern's alleged male lover was very much alive, so "he married the Baby as a cover. I don't think she ever knew." If not, she may have suspected it: decades later, Dr. Harold Barnard divulged that, in a confidential conversation, Harlow acknowledged that Bern had "attempted something along the homosexual line, some kind of deviation." Since he declined to elaborate, Dr. Barnard's definition of "deviation"—formed in an era when Charles Chaplin's teenage wife divorced him for demanding fellatio—may have included acts now considered normal. Like so much about Bern's sexuality, the truth will never be known.

Its consequences are clear. By the time he met Harlow, Bern was incapable of consummating a marriage; that he would wed her anyway was madness. "There's something of Bern in *The Barefoot Contessa*," confessed writer-director Joseph L. Mankiewicz of his film about a movie star's tragic marriage to an impotent man. "He loved beautiful women with whom he could do nothing. That's the dreadful thing about impotence: you can only go so far, and then the woman expects you to . . . and you *can't*. What follows is a great humiliation, which Freud would say you wanted all along.

"His mistake was to marry Harlow; it took his masquerade too far. To have a symbol of sex as a wife and be unable to . . . If you have any sensitivity—which Paul certainly did—it would be devastating."

To those familiar with his family history and personal problems, Bern's suicide seemed a foregone conclusion. The question was not "if" but *when*, with Harlow an unwitting answer. As a sexual symbol married to a sexual imposter, she placed her husband in an excruciating plight that presumably hastened his suicide. The surprise appearance of Dorothy Millette supplied a second motive: bigamy. Though it was illegal in California, the state of New York recognized common-law marriage, which made Bern a bigamist if Millette chose to press charges.

Bern's two wives sealed his fate. After renouncing both ("He wants me out of here," Harlow sobbed to Blanche Williams; "Get out of my life!" Winifred Carmichael overheard Bern tell Millette), he went to his dressing room, removed his clothes, reached for the gun he always carried but never fired, regarded his "undersized" member in a mirror, and used his weapon for the first and final time. Anita Loos called it "the very apotheosis of masochism," though it was viciously sadistic as well: in the last act of his lifelong psychodrama, Bern pulled the trigger *after Harlow's arrival* that Labor Day morning, causing her to find his corpse and face the consequences. "She was in the house when he died," confirms Elaine St. Johns. "Howard Strickling told me so himself. He said she called him in a state of hysteria and said, 'Paul just killed himself.'" Strickling rushed to Easton Drive, and although Adela Rogers St. Johns claimed she accompanied him, her daughter doubts it. "Howard never said she did, and he was extremely close to me. So I don't believe Mom was there."

Strickling spirited Harlow to Club View Drive, apprised Mother Jean of the situation, then summoned Whitey Hendry and Virgil Apger to the studio. Meanwhile Mother Jean alerted Mayer in Santa Monica and ordered her daughter to feign shock at Bern's death. Harlow followed direction so dutifully that when Thalberg arrived to break the "news," she gave "the performance of her life."

As Henry Hathaway suspected and Howard Strickling later admitted, the "suicide note" in Bern's guest book was actually an apology to Harlow, whose chance meeting with Millette "last night was only a comedy." Had he lived, Bern's words would have been sent with a bouquet ("the only way to make good the frightful wrong I have done you") to Harlow's studio dressing room, where Sada's Flowers of Culver City made daily deliveries. After his suicide, the note assumed a significance it was never intended to have.

So did Dorothy Millette, whose suicide honored her 1920 vow to join God like Henrietta Levy. Before she mimicked Bern's mother and drowned, Millette lived in anonymity. She did not expect her death to be different.

I'd have liked to have gone to bed with Jean Harlow. She was a beautiful broad. The fellow who married her was impotent and he killed himself. I would have done the same thing.

—*Groucho Marx*

What a Marx brother found funny was no joke to Harlow, who weathered a crisis with dignity and courage. Irene Mayer Selznick called her a heroine, and soon others followed suit. "Hollywood is extremely proud of Jean Harlow," a fan magazine announced. "How many twenty-one-year-old girls could stand the grueling test of character Jean has endured and come out with flying colors?"

The outcome was unprecedented. Six weeks after Bern's suicide, *Red Dust* opened to critical raves and record-breaking business. *Time* knew why: "The best lines go to Harlow. She bathes hilariously in a rain barrel and reads Gable a bedtime story about a chipmunk and a rabbit ["Say, I wonder how *this* comes out?" her character wisecracks]. Her effortless vulgarity, humor, and slovenliness make a noteworthy characterization, as good in the genre as the late Jeanne Eagels' Sadie Thompson." Comparison to a legendary stage star like Eagels was heady praise for Harlow, a former subject of critical scorn. No one mocked her now.

A key-city survey during *Red Dust*'s release reflects theater exhibitors' awe and relief that, amid the Depression, a movie could still "clean up" in Kansas City, "get the dough" in Seattle, "top the town" in New Haven, and do "wow biz" in Detroit. *Red Dust* was "a winner" in Portland, "a smash" in San Francisco, "the current box-office champ" in Cincinnati, and "b.o. dynamite" in Minneapolis, whose "populace is whispering about it as the last word in red-hot sexiness."

"*Red Dust* is gold dust," exulted a Pittsburgh exhibitor. "Gable and Harlow spell swell b.o." And although Gable was billed above her, "Harlow's draw is stronger," as was her impact. Watching *Red Dust* in a 5,400-seat theater, a New York *Times* critic noted "platinum blondes on all sides" studying their idol on-screen.

Red Dust grossed $1.2 million, triple its $408,000 cost; *Motion Picture Herald* named it the season's number-one draw; and Loew's chairman Nick Schenck promised stockholders another Harlow-Gable vehicle as soon as possible.

In retrospect, the movie's most remarkable feat went unrecorded: for the first time in film history, a star had not only survived a scandal, but emerged more popular than ever. Instead of destroying Harlow's career, Bern's suicide strengthened it, transforming her image from immoral siren to innocent victim. In an only-in-Hollywood irony, tragedy and disgrace brought Harlow admiration and respect. Now she was no longer a national joke.

Absolved of Bern's death, Harlow blamed herself anyway. Her late husband's history of mental illness, manic-depressive mood swings, and manipulation of beautiful but insecure women meant nothing to a twenty-one-year-old who romanticized her relationships. So what if he had sexual problems? Who cared if he staged his suicide so she would find his body, face a scandal, endanger her career, and assume his debts? Bern's bizarre neuroses had no effect on Harlow, who truly believed that trust had brought them together and sex had torn them apart—and sex, of course, was what she symbolized. The result: she was the sinner to Bern's saint, the sadist to his masochist. Actually, it was the other way around.

That winter Harlow attended a dinner party hosted by Irving Thalberg and Norma Shearer. Rising to greet her, Irene Mayer Selznick was stunned by her reaction. "You don't have to," Harlow murmured. "I understand how you must feel." In fact, it was how *she* felt. Selznick offered sympathy and support; Harlow thought herself unworthy of either.

The situation worsened when Thalberg suffered his second heart attack (M-G-M called it "influenza") on

Christmas morning at age thirty-three. Usually unemotional, Thalberg had sobbed throughout Bern's funeral service, and though his cardiac condition was well known, many attributed this seizure to his closest friend's suicide. Aware of this, Harlow showed her guilt by drowning her sorrows. At a holiday party on the M-G-M lot, script clerk Willard Sheldon saw "a girl lying on the ground. It was the Baby. People were just passing by, so I picked her up and helped her inside." Though heavy drinking was almost an occupational hazard in Hollywood, "the Baby" seemed just that. Sheldon was shocked.

To her mother's horror, Harlow's new habit was soon an open secret. Though she played the teetotaler with certain people—"I just don't like the taste of it," Harlow told Virginia Conway—her bouts of depression precipitated alcoholic binges. "After Paul's death, she began drinking," states Jacqueline Smith, Harlow's stand-in and practitioner Genevieve Smith's daughter, "which was not something Christian Science approved of. But she *liked* to drink; it was her escape from unhappiness." So was Agua Caliente, a posh Tijuana resort where liquor and gambling were widespread and legal. "She *loved* craps," Barbara Brown recalls. "When we went to Caliente, she wouldn't let anybody stand behind her but me." On the New Year's Eve after Bern's death and Thalberg's heart attack, Mother Jean accompanied Harlow to Caliente but could not control her drinking. It was the start of a serious problem.

Later, in the guise of fiction, Harlow described her dependency. *I've got to have a drink*, she wrote. *I wonder if I'm getting to be a real drunkard? No. I'm drinking only because I have to have something to keep me going. If I were leading a normal life, I'd drink only to be sociable.* Since normalcy seemed inconceivable to a bride at sixteen, a bit player at seventeen, a star at eighteen, a divorcée at nineteen, a mobster's mistress at twenty, then a bride once again at twenty-one (and a widow two months later), Harlow sought solace in liquor. She could not find it anywhere else.

Part Four

Bombshell

Chapter Twelve

$\mathcal{B}$y 1933, the Depression had hit even Hollywood. A third of the nation's movie theaters closed; ticket sales plummeted from 110 million to 60 million per week; Columbia, Universal, and Warner Brothers suffered crippling losses; and Fox, Paramount, and RKO went into bankruptcy or receivership. Only M-G-M posted an $8 million profit, and when President Franklin D. Roosevelt declared a nationwide "bank holiday" in March, it was the sole movie studio not only to meet its payroll, but to compensate its workers in cash.

Invoking a "national emergency" clause in employee contracts, Hollywood studios slashed salaries in half. It was an act of desperation everywhere except at M-G-M, which promoted the policy as patriotism: not only had Roosevelt called movie-star salaries "unconscionable," but compared to the average family income of $1,600 a year, Harlow's $1,500 per week did seem obscene. With this in mind, Louis B. Mayer assembled M-G-M workers on March 9 and announced a "voluntary" 50 percent pay cut, to take effect immediately and to last for eight weeks. Later such inequities would lead to unionization, but for now no one dared oppose him. The studio withheld full wages for a month.

The next day a literal shock shook the studio: late that afternoon an earthquake struck southern California, killing hundreds and leveling Long Beach, the city at its epicenter. In nearby Culver City, M-G-M gate columns "were waving like spaghetti" as frantic executives, stars, and crew members sought safety in doorways. "I was walking across the lot to take a dancing lesson," recalled Harlow. "My first thought was of my mother's safety." Busy building a mansion with her daughter's money, Mother Jean disregarded the disaster.

Harlow's dancing lessons were for *The Hollywood Revue of 1933*, an all-star extravaganza with a score by Richard Rodgers and Lorenz Hart. Both men liked Harlow—"she taught my wife to shoot craps," Rodgers remembered—but bemoaned her total lack of musical talent. "Jean Harlow can't sing a lick," revealed the *Hollywood Reporter*. "When Rodgers and Hart listened to the platinum blonde do the scales, they raised their hands in horror." Eventually the duo composed "A Prayer," a switchboard operator's plea for stardom. "Gauged to fit Harlow's voice, the whole tune, verse and chorus, only covers a range of six notes," the *Reporter* continued. When even this proved too taxing, Mayer withdrew Harlow from the film. Rodgers and Hart gave "A Prayer" new lyrics and another title: "Blue Moon."

Before sailing to Europe for an extended convalescence, Irving Thalberg had hired Anita Loos to write a sex comedy for Harlow and Gable. Loos obliged with *Black*

Orange Blossoms, a rowdy tale of two con artists struggling to survive the Depression. Like *Red-Headed Woman* and *Red Dust,* the heroine of *Black Orange Blossoms* had unpunished premarital sex, a plot point which Mayer, who had story approval during Thalberg's absence, would not permit. Public furor over Harlow's films had already forced the Hays Office to tighten its Production Code, so when Mayer demanded that all "fallen" women reform by the fade-out, Loos took orders literally and ended *Black Orange Blossoms* in—where else?—reform school, where Harlow paid for her sins before winning Gable, who also went straight, in the final reel. And since Mayer would not name an M-G-M movie after an alcoholic beverage, *Black Orange Blossoms* became *Hold Your Man.*

Without Thalberg to oversee its structure and characterization, *Hold Your Man* suffered a split personality: after a bawdy beginning, Harlow and Gable are duly, dully rehabilitated in a finish unsuited to its start. And despite her vocal debacle with Rodgers and Hart, Harlow performed *Hold Your Man*'s title song on-screen. "They have me singing in a reformatory!" she warned reporters. "My singing would be enough to get me in, but I'd never be able to sing my way out."

It hardly mattered. Ignoring tepid reviews, audiences embraced *Hold Your Man* in huge numbers. "The popularity of the Harlow-Gable combination cannot be questioned," the New York *Times* noted. "Virtually every seat in the Capitol Theater was taken after its doors opened for the first showing of *Hold Your Man.*" Amid the most serious slump in film history, *Variety* called Harlow's latest release "the most promising money picture in months," a prediction which proved correct. *Hold Your Man* cost $266,000 and grossed $1.1 million, a 400 percent profit.

In a single year, Harlow's three M-G-M films had made $3 million. Only Marie Dressler, a sixty-three-year-old comic who was the studio's most popular star, could claim such success, which led to yet another advancement: like Dressler, Harlow was deemed commercial enough to carry a movie without an established leading man. Greta Garbo and Norma Shearer also shared this honor, but each made only one production per year; after *Hold Your Man*, exhibitors demanded *five* Harlow films in the same period, more than any other M-G-M actress. "On the verge of ruin" after two colossal flops, Joan Crawford was not even in the same category.

Crawford hated Harlow. "Joan was quite jealous," reveals journalist Dorothy Manners, who had known Crawford since her arrival in Hollywood eight years earlier. "She'd been the sexpot of the M-G-M lot for years, and then they brought in the Baby." Decades later Crawford would call Harlow "one of Metro's real biggies, but a more tragic person you can't imagine," but at the time she had no sympathy whatsoever. Crawford's then-husband, Douglas Fairbanks, Jr., termed her attitude toward Harlow a "controlled detestation."

"The Baby and I became friends immediately," continues Dorothy Manners. "When Joan found out, she let me have it. 'If you're going to see *her*, you'll have to give up *me*.'" Cowed by Crawford ("Joan was strong; we *minded* Joan") but loyal to Harlow, Manners saw her new pal in secret.

Another of Crawford's outbursts occurred during

Dancing Lady, a musical she considered beneath her dramatic skills. Aware of this, producer David O. Selznick provoked Crawford on purpose. "Joan, I don't know if you can play this part," Selznick told her. "It's kind of tarty. I think it's more Jean Harlow's style."

Crawford bristled. "Look, Mr. Selznick," she snapped, "I was playing hookers before Harlow knew what they were, so let's not hear any talk about style because I know more about that than she ever will." Selznick held his laughter until Crawford left his office.

Prior to *Hold Your Man,* Selznick demanded Harlow for *Dinner at Eight,* an all-star adaptation of the hit Broadway play. In a cast which included Marie Dressler, John and Lionel Barrymore, Wallace Beery, and Billie Burke—veteran troupers with more than a century of experience between them—Harlow was a neophyte, and she knew it. "She was so insecure about working with these people," states Selznick's assistant, Marcella Rabwin. "She would come into my office and say, 'Do you think I can talk to Mr. Selznick?' She didn't realize she was important! She had no idea." It was a welcome contrast to Crawford, whose sense of self-importance was all too apparent.

In *Dinner at Eight,* Harlow played "Kitty Packard," the tarty wife of a *nouveau riche* tycoon (Wallace Beery) who spends her days in bed, eating bonbons and awaiting house calls from her doctor-lover. When her husband wins a prestigious Cabinet position in Washington, Kitty refuses to relocate and ruin her chance to crash New York society. "You're not gonna drag *me* down to that graveyard," she snarls. "Pinning medals on Girl Scouts and pouring tea for the D.A.R.s and rolling Easter eggs on the White House lawn—a swell lotta fun *I'd* have." The *Red-Headed Woman* was classy by comparison, and like all who knew her, Marcella Rabwin stresses the disparity between Harlow and her role. "It's ironic, because today Kitty Packard is all people see, and that isn't the Baby at all. She wasn't flashy, she was *shy*. Kitty Packard is the actress, not the person."

Normally Harlow never studied herself during shooting, but during *Dinner at Eight* she asked to see dailies in Selznick's private projection room. Rabwin arranged it and received "a big bottle" of *L'Heure Bleu,* Harlow's favorite perfume, in return. Though touched by the gesture, Rabwin felt it indicated Harlow's "severe inferiority complex. If anyone did anything for her, she'd give them a present. She was expressing gratitude for practically *nothing.*"

Harlow was especially grateful to *Dinner at Eight* director George Cukor, whom Selznick had brought from RKO especially for the film. "Cukor gave her a lot of aid," says assistant director Joseph Newman. "He gave her an understanding of the role, which was the exact opposite of her personality."

Cukor himself declined all credit. "When I first saw her in *Hell's Angels,* she was so bad she was comic," he recalled. "People laughed at her; she got big laughs where she didn't want them. Then she did *Red-Headed Woman* and *Red Dust* and was marvelous. She was unique among actresses; she had that rare quality of speaking lines as though she didn't quite understand them." On *Dinner at Eight,* Cukor realized that Harlow "knew exactly what she was doing" and let her do it. "I don't think you can teach people how to be funny," he explained. "You can make suggestions about how to speak a line or get a laugh, but it has to be in them." Harlow, concluded Cukor, "played comedy as naturally as a hen lays an egg."

Although she worked only ten days on *Dinner at Eight*, Harlow's scenes caused tremendous technical difficulties. To match her trademark hair and wardrobe, art directors Hobe Erwin and Fred Hope had designed Kitty Packard's boudoir in eleven shades of white. "They said it couldn't be done," boasts Hope's widow, "because there'd be no contrast in values. But my husband and Hobe used shadows for contrast." Against such a blinding background, even the smallest shadow appeared on-camera, including one cast by Harlow's pubic hair. To hide it, the "Platinum Blonde" was bleached both above and below, and when even this was not enough, studio hairdresser Edith Hubner affixed a snow-white "wiglet" to Harlow's head and cameraman William Daniels shot her close-ups through strips of gauze.

Dissatisfied with *Dinner at Eight*'s original, downbeat ending, Selznick hired humorist Donald Ogden Stewart to devise a different one. Stewart, who had created *Red Dust*'s racy coda, surpassed it by having Kitty Packard inform "Carlotta Vance" (Marie Dressler) that she "was reading a book the other day."

Carlotta does a double take. "Reading a book?" she asks in astonishment.

Kitty, oblivious, continues. "Yes, it's all about civilization or something, a *nutty* kind of a book," she chatters. "Do you know that the guy said that machinery is going to take the place of *every profession*?"

Carlotta eyes Kitty from top to bottom. "Oh, my dear," she murmurs, "that's something *you* need never worry about." Ignorant of the insult, Kitty follows her into the dining room as the film ends.

Shot on its final day of production, *Dinner at Eight*'s last scene attracted a large crowd of onlookers. "The Baby and Dressler had a great time doing it," remembered assistant editor Chester Schaeffer. As usual, Harlow did not hide her gratitude. "Being in the same cast with Marie was a break for me," she told reporters. "She's one trouper I'd never try to steal a scene from. It'd be like trying to carry Italy against Mussolini." Nonetheless she considered Kitty Packard "my best performance," and when, after her dialogue with Dressler, George Cukor called "Cut!" and the crew laughed and cheered, Harlow rushed to her dressing room and cried. She had never been so proud.

To separate Harlow from her screen characters, the M-G-M publicity department enhanced her original surname from Carpenter (too common) to "Carpentier" (*tres chic*) and claimed Edgar Allan Poe as an ancestor of her maternal great-grandmother, Matilda Poe Harlow, although no connection could be traced. The studio also supplied fan magazines with photographs of Harlow "devoting her spare time to charity work" while Adela Rogers St. Johns wrote a whitewashed account of Bern's death portraying his devastated widow as an innocent dupe.

Although this was accurate, strangers still thought Harlow a hoyden and treated her as such. Gossip spread among unlikely sources: in a letter to former Supreme Court Justice Oliver Wendell Holmes, diplomat Lewis Einstein described a *Dinner at Eight*-esque encounter between Harlow and acid-tongued Margot Asquith, the Countess of Oxford and widow of former Prime Minister H. H. Asquith. "I must relate to you Lady Oxford's latest," Einstein wrote Holmes. "Having met Jean Harlow (the original platinum blonde) at a party, the latter exuberantly began to call her 'Margott,' stressing the final 't.' Margot (severely): 'The final "t" in my Christian name is silent, unlike *your* family name." Like a character in her current movie, the real-life countess not only called Harlow a harlot, but mocked her most vulnerable area: her mind.

That she was actually a smart woman who "played dumb" did not seem possible. At another Hollywood party, a witty remark by Harlow led a listener to wonder aloud, "Who did you hear say that?"

Harlow bowed her head. "My God," she muttered. "Must I always wear a low-cut dress to be important?"

That spring Mayer slated Harlow and Gable for *The Prizefighter and the Lady* with director Howard Hawks. Unhappily married to Norma Shearer's schizophrenic sister, Hawks supervised Harlow's costume fittings for the film. "There she was," he said later, "in a shiny satin dress with nothing at all underneath. I said to the wardrobe woman, 'For God's sake, do something. You can't have that movement under her dress.'

"Forty minutes later they came back. I said, 'Let's see you walk.' She did. The wardrobe woman shook her head and sighed. 'I've taped her [breasts] and everything, but when she goes north, they go south.'" Hawks, who preferred taller, rangier types—Lauren Bacall was his discovery and ideal—left without a word.

Harlow followed. "Do you always walk out like that?" she wondered.

"Look," Hawks told her. "You're not my type."

"How do you know?"

"Well, look at you. The makeup, the hair, the dress, *everything.*"

"I'm not like that," said Harlow. "This isn't me."

Hawks arranged a golf game. Harlow asked to join him. "I'll wash off the warpaint and put on a shirt and pants," she promised—"and by the time she came back," Hawks marveled, "she was just *adorable.* That other facade had nothing to do with the real girl." Hawks slept with Harlow that same night, but their relationship did not progress further. Neither did their work on *The Prizefighter and the Lady*, which was made that summer with a different director and more appropriate star: boxer Max Baer.

The son of a hog butcher, Baer's awesome strength came from swinging a cleaver in his father's slaughterhouse for fourteen hours a day. By adulthood he was a 6' 2", 200-pound contender whose massive shoulders, supple arms, sturdy legs, and lethal right hand resulted in nineteen straight knockouts, then one fatality: after five rounds with Baer, his twentieth opponent died the next day. "He was a tremendous showman, could punch like a mule, and people liked him," says his son, Max Baer, Jr. "If there was a guy like my dad today, he'd be doing $100 million a fight." On June 8, 1933, in a sold-out bout at Yankee Stadium, this twenty-four-year-old Jew from Livermore, California, launched "a sweeping, brutal, berserk attack" on German heavyweight Max Schmeling, a Nazi symbol of Aryan supremacy. "While Germany persecuted the Jews, my father

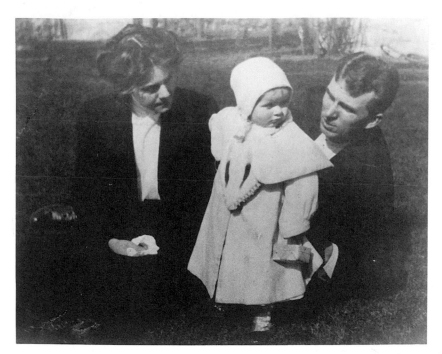

Kansas City, 1912: Mont and "Mother Jean" Carpenter dote on "the Baby."
(Bill Forbriger Collection)

Hollywood School for Girls, 1925:
eighth-grader Harlean Carpenter
(lower left) already displays allure.

Harlean at Camp
Cha-Ton-Ka, where
she contracted
scarlet fever in
the summer of 1926.
(Fred Lee Collection)

David "Thor" Arnold *(far right)* that same summer. (Fred Lee Collection)

Charles McGrew II married Harlean in 1927. He was twenty. She was sixteen. (courtesy of Margo McGrew)

TO MY MOST PRECIOUS JEWELL [*sic*] MY JEAN, signed Marino Bello to Mother Jean. I DO LOVE YOU LIKE A TIGRE [*sic*]. I WILL PROTECT YOU LIKE A LION AND WILL OBEY YOU LIKE A LAMB BUT NEED YOUR LOVE TO LIVE. YOUR MARINO. (Brian Bundy Collection)

In 1928 her husband photographed Harlean at Griffith
Park in Los Angeles . . .
(courtesy of Margo McGrew)

... where she returned a year later with Edwin Bower Hesser—and dramatically different results.

Bit player "Jean Harlow" with Laurel & Hardy in *Double Whoopee.* (Photofest)

Howard Hughes directs Harlow and Ben Lyon in *Hell's Angels.*

Abner "Longy" Zwillman, "the Al Capone of New Jersey." His affair with Harlow advanced her career.

Undressing for success in *The Iron Man.* "She'll probably always have to play these kind of roles," noted *Variety* of Harlow, "but nobody ever starved possessing what she's got." (Culver Pictures)

Mother Jean nurses Harlow after her 1931 collapse. Note the medicine nearby.

The "Platinum Blonde" in her favorite offscreen outfit: sweater and slacks, but no bra or panties.

Harlow married Paul Bern on July 2, 1932. *Left to right,* "Aunt Jetty" Chadsey, Mother Jean, Miriam Bern, Friederike Bern Marcus, Henry Bern, the groom, Judge Leon Yankwich, the bride, Donald Roberson, Marino Bello. (Ed Baker Collection)

A widow (and murder suspect) two months later, Harlow attends Bern's funeral with Bello and Willis Goldbeck.

Dorothy Millette, Bern's "mystery wife." (UPI/Bettmann)

beat Schmeling," states Max Baer, Jr. "He was the 'Jewish Savior.'"

He was also a "Jewish Adonis" who reveled in his reputation. "He has a satyrlike quality which seems irresistible," *The New Yorker* noted, and smitten women agreed. "Dad was like a big kid," his son explains. "He'd run around with every dame and say, 'Aw, she don't mean a thing to me.'" Baer bought his conquests mink coats "not to keep 'em warm, but to keep 'em quiet!" Most stayed silent, but when a waitress brought a $250,000 "breach-of-promise" suit against Baer, his outraged wife, actress Dorothy Dunbar, threatened divorce. "She threw things at him," laughs Baer's son. "Dad said she was harder to get out of the way than Joe Louis."

"I didn't care then, and I don't care now," declared Dorothy Dunbar Baer six decades later. Neither did her husband, especially when M-G-M offered him $3,000 a week—twice Harlow's salary—to appear in *The Prizefighter and the Lady*. "This is pie," said Baer of his screen debut. "It calls for a two-fisted guy who likes himself. All I gotta do is be me and I'm in character."

Being himself was Baer's specialty. "Hello, Baby!" he hailed Joan Crawford, who stalked off the set and never spoke to him again. Undaunted, Baer accosted Harlow. "Are you free tonight, or are you reasonable?" he asked. Apparently she was both, for their affair began shortly thereafter. So did her best film to date.

Chapter Thirteen

Bombshell was an unproduced play about this poor girl who became a big star," stated screenwriter John Lee Mahin. "Nobody understood her, everybody used her, she worked all the time ... It was tragic." In a story conference with producer Hunt Stromberg and director Victor Fleming, Mahin, who had just cowritten *The Prizefighter and the Lady*, had an inspiration. "I said, 'Let's turn this into a comedy. It's *funny*. Vic, you must have known people in the early days ...' "

"I know one right now," Fleming realized. "Clara Bow. She used to be my girl. You'd go to her house, and there'd be a beautiful Oriental rug with coffee stains, and dog shit all over the floor, and her father would come in drunk, and her secretary was stealing from her—"

"That's enough," exclaimed Stromberg. "We got it."

With Clara Bow as their basis, Mahin and cowriter Jules Furthman created "Lola Burns," *Bombshell*'s beloved, beleaguered heroine. Known to 110 million moviegoers as "The 'If' Girl" (Clara Bow was "The 'It' Girl"),

Lola toils at "Monarch Studios" to support her drunken father, dissolute brother, and corrupt secretary, all of whom share her Beverly Hills mansion with a trio of over-sized sheepdogs (Clara Bow kept Great Danes) and a retinue of servants. Despite her "blonde bombshell" image, Lola is actually a guileless girl from Peoria whose dream role is Alice in Wonderland. Appalled by her notoriety, she appeals to silver-tongued studio publicity chief "Space Hanlon" (Lee Tracy), a spoof of Howard Strickling:

LOLA

We used to have a lot of fun, but ever since I began to make a name for myself, you've been double-crossing me with your rotten publicity—

HANLON

—and seen to it that Lola Burns is a family slogan from Kokomo, Indiana, to the Khyber Pass! Strong men take one look at your picture and go home and kiss their wives for the first time in ten years! You're an international tonic! You're a boon to repopulation in a world thinned out by war and famine! You're—

LOLA

That's all very funny, but how do you think *I* enjoy reading all that scandal that hasn't an *ounce* of truth in it?

HANLON

I've told you, sugar: it isn't what *you* like to read, it's what the *public* likes to read. They see you in these scarlet letter, lily-of-the-street parts—

LOLA

Well, I'm getting sick and tired of playing un-
ladylike parts and of your undignified publicity—
and I'm gonna tell Mr. Gillette about it!

Unlike Louis B. Mayer, Monarch monarch "H. E. Gillette"
is a benevolent Gentile concerned with the emotional wel-
fare of his stars. Hanlon is not. "That's the swell item about
Burns," he tells Gillette. "She's great copy because she don't
know what she wants, and she wants something different every day." One day Lola wants a baby, which she tries to adopt
from a local orphanage. "You think I want my bombshell
turned into a rubber nipple?" wails Hanlon, who stages a
scandal in Lola's home to horrify orphanage officials. Truly
upset, she flees to a desert ranch and meets dashing "Gifford
Middleton" (Franchot Tone), a Boston patrician who writes
lyric poetry. "Your hair is like a field of silver daisies," he
declares. "I'd like to run barefoot through your hair."

 Lola loves it. "Not even Norma Shearer or Helen
Hayes in their nicest pictures were spoken to like that," she
sighs, then accepts Gifford's proposal although they've just
met. The next day his parents discover her stardom and
forbid the marriage. "Gifford, you see, is a Middleton,"
huffs his mother.

 "Gifford's a sap!" explodes Lola. "And if you're a lady,
I'm Aimee Semple McHutton [sic] on a raft! You can take
your Bostons and your bloodlines and your Bunker Hills
and stuff a codfish with 'em—and then you know what you
can do with the codfish!" Proud of her profession, Lola
returns to Hollywood and learns that the Middletons were
actually ham actors hired by Hanlon. *Bombshell* ends with

yet another battle between them as Lola continues her madcap career.

Bombshell began shooting in August 1933. To fit its 160-page script into a 95-minute movie, Fleming directed scenes at breakneck speed. At the time, the notion of nonstop, overlapping dialogue was still novel and considered more suitable to theater than film. A veteran of each, Lee Tracy had no trouble; to his amazement, neither did Harlow. "She has a natural sense of timing," he noted, and nowhere was this more apparent than *Bombshell*'s best scene. Exploited by her father, brother, secretary, and studio, the easygoing "If" Girl finally loses her temper:

LOLA
(*rapid-fire*)
Oh, get away from me, all of you! You're nothing but a pack of leeches!
(*points to Hanlon*)
At least he was right in one thing—I don't know how I *ever* expected to bring a baby in here, with an old fool for his grandfather that's half-drunk all the time!

POPS
(*sputtering*)
After the way I've worked to handle your affairs—

LOLA
Well, what *about* my affairs? Where *are* they? Why aren't my bills paid? Where does my money go? *I* never see any of it!

SECRETARY

Lola—you're exciting yourself—

LOLA

And what're *you* mewing about? Don't think I don't know about you and your stealing, and the cuts you get from the stores—

BROTHER

Now listen, Sis—

LOLA

(*whirls on him*)

And *you,* who haven't had a job to your name for three years! And bringing *her* [a hooker] in here like it was a hotel for traveling salesmen!

(*back to All*)

I've only stood it because it's the only home and family I've got, but I'm getting sick of it, do you understand? There's only [her maid] Loretta and the dogs that ever do a single thing for me. All the rest of you are just out for what you can get, and I'm getting pretty tired of being a golden goose, or whatever ya call it!

HANLON

Atta girl, sugar!

LOLA

(*turns on him*)

Don't "atta girl" *me!* I never want to see *you* again as long as I breathe! You're worse than all the *rest* of 'em!

HANLON

But, Lola—

LOLA

(*quotes headlines about her*)

"Stone Age Stuff"! "Mad with Desire"! "Lovers' Brawl"! Is that the way you prove you "just more than care for me"? Treating me like a strip act in a burlesque show! "A glamorous bombshell," eh? A glorified *chump,* that's what I've been!

(*shouting*)

Well, I'm *through,* do you understand? With the business, with everybody! You can get another "If" Girl, or "But" Girl, or "How, When, and Where" Girl—*I'm* clearing out!

(*to family*)

And you can all stay here in this half-paid-for car barn and get somebody *else* to pull the apple cart! *I'm* going to get some peace and quiet, and if any of you try to interfere with me, I'll—I'll complain to the authorities!

By now Harlow's comic knack and her combination of sexuality and vulnerability were well known. This tantrum, however, featured further talents: a gift for mimicry; innate sense of pitch, sound, and rhythm; and incredible breath control, all of which made Lola's tirade both comprehensible and convincing. The advent of "screwball comedy" would soon make such skills mandatory, but *Bombshell* preceded the trend, and Harlow set its tone. No actress was as fast, or as funny.

Her photographic memory helped. 'She never ran lines," Barbara Brown reveals. "I'd have lunch with her every day, and *not once* would she rehearse. She'd look over the script, then come out of her dressing room and do it perfectly, take after take. And I'd wonder, 'When does she learn her dialogue?' "

During shooting on *Bombshell,* crew members compared Harlow's mother and Bello to Lola Burns' greedy clan. "I felt sorry for the Baby," said script clerk Morris Abrams. "All she did was work while her family took her money, just like the girl in the movie. She would come in at 6 A.M. each morning for makeup and hair and wardrobe and rehearsal, then shoot 'til dinner or later—and in they'd stroll in the middle of the day, dressed to the nines and riding high. They were parasites."

Although he seemed unaware of it, *Bombshell* satirized "leeches" like Bello, who passed idle days at his stepdaughter's studio, boasting of criminal connections and vast personal wealth. "He was a loudmouth and a braggart," says second assistant director Willard Sheldon. "He would brag about being the Baby's manager and pretend her money was his." Bello also promised young hopefuls a shot at stardom in exchange for sexual favors. "He hung around the studio chasing women," recalls Marcella Rabwin. "He was sleeping with every extra girl he could." Fancying himself an actor, Bello even played a villain in M-G-M's Italian version of *Men of the North.* "He would strut around the lot bragging about his work in it," sneers Sheldon, "and I can't *tell* you how bad he was. Unbelievable."

By now Harlow despised her stepfather, referring to

him curtly as "Bello" or, among friends, "the Sicilian pimp." Given her feelings, unfounded rumors that he was "more than a stepfather" to her were outrageous and disgusting. "Pimp" was indeed the best word for Bello, especially when he urged Harlow to marry Max Baer so that he could manage them both.

Harlow could not seek maternal comfort. "Boy, was *she* a character," says Dean Dorn of Mother Jean. "We could not *believe* she was the Baby's mother. There was absolutely no connection between the two; everything about them was entirely different.

"The Baby was meek and tiny, while Mother Jean was this big, imposing woman, a real pain in the ass. When things didn't go the way she felt they should, she made a commotion, and the Baby never made a commotion about *anything.*" Admitting that she could rant "like a wild woman, venting my venom," Mother Jean recalled Harlow's playful response. "Now why waste all that effort when you could get $3,000 a week for it?" she joked. "Just don't do it for nothing."

Mother Jean took her seriously and arranged for a screen test. "Please don't make me ashamed of you," Harlow pleaded. The test was not made.

Like the Burns family in *Bombshell*, the Bellos built a garish mansion with Harlow's money. Located at 214 South Beverly Glen Boulevard in tony Holmby Hills, the two-story, four-bedroom "Whitest House in the World" had a Georgian facade, French interior, and outdoor pool with two dressing rooms. Furnishings alone cost $25,000 and included a walk-in refrigerator, polar bear rug, portrait of Mother Jean, and ermine-covered toilet seats with tassels. Even the headboard of Harlow's bed was upholstered in white ermine.

Her new home befit Lola Burns, and Harlow knew it. "She told me she wasn't too crazy about this big house, but her mother and Bello liked it," explains Anita Page. Like Lola, Harlow considered her "half-paid-for car barn" a joke and treated it accordingly. "Get a load of this!" she giggled before showing actress Judith Wood her white-on-white bedroom. Wood did not see the adjoining sitting room, which Harlow filled with her favorite books. Who would believe she read them?

On August 29, midway through shooting on *Bombshell*, *Dinner at Eight* premiered at Grauman's Chinese Theatre. "Acting honors go to Harlow," hailed *Variety*, "taking hold of her fat role and making it stand out even in this distinguished company. By long odds the best thing she has done to date." Besides her performance, Harlow's white hair, wardrobe, and boudoir became icons of her era, and while rival studios struggled to survive, *Dinner at Eight* earned $2.1 million, an enormous sum during the Depression. It was Harlow's biggest hit yet.

Her private life was less successful. "Too much brain work," griped Max Baer of *The Prizefighter and the Lady*. "I haven't had to think so hard since I left high school." Harlow also disenchanted him. "Dad liked her, but she was just another broad," explains his son. "He was excited because she was Jean Harlow, but once he was in there, there wasn't much happening. He said the person she was in the press and the movies wasn't her at all." Compared to her public image, Baer found Harlow "boring" and began "ducking" her. "She'd sit in her car outside his house, so he'd slip out the back door. He took off to Santa Barbara with Garbo."

After praising Harlow's performance in *Dinner at Eight* as "the best work of her career," powerful columnist Louella Parsons alluded to her current affair. "Jean Harlow parked inside the fight ring on the Max Baer set, her eyes focused on the handsome prizefighter," wrote Parsons, then went to Baer's wife. "Max may be in love with her," Dorothy Baer conceded. "I suppose he is. He loves glamour." Parsons provided grounds for divorce: adultery, with Harlow cited as "co-respondent."

This posed a serious problem. September 5 marked the first anniversary of Paul Bern's suicide, and here was his widow, involved with a married prizefighter and implicated in his imminent divorce. Harlow had withstood one scandal; she could not survive another. When the *Bombshell* company went on location to Tucson a week later, the strain showed. "She seemed harassed," said Morris Abrams. "Something was bothering the hell out of her, and she seemed unable to handle it."

Pressure mounted when Harlow returned to Hollywood on September 14. "I remember sitting at dinner when the phone rang for Grandmother," Leatrice Gilbert recalls. "It was Jean Harlow asking for help with a problem." Before the retired practitioner could perform a healing, Mother Jean steered Harlow from Christian Science to Howard Strickling, with Mayer informed of their actions. "My father wasn't busy busting up marriages, but to avert possible scandals, he *would* take steps," admitted Irene Mayer Selznick. In this instance, taking steps meant protecting Harlow. She must be married at once.

Finding a mate was a complex mission. Harlow's third husband had to be ready, willing, and, most important, able; after her last unconsummated union, no marriage could appear arranged. She also had to like, if not love her new spouse enough to live with him—perhaps not forever, but presumably longer than his predecessors. And bridal stipulations aside, most eligible bachelors were not available on such short notice, nor were they willing to wed a star whose life made Lola Burns seem uncomplicated by comparison.

The search ended, fittingly enough, on *Bombshell*'s set. Harlow proposed, her stunned choice accepted, and Strickling, who had convinced Dorothy Baer to delay her divorce, made the necessary arrangements. At 4 A.M. on Monday, September 18, 1933, a chartered plane landed in Yuma, Arizona, and its two passengers proceeded to a local justice of the peace, whose eleven-year-old daughter awoke him. "Who is it?" he wondered. "What's happening?"

"Nothing important," the girl replied. "It's just Jean Harlow, and she wants to get married."

Her groom was Hal Rosson.

Chapter Fourteen

By the time he married Harlow, Hal Rosson was a Hollywood pioneer. Born in 1895, he had migrated from New York to California as a teenager, ascended from bit player to cameraman by age twenty, and shot over fifty films during the ensuing decade. A meticulous craftsman with a finicky manner—crews called him "Putt-Putt," though never to his face—Rosson thrived at M-G-M, which prized his perfectionism and put him under contract in 1930. Two years later he met Harlow on *Red-Headed Woman*, then photographed her in *Red Dust, Hold Your Man,* and *Bombshell.* At no time did rumors of a romance arise.

Like Bern before him, Rosson's marriage to Harlow "came as a total surprise." Front-page stories detailed their similarities: both men were older (at thirty-eight, Rosson was sixteen years Harlow's senior), both were employed by M-G-M, and both, according to newspaper accounts, looked uncannily alike. "Hal Rosson might be taken for the brother of Paul Bern," observed reporters, though in truth their resemblance was slight. Bern had been sallow and paunchy; Rosson was dark and compact. Bern sulked and brooded; Rosson had "a tremendous sense of humor." Bern's sexual anguish led to suicide; Rosson displayed no such neuroses. "Hal *loved* women," states his nephew, Robert Terry. "He called them his *'hors d'oeuvres.'*" One such appetizer, Ziegfeld *Follies* showgirl Nina Betts, married Rosson in 1925. They divorced three years later.

A final contrast was unfit to print: Bern had an "undersized" organ, but Rosson's crew called him "Long Dong" behind his back. "I was in the gym with him several times," says Bill Edmondson, "and he really did have a big one for his size. He was about 5′ 5″, and it was seven or eight inches long."

Harlow's rapport with Rosson had long been apparent. "I used to see them on the set together, kidding and fooling around," remembers Dean Dorn. "He made her laugh; he always had something funny to tell her." He was also an important ally. "Sometimes he'd see her through the camera, and if she didn't look so good, he'd go over and get her sparkle going." In an era when directors were more preoccupied with production schedules than stars, a caring cameraman was a godsend to Harlow, whose studio expected her to "sparkle" six days a week. Rosson made sure she did, and though their relationship had never been amorous, it was always amicable. "To me, love has always meant friendship," Harlow stated. Her marriage to Rosson seemed proof of it.

In truth it was "a studio wedding," and M-G-M workers knew why. "She only married him to offset a scandal with Max Baer," says Jacqueline Smith. "The Baby and Hal were great pals, but it was never a big romance." Ted

Tetrick assumes Rosson "fell for the gag. I think *anybody* would have; if Jean Harlow asked a guy, 'Will you marry me?' he would've thought she was kidding! But in this case she wasn't." Infatuated with Harlow, Rosson had settled for friendship until her sudden proposal. "Poor Hal," sighs still photographer Ted Allan. "He was used. He didn't realize the studio set it up. I worked with him right after that, and he had no idea. He was in love."

Following their Yuma wedding, Harlow and Rosson flew back to Hollywood for a press conference by the pool of her Beverly Glen home. As the newlyweds answered questions and posed for pictures, Rosson appeared dazed. "It doesn't seem real," he repeated. "It can't be true ... she really belongs to me."

Desperate for a fulfilling relationship, Harlow had already romanticized her arranged marriage. "Our decision to elope came suddenly, but we'd been planning the .marriage for months," she said despite her proposal only days earlier. "Isn't he a precious? I asked him to marry me!"

Rosson blushed. "I'm not a handsome guy," he muttered.

"You *are* a handsome guy," admonished Harlow. "I know it's trite," she told reporters, "but I want to go on record that ours is one Hollywood marriage that will last!"

It hardly seemed likely. "As long as I have been covering Hollywood stories, I don't believe I ever covered a stranger one than that wedding," wrote Louella Parsons, whose meddling had caused it. Informed of her presence at the press conference in Harlow's home, Joan Crawford accused Dorothy Manners of treason. "How could you?"

shrieked Crawford. "You promised!" She did not speak to Manners for years.

Harlow's latest marriage mirrored her current movie, only this was no comedy—and unlike Lola Burns' family, the Bellos wanted more than money. While Harlow finished *Bombshell,* her mother and stepfather seized title to Beverly Glen and made Rosson sign a postnuptial agreement relinquishing all "community property" rights. In return, he issued an ultimatum. *"They* go or *we* go," Rosson told Harlow, and because the Bellos now owned Beverly Glen, her choice was a foregone conclusion. Nine days after their wedding, Harlow and Rosson moved to adjoining third-floor suites at the Chateau Marmont, a small hotel on Sunset Boulevard. Harlow brought her books.

That same day Dorothy Baer filed for divorce. Harlow was not named. As hoped, her sudden marriage had averted scandal.

Two days later, on September 29, 1933, Harlow placed her palms and feet in wet cement at Grauman's Chinese Theatre, an honorary custom for established stars. A prior, onstage ceremony had failed when the cement dried and shattered, so this time she repeated the process in the theater's forecourt, then returned that evening for *Bombshell*'s premiere.

Miraculously, editor Margaret Booth had assembled the film in a week, though few had faith in the result. "When we took *Bombshell* out, we thought it was a dud," she remembers. "I cut it very snappy, which was unusual then. Nobody had ever cut a film that fast." Booth had one hope: Harlow. "I used a lot of close-ups, because she was unusual-looking and had this great, expressive face. But everybody at the studio said, 'This isn't going to be any good.'"

They were wrong. *Bombshell*'s "snappy" cutting and wisecracks "as rapid as a tommy gun" delighted audiences, as did Harlow. "She is Clara Bow and herself all rolled into one grand role," declared the New York *Daily News*. "Jean's performance is so good that she outshines Lee Tracy."

Eminent critic Richard Watts, Jr., agreed. "*Bombshell* provides the first full-length portrait of this amazing young woman's increasingly impressive acting talent. Miss Harlow reveals again that gift for an amalgamation of sophisticated sex comedy with curiously honest innocence which is the secret of her individuality." Two years earlier Watts had claimed Harlow "completely ruins [a] scene" in *The Public Enemy*, so her subsequent transformation astonished him. "There can be no doubt now that she is a distinguished performer," Watts proclaimed. "*Bombshell* is another step in Miss Harlow's brilliant career." For the rest of her life it remained her favorite movie.

The morning after its premiere, Mother Jean sent a letter to Arthur Landau, whom she called "Pops." Filled with pride, pettiness, and paranoia, its contents capture her vividly. Her emphases appear as written.

> Pops, darling, this will please you:
> *Bombshell* was a SENSATION, a WOW, a SUCCESS, and what an evening. The wires poured in and Hunt Stromberg sent the Baby a huge box of roses with this note: "To my favorite actress, with my appreciation for a perfect performance. Love, Hunt." Which made

the Baby cry with gratitude. A huge box of cut orchids from Jules Furthman (from his own greenhouse) [arrived] with an exquisite note of appreciation for the most perfect performance he had ever seen and that NO one could have done what "Harlow" did, and how proud he was to have his name on the [advertising] sheet with hers. Wasent *[sic]* that lovely?

We are so grateful and happy for the Baby.

L.B. [Mayer] sat in front of us and when he and [M-G-M vice-president Eddie] Mannix came in, they did not EVEN speak to the Baby, ONLY nodded. When it was over and the audience was WILD, L.B. stopped at the Baby's side and started to explode, [then] caught himself and said, "God, [Lee] Tracy has great lines." Now Pops, if I had not heard it I could NOT have believed that. Not even, "Jean, your work was nice." Not one word except JUST what I have told you. CAN you imagine such a fool as to think he could intimidate three people like us with such childish tactics? Really, those people must think we are of very limited intelligence and of very lowly birth to accept such childish tactics. BUT Pops, if I have anything to do with the situation I would make that gentleman pay in blood for the insult.

Yesterday the Baby finished the concrete at the CHINESE [theater] and we are so proud to have her name among the biggest of the industry.

Tell Mrs. Landau when she returns I will have to hear about all the pretty new styles . . .

Mother

Her own style speaks for itself.

On October 15 Harlow and Rosson attended a University of Southern California football game at the Los Angeles Coliseum, dined with the Bellos at Beverly Glen, and returned to the Chateau Marmont. Harlow had complained of abdominal pains all day, and by 3 A.M. she was in such agony that Rosson summoned Dr. Sidney Burnap, who diagnosed appendicitis and rushed her to Good Samaritan Hospital.

At the time it was cause for concern. Two years earlier *Platinum Blonde* star Robert Williams had died after an appendectomy, and though Harlow's surgery went smoothly, her condition made headlines. BABY PROGRESSING RAPIDLY, Bello wired Arthur Landau. EXPECTING HER HOME IN TEN DAYS. AS USUAL, SHE WAS A BRICK. AS SOON AS SHE OPENED HER EYES AFTER THE EFFECT OF THE ANESTHETIC VANISHED, SHE STARTED TO MAKE FUN OF US AND WISECRACK. Another detail went undisclosed: during the operation, Dr. Burnap detected a past history of gonorrhea in Harlow's pelvis. Its source was unknown.

Discharged from Good Samaritan on October 30, Harlow returned to Beverly Glen so Mother Jean could supervise her recuperation. "The Baby is weak and confused," she insisted despite Harlow's clean bill of health. "She could stay in the hospital forever and never receive the attention she needs." Rosson remained at the Chateau Marmont.

Shortly thereafter Harlow appeared at Dorothy Manners' doorstep with several cases of assorted liquors. "What are you doing?" Manners wondered. "We have booze here."

"Mommie doesn't want me drinking," Harlow told her. "She says I have a problem." Rather than argue, Harlow had agreed to abstain, then sneaked her spirits to Manners "so she could drop by and drink" without Mother Jean's knowledge. "I don't believe her," Harlow added. "I don't have a problem. I don't drink any more than anyone else."

Manners sympathized. "We *all* drank a good deal," she says today. "The Baby had a lot of hangovers, but who didn't?" Like Harlow, Manners assumed "Mother Jean, who watched over her like a hawk, was just trying to scare her."

If so, the strategy failed. "I'm not going to drink around her," Harlow confided, "but I *am* going to drink."

M-G-M wanted her at work. Though too sophisticated for mass audiences, *Bombshell* had made $761,000, a modest sum after *Dinner at Eight* but more than twice its $344,000 cost. To her studio's surprise, Harlow had become Hollywood's rarest commodity: a homegrown star with worldwide appeal. "A 'Jeanne Harlow' picture is always a surefire hit in Paris," reported the New York *Times* of "*la blonde platinée.*" "*Bombshell* is still drawing crowds." Domestically, Harlow placed third in exhibitor polls of female stars, trailing Marie Dressler and Janet Gaynor due to rural resistance. Harlow was more popular in major cities, but small-town conservatives preferred Dressler's dowagers and Gaynor's ingenues to Kitty Packard or Lola Burns.

Her image ashamed Harlow. "I don't want to keep on playing that kind of woman," she said of a proposed *Red-Headed Woman* sequel. "I think I've established myself as an *actress*, don't you?'' She was more concerned with her screen characters than her salary, though compared to Crawford's $4,500 a week or Garbo's $250,000 and Shearer's $110,000 per picture, Harlow's $1,500 a week was a pittance. It did not matter. "I never in my life heard the Baby complain that she wasn't making enough money," states Dorothy Manners. "She wasn't in it for the money."

Bello was, and after *Bombshell* he offered his step-daughter's services to M-G-M for $5,000 a week. Mayer informed him that Harlow was already under contract and hence he "had nothing to sell." Bello threatened to with-hold her from *The Age of Larceny*, an Anita Loos and John Emerson script already in pre-production. Mayer "told him emphatically that it might as well be determined now whether she intended to fulfill her present contract or refuse to do so, in which event we [M-G-M] would see just how good our contract was." Caught in the middle, Harlow obeyed her stepfather and refused to report to the studio. On November 13, she was put on suspension.

At the height of the Depression, the salary demands of a twenty-two-year-old star were not seen with sympathy. *Variety* deemed Harlow "unappreciative of M-G-M elevat-ing her to stardom," *Picturegoer* accused her of "walking out on the job," and *Photoplay* presumed that "the dog house has a ladies' entrance, too." Only Dorothy Manners defended her. Titled "Is Jean Harlow Hollywood's Most Underpaid Star?," her *Motion Picture* piece juxtaposed Harlow's earnings with higher-paid, lower-ranked ac-tresses and denounced the discrepancy.

Harlow herself denied the dispute. "You can't fight with your friends, and Louis B. Mayer is the best friend any girl in the world could have," she contended. Whether or not she believed it was beside the point: "never a complainer or agitator," Harlow hated her strike and blamed Bello for it. After six weeks of inactivity, she began giving interviews, reading revisions of *Eadie Was a Lady* (formerly *The Age of Larceny*), and posing for glamour photographer George Hurrell.

Hurrell had met Harlow on *The Secret Six,* then shot her for *Red-Headed Woman* and *Bombshell.* "We were on the same wavelength from the beginning," he said, though at first her straightforwardness startled him. "She would drop her dress and be nude underneath! Not in a seductive way; she just had no shame or inhibition about her body." From the start Hurrell "genuinely liked" Harlow, who stayed the same despite her stardom. "She never changed personally. She was one star who never, ever believed her publicity."

Hurrell found Harlow "extremely photogenic" but physically imperfect. "I always positioned my lights at a low angle, because a top light exaggerated her deep-set eyes, which literally vanished in the camera," he revealed. "Her high forehead and short chin were also a consideration in lighting her, though the cleft in her chin was an asset because it balanced her forehead." Feature for feature, Mother Jean was more impressive. "She was a good-looking woman," said Hurrell. "You could tell she'd been a beauty in her day." Harlow, however, was an ideal model. "She took direction superbly. Never got tense, never forgot a position. I don't think she knew how to be awkward.

"She was not frightened by the camera; she reacted to it, and in some strange way, I was the third party—*they* were the conspirators." Taken at Beverly Glen during her salary strike, Hurrell's portrait of Harlow on her polar bear rug still captures the conspiracy.

Like all who knew her, Hurrell noted the contrast between his on-camera subject and her actual self. "When you got her alone, she became sweet and shy. It was like she didn't have to be 'Jean Harlow' anymore." Also apparent was the difference between mother and daughter. "Mother Jean was *strong*. She had *will*. She had willpower, and the Baby didn't."

Forbidden by the Bellos from drinking or working, Harlow devised *Today Is Tonight*, the saga of a New York society couple, Peter and Judy Landsdowne, whose married bliss ends when he is accidentally blinded, then goes broke in the stock market crash. Without his eyesight or money, Peter becomes bitter and reclusive; resolving to help him, Judy risks her reputation to appear as Lady Godiva onstage, turning day into night so her unwitting husband will think she works for a charity foundation. Eventually he discovers her ruse and realizes her devotion. The tale ends with their true love affirmed.

Harlow's story indicates her sensibility: poignant, tender, and impossibly romantic. "She's a girl with lots of love who weakens now and then, but clings to an ideal that finally comes through triumphant," she said of the heroine she had based on herself. More like Judy Landsdowne than any part she had played, Harlow created *Today Is Tonight* to include her dream role, which she would portray onscreen. Meanwhile Bello took a $22,500 "chattel mortgage" on Beverly Glen's furnishings, and when even that did not suffice, he announced that the "Platinum Blonde" was writing a book. Worldwide publication offers followed, so Bello paid fledgling publicist Tony Beacon $500 to supply a 70,000-word text.

Beacon loved Harlow. "The first time we met, she said, 'Call me "Baby"; that's what my friends call me,'" he recounts. "She was the warmest human being I ever knew." As for *Today Is Tonight*, "her idea was good, and it *was* her idea." Beacon also found Harlow "very intelligent. A retentive memory. A voracious reader. She loved to read, especially historical novels and detective stories."

Like Hurrell, Beacon beheld Harlow's lack of inhibition. "She had a beautiful body, and she wasn't ashamed of it. She wasn't being provocative, she was being *natural*. I never met a woman more natural than the Baby."

Not everyone admired her attitude. At a Hollywood party, Beacon watched "the hostess, who didn't like the Baby at all," note Harlow's plunging neckline. "Why, dear," she scolded, "that dress is down to your waist!"

Without a word Harlow slipped her gown from her shoulders, exposing her breasts and stomach. "Could I have more coffee?" she asked politely as guests gasped and applauded. Struck by the incident, Beacon used it in *Today Is Tonight*.

The novel's other references to real life are not as amusing. When her husband attempts suicide, Judy cries, "Cut the comedy!" a blatant paraphrase of Paul Bern. "What do you think I did today?" she jokes on another occasion. "I had an affair with a prizefighter!" The reference to Max Baer is flagrant and authentic, as are *Today Is Tonight*'s incessant discussions of drinking. Judy wonders whether she is "a good drinker," worries that she "is drinking too much," and finally faces the truth. "I'll be honest," she tells herself. "I'm taking this drink because I want it very badly, and I won't make any promises about not taking another. I know I will take another ..." As her intimates knew, this credo was Harlow's.

To secure a movie sale before publication, Bello submitted *Today Is Tonight* to every studio except M-G-M, which still had Harlow on suspension. Apprised of this, Mayer invoked a clause in her contract prohibiting Harlow from "rendering any services to any person, firm, or corporation other than [M-G-M] without written consent." Harlow's novel could not be published without Mayer's permission, and to get back at Bello, he angrily withheld it. A disillusioned Beacon left Hollywood forever, and though screenwriter Carey Wilson polished its prose as a favor to Harlow, he could not convince Mayer to approve *Today Is Tonight*'s publication or adapt it to the screen. Bello's blunder had dashed her dream role.

By the spring of 1934, exhibitors were frantic. Promised five Harlow films per year, they had yet to play one and reap certain profits. Audiences also protested her absence, so after a six-month stalemate, M-G-M bowed to pressure and signed Harlow to a new seven-year contract starting at $3,000 a week. Now she could resume her career and end her marriage to Hal Rosson without risking scandal. On May 5, 1934, seven months and seventeen days after eloping to Yuma, they formally separated. Neither notified the press.

The next day Harlow served as matron of honor at the wedding of Carey Wilson and actress Carmelita Geraghty. Walking down the aisle during the ceremony, she suddenly turned to a group of reporters. "Did you guys know I'm getting a divorce?" Harlow whispered.

The result was "pandemonium," remembered Joseph L. Mankiewicz. "The reporters rose to their feet and ran to the telephones, which of course were in the opposite direction of the ceremony. There was tremendous disarray." Harlow apologized for her behavior, completed the ceremony, then elaborated to Louella Parsons. "Our marriage is finished," she told the columnist who instigated it. "There will be no reconciliation." Her grounds for divorce: "incompatibility."

"I don't want to make a 'heavy' of Hal," Harlow added. "We simply were not meant for each other." For the rest of his life Rosson refused to discuss the marriage, though privately he called Harlow "a captive daughter" of Mother Jean and Bello, the "greedy, voracious prison keepers" who had "kidnapped" his wife from the hospital after her appendectomy and "ferreted her off" to Beverly Glen. "Hal said he never really got her back after that," relates Robert Terry. "He said her mother broke up the marriage." Like Harlow's last two husbands, Rosson had tried to liberate her from Mother Jean but lost the battle. Her hold was too strong.

Although she would mock them as "marriages of inconvenience," Harlow's failed relationships with Chuck McGrew, Paul Bern, and Hal Rosson were no laughing matter, and she knew it. "What's lacking in me?" she asked John Lee Mahin. "The right man," he replied. A three-time loser at age twenty-three, Harlow had despaired of finding him.

That same month, she did.

Chapter Fifteen

At the time of Harlean Carpenter's birth in Kansas City, eighteen-year-old William Powell lived a few blocks away. Nonetheless he did not know her family, and within a year Powell had left for New York to enroll in the American Academy of Dramatic Arts. Debuting on Broadway in 1912, he toured onstage for ten years, then made his first film in 1922, playing the maniacal "Professor Moriarty" to John Barrymore's *Sherlock Holmes.* For the rest of the silent era, Powell specialized in villainous supporting roles, and when "talkies" amplified his perfect diction and debonair poise, Paramount featured him as society sleuth "Philo Vance" in a series of mysteries. Stardom followed, with Powell defecting to Warner Brothers for $6,000 a week and divorcing his first wife for actress Carole Lombard. Their two-year marriage ended in 1933, and when he refused to accept a wage cut, Warners canceled Powell's contract. A confidential memo called him "washed up" in Hollywood.

Powell's agent, Myron Selznick, was David O. Selz-

nick's brother, so in 1934 the latter Selznick hired Powell—
"against everyone's protest, including [Louis B. Mayer's]
own"—for *Manhattan Melodrama* with Myrna Loy. Afterward M-G-M reteamed them in *The Thin Man,* a low-
budget mystery based on Dashiell Hammett's book. As
"Nick and Nora Charles," a high-living, hard-drinking ex-
detective and his heiress wife, Powell and Loy personified
wit, class, and sophistication, making *The Thin Man* a surprise sensation and its forty-one-year-old, supposedly
"washed-up" star more popular than ever. Now he had an
Academy Award nomination and a ten-film, $500,000 con-
tract.

By all accounts, the off-camera Powell was an incarna-
tion of his *Thin Man* character. Anita Loos thought him "a
real gentleman—urbane, witty, and charming," Irene
Mayer Selznick found him "an attractive, interesting, darling fellow," George Hurrell regarded him as "the most
impeccably groomed man I ever met," and Powell's widow
describes him as "the same person in life as he was on-
screen." Judith Wood, whose affair with Powell was brief
but memorable, states it succinctly: "He *was* Nick Charles,
and he was *good.*"

Though M-G-M press releases claimed Harlow met
Powell after her separation from Rosson, photographs of
them on the *Manhattan Melodrama* set prove otherwise.
Powell later admitted he knew Harlow casually but "never
had any dates with her 'til I learned she was leaving Hal."
On their first date, a Sunday night dinner in Santa Barbara,
Harlow seemed unaware of Powell's stature and fell asleep
en route. It was the same sort of unpretentiousness he had
loved in Lombard, whose foul mouth and down-to-earth

manner deflated his ego. Sensing similar qualities in Harlow, he pursued her.

Powell had Paul Bern's intellect and Hal Rosson's humor, and though his six-foot height dwarfed both, all three resembled Mont Carpenter, whom Harlow had lost at a formative age and still sought to replace. "She worked Bill Powell into a father image," figured Joseph L. Mankiewicz. "She was looking for a father, and he was smart enough to see it. He knew his role." The Baby had a "Poppy," Harlow's pet name for Powell. "I've found him," she told friends excitedly. "I never thought this would happen to me."

Before their separation, Harlow and Rosson had been shooting *Born to Be Kissed,* the latest name of *Eadie Was a Lady.* Afterward, to avoid discomfort, cameraman Ray June replaced Rosson, who was then stricken by polio and placed in quarantine. Harlow's daily calls prompted rumors of a reconciliation until Rosson recovered and asked for a foreign assignment. M-G-M sent him to London and Harlow filed for divorce, charging that Rosson had "read in their bedchamber to a late hour." For a smart actress anxious to shed her screen image, it was not a wise move. A British journalist termed Harlow's statement "one of the most ill-advised pieces of testimony a star could give."

Born to Be Kissed had a different dilemma: that spring, the Roman Catholic Church had established a "Legion of Decency" to abolish "immoral pictures." Dismissed by Hollywood studios as a bush-league Hays Office, the Legion of Decency swiftly expanded from its Catholic constituents to other denominations. Three months after its inception and during shooting on *Born to Be Kissed,* a whop-

ping 65 million moviegoers—half the U.S. population—
had agreed to heed Legion of Decency directives to shun
"indecent and un-Christian films." Contending that it glorified gangsters, the Legion of Decency even condemned a
reissue of *The Public Enemy*, which was withdrawn for the
next twenty years.

From its founding the Legion of Decency had targeted
Harlow and fellow sensation Mae West as "a two-woman
campaign of sex-ridicule" whose credo was best expressed
by West: "When women go wrong, men go right after
them." Worse than West's *double entendres* ("I'm the girl
that works at Paramount all day and Fox all night") and
Harlow's harlots was that each enjoyed sex without shame
or embarrassment. Fearing audiences would follow suit,
the Legion of Decency ordered both to play virtuous characters or face nationwide boycotts. Its threat caused "temporary hysteria" in Hollywood, where Hays Office "morals
director" Joseph Breen unofficially banned *Born to Be
Kissed* as "one of the most torrid efforts to emanate from any
studio at any time." Not even a proposed new title of *100%
Pure* could change Breen's mind.

Because ten months had elapsed since *Bombshell*'s release, exhibitors clamored for *The Girl from Missouri*, the
fifth and final title of Harlow's current movie. When
M-G-M persuaded Breen and the Legion of Decency to
approve it, its contents proved tame: forced by her stepfather
to work in a roadside "booze house," sexy "Eadie Chapman" goes to New York in search of a sugar daddy. Despite
her "hotsy-totsy" looks, Eadie is 100 percent pure and plans
to stay so. "Nobody ever believes I have ideals, but I have,
and I'll show 'em I have," she vows. Her golddigging makes

this difficult, especially when a tycoon commits suicide at a stag party and Eadie discovers his corpse. Pursuing another millionaire to Palm Beach, she falls for his son but holds out for marriage. Several obstacles later, she obtains it.

Compared to Harlow's prior M-G-M movies, *The Girl from Missouri* was a mild disappointment. She was not. "Miss Harlow, who simply must be accepted as a fine comedienne, plays her laughs too shrewdly to warrant the frequently heard opinion that not all of her humor is intentional," maintained the New York *Times*. Others questioned the film's "torrid" reputation. "There is nothing," *Variety* noted, "to which objection may honestly be offered."

Harlow disagreed, so when a seven-year-old girl approached her on Hollywood Boulevard to say, "I'm going to *The Girl from Missouri*!" she was horrified. "Honey, I don't believe that is quite the film for you to see," Harlow counseled. "I'd much rather you wait for my next one." Her discomfort did not hurt business. *The Girl from Missouri* grossed $1.1 million, twice its $511,000 cost.

A week before it opened, Harlow and Powell drove to the Del Monte Lodge on the Monterey peninsula. Sighted together, they issued a routine disclaimer: "We're just good friends." No one believed it, and their subsequent presence at places like the Trocadero, a Sunset Strip nightclub, and Max Reinhardt's staging of *A Midsummer Night's Dream* at the Hollywood Bowl confirmed their affair. To promote it, Mayer removed Joan Crawford from *A Woman Called Cheap*, replaced her with Harlow, made Powell its hero, and retitled it *Reckless*.

The marquee value of Harlow and Powell in *Reckless*

seemed surefire. Its material was another matter. "I certainly never would have planned a musical for Jean Harlow," said David O. Selznick, especially one in which the "Platinum Blonde" played an actress whose husband shoots himself. Though based on the marriage of Broadway star Libby Holman (who threatened to sue), the film's allusions to Harlow and Bern were blatant and grotesque. Scenes of her hearing a gunshot and then finding the body, followed by lurid headlines, a coroner's inquest, and a district attorney's assertion that "technically, it was suicide, but morally, it was murder," forced Harlow to reenact the most traumatic event of her life.

Exploitative elements aside, Harlow's presence in a musical was preposterous, and although Virginia Verrill dubbed her voice and Betty Halsey doubled her dancing, she had to learn every song and step. It was an overwhelming assignment, and Mother Jean was merciless. "She was on the set all the time," says dancer Loie Tilton. "The Baby was under so much pressure, but she went along with whatever her mother said." Harlow had gained weight while on strike, and though it was gone by *The Girl from Missouri*, Mother Jean wanted no recurrence on *Reckless*. "She wouldn't let her eat," continues Tilton. "During rehearsals, we'd get hungry and have a candy bar, but the Baby never could because her mother wouldn't let her." Allotted only a slice of pineapple, shredded carrot, and a scoop of cottage cheese per day, the famished star would sneak off the set and find Movita, a Mexican beauty signed for *Mutiny on the Bounty*. "C'mon!" she would coax. "Let's get a goody!" The two would run to the M-G-M commissary, devour an ice-cream cone or slice of cake, and return to work.

Four days after Paul Bern's funeral, Harlow bathed nude in *Red Dust*. Co-star Clark Gable admires the view.

Left to right, Harold Rosson, Victor Fleming, Mary Astor, and Gable watch Harlow at work in *Red Dust*.

(Ed Baker Collection)

By popular demand, M-G-M reteamed Harlow and Gable in *Hold Your Man* . . .

. . . but made sure they reformed by the final reel. In surviving prints, a black preacher performs the ceremony (*right*)—but as this rare still (*opposite*) shows, *Hold Your Man*'s "Southern version" cast a white clergyman instead. Barbara Barondess stands second from left.

Harlow and George Cukor on the *Dinner at Eight* set. "She played comedy," he recalled, "as naturally as a hen lays an egg." (Photofest)

To hide
Harlow's drinking,
Mother Jean wrote
"NOT FOR
PUBLICATION"
on the rear
of this photo.
Also pictured: Bello,
bandleader
Johnny Hamp,
and Ruth Hamp.
(Ed Baker Collection)

On the *Bombshell* set
with John Lee Mahin
and Victor Fleming.
Harlow's performance
was hailed as her best.
(Ed Baker Collection)

On a break from *Bombshell*,
Harlow drinks beer with
Howard Hawks and Max Baer.
Both were her lovers at the
time. (Ed Baker Collection)

"I know it's trite," Harlow told reporters (*above*) after eloping with Hal Rosson in 1933 (*below*), "but I want to go on record that ours is one Hollywood marriage that will last!" Eight months later it was over. (Culver Pictures)

Harlow at home in 1934. "She was not frightened by the camera," recalled George Hurrell. "She reacted to it, and in some strange way, I was the third party—*they* were the conspirators." (courtesy of George Hurrell)

Mother and daughter in
1933. "The grip she had
on that girl," Myrna Loy
wrote, "was unbelievable."

"The Whitest House in
Hollywood," which
Mother Jean built with
Harlow's money.
Even its toilet seats
had ermine covers.
(AMPAS)

With Louis B. Mayer,
who loathed Harlow's
persona but liked her
personally.

"I've found him," said Harlow of lover William Powell. "I never thought this would happen to me."

Movita considered Harlow "like a child. Talking to her was like talking to a little kid." She soon learned why. "Her mother was very possessive; she *treated* her like a child. I wondered how she could stand it."

Today it is difficult to imagine the "Platinum Blonde" as "the Baby," yet without her "warpaint," Harlow could appear as childlike as her conduct. *Reckless* actress Rosalind Russell never forgot their first meeting. "I remember sitting under a hair dryer," wrote Russell, "and sitting next to me was a child, also under a dryer. She was wearing shorts, and her little baby legs, perfectly formed, rested against the back of her chair while the nails of her little baby hands were being manicured.

"My word, I thought, a ten- or eleven-year-old having that bright red polish put on, and suddenly the hood of the dryer went back and the child stood up and it was Jean. She was probably twenty-three at the time, but without any makeup and no eyebrows, she looked exactly like a little kid."

Russell's encounter with Mother Jean was equally memorable. "One night her mother phoned and asked me to please come over, it was important. So I went, and when I got there, Jean wasn't even home. Her mother kept bab-bling about how she wanted Jean and me to be good friends, while I wondered what in the world I was doing in that place." When Harlow arrived, Russell found a "very warm, very friendly, very lonely little creature. She just seemed lost."

During production on *Reckless,* a crisis arose. After years of weekly bleaching, Harlow's hair had become so brittle that it broke off her head. "It was awful," reveals

Marcel Machu, a "wave and dye specialist" summoned to M-G-M. "They'd ruined her hair. It was falling out all over the place. It was completely destroyed."

Machu found Harlow "dying of worry, not only for herself, but her movie, because if the studio shut it down in the middle of shooting, it would have been a disaster." At first this seemed inevitable. "If you expect this woman to work today, tomorrow, or the next day, you're crazy," Machu informed director Victor Fleming. "If they touch her again, she'll have no hair at all."

Since the possibility of the "Platinum Blonde" going bald was "a huge secret," M-G-M sequestered Harlow in a studio bungalow and Machu assessed the damage. "They'd been overbleaching her," he discovered, "and they were mixing peroxide, which wasn't so bad by itself, with ammonia, which was a *killer*." The other two ingredients, Clorox and Lux flakes, made it even more lethal.

"It was too late to save her hair," states Machu. "All I could do was get her through the movie." For the next three days, he massaged Harlow's head with olive oil "until her scalp absorbed it and her hair didn't break anymore," then gave her "a very light permanent which made a finger wave stay." Meanwhile studio hairdresser Sydney Guilaroff ordered custom-made wigs from New York which Harlow wore for the remainder of *Reckless*.

Released in April 1935, her musical debut perplexed critics and frustrated fans. "Metro-Goldwyn-Mayer has taken the screen's liveliest comedienne and chased her through a stale and profitless meringue of backstage routines and high-society amour," griped the New York *Times*. "*Reckless* is a good title," conceded *Variety*, "but it'll need all the box-office potency of Harlow and Powell to offset the ingredients." As hoped, the real-life lovers lured audiences to *Reckless*, though a lack of repeat business resulted in a $125,000 loss. It was Harlow's first failure since her arrival at M-G-M.

By now she was shooting *China Seas*, an all-star "super-special" from Irving Thalberg, whose precarious health limited his workload to a few top projects. In development for four years, the film's final script was the uncredited work of John Lee Mahin, who borrowed freely from *Red Dust* for his surefire plot: on a voyage from Hong Kong to Singapore, a virile steamship captain (Gable) spurns his brassy blonde mistress (Harlow) for a refined British widow (Rosalind Russell). Hurt and heartbroken, she helps a venal pirate (Wallace Beery) plunder the vessel. Gable foils the raid, saves the ship, forsakes Russell, and forgives Harlow, whom he has loved all along.

A comparison between *Red Dust* and *China Seas* shows how thoroughly the Hays Office and the Legion of Decency homogenized Hollywood movies. In *Red Dust*, Harlow's heroine was a brazen hooker who bathed nude in a rain barrel; in *China Seas*, she is "a professional entertainer" whose custom-made brassiere had fur-lined tin tips. *Red Dust* let Gable bed both Harlow and Mary Astor; *China Seas* forced him to eschew sex despite his randiness, Harlow's readiness, and Russell's widowhood. Finally, *Red Dust*'s "last scene is a pat on Harlow's fanny and a quick fade," producer Hunt Stromberg had instructed. "She'll go on sleeping and living with Gable and making him happy without getting married." It was a far cry from *China Seas*, which concludes with Gable's proposal. "You'd marry *me*?"

cries Harlow, whose amazement is appropriate. Salty as *China Seas* was, its wholesome conclusion seemed motivated by its censors, not its characters. No wonder *Red Dust* was yanked from distribution at the Legion of Decency's demand.

After *China Seas* finished shooting, Harlow observed "the most important day of the year" with a handwritten note:

May 12, 1935

Dearest of all mothers:

This is Mother's Day to lots of people, but to me it's God's loveliest gift to humanity. You are God's finest conception of motherhood and I will always be eternally grateful He allowed me the privilege of belonging to *you.*

I love you for now and forever—

me

On her eighth birthday in 1919, Harlean Carpenter had sent a similar letter. Sixteen years later her sentiments remained slavish, and Harlow was humorless about them. At a Hollywood party, she rose to toast "the people who are responsible for what little success I have: my mother and God."

"Gee, Baby, at least give Him top billing," quipped John Lee Mahin. Harlow did not speak to him for a year.

She could not shun Bill Powell, who despised the Bellos. "Few people were as badly used by relatives," he said later, and since Powell refused even to eat with Harlow's mother and stepfather, she shuttled between Beverly Glen and his Beverly Hills mansion.

At the end of May, the couple celebrated the first anniversary of their first date at San Simeon, the coastal castle of William Randolph Hearst and his movie-star mistress, Marion Davies. "Jean Harlow was crazy about Bill Powell," Davies discovered. "She waited on him hand and foot." DARLING, Harlow wired her mother from San Simeon, HAVING DIVINE TIME. NEVER HAPPIER. LOVE TO ALL. ME.

A month later she flew to Wyntoon, Hearst's 67,000-acre estate on the McCloud River. "Will you please tell Miss Harlow," Hearst hissed to Davies at dinner, "to go to her room and get dressed?"

"But she has an evening gown on," Davies replied.

"To me it looks like a *night*gown."

Davies took Harlow aside. "Do you realize," she murmured, "your dress is . . ."

"So what?" said Harlow.

"Well, W.R. [Davies' nickname for Hearst] doesn't like it. Couldn't you change and put on something else?"

"Alright," shrugged Harlow, who left the table and returned in a coat "which she wore all during dinner," recalled Davies. "She wouldn't change her dress."

Since her host forbid unmarried couples from cohabiting, Harlow shared a room at Wyntoon with actress Aileen Pringle. "Would you get in bed with me?" she asked the first night.

Pringle panicked. Harlow continued. "I can't fall asleep without putting my head on someone's shoulder, and without my mother or Bill . . ." Charmed and touched,

Pringle held Harlow until she slept. "She was a sweet, innocent child," Pringle sighs.

"I found her absolutely adorable," agrees Maureen O'Sullivan, Harlow's roommate at Hill Haven, the Lake Arrowhead lodge of Myron Selznick. "She would get up early and shut the windows so I'd be warm, and since she slept in the raw, she would get a nightgown, rumple it up, and put it on the bed so the maid wouldn't be shocked! She was so cute.

"She didn't bother with underwear," O'Sullivan adds. "She just wore flaring white slacks and a white sweater, combed her hair, sprayed herself from head to toe with a long tube of perfume, and was off for the day." At Hill Haven, Harlow confided her love for Powell and called Mont Carpenter in Kansas City. She could not do either at home.

By the summer's end, nationwide ticket sales had rebounded from 60 million, a 1933 nadir, to 80 million per week. No new release was more widely awaited than *China Seas*, which *Time* called "first-rate, lively, funny, and convincing" and whose "premiere seemed to presage box-office records and a banner year, as usual, for the most ingratiating member of its cast, Jean Harlow." Pronouncing her "the foremost U.S. embodiment of sex appeal [who] has paradoxically made herself a symbol for the kind of allure which her appearance naturally suggests by ridiculing it," *Time* put Harlow on its August 19, 1935, cover. She wore a white negligee with ostrich-trimmed sleeves. *Time*'s caption: "Fine feathers make fine fans."

Besides its publicity value and prestige, *Time*'s profile of Harlow contained more truth than most contemporary accounts. For the first time, readers were told that Mother

Jean "had always wanted to be an actress" until she "began to see that her dreams for her own career might finally be realized vicariously" through her daughter. *Time* also noted Harlow's "habit of speaking of herself in the third person, which seems to confirm her mother's impression that the cinema star, Jean Harlow, is their joint creation." In the same vein, "the mysterious Marino Bello" was snidely described as "the owner of some mines to which he is usually just going or from which he has just returned."

The mystery of Bello's mines was solved by Powell, who read *Time*'s story and hired a private detective to investigate them. "Bello had a confederate in Mexico who would send him reports about a gold mine," learned Powell, "which he'd show to the Baby and take 25 percent of her salary to invest." In fact, "there was no mine at all. It was fiction." Bello's "business investments" included a Mexican mistress supported by his stepdaughter's salary.

"She was taking an awful rooking," Powell remembered. "If ever a gal was used . . ."

Legend has Mother Jean so besotted by Bello that she condoned his chronic adultery. Actually, she had tried to divorce him five years earlier but failed when Bello used Edwin Bower Hesser's nude photographs of Harlow as blackmail. These threats had kept them together, and though Mother Jean was aware of Bello's affairs, she overlooked them until Powell intervened. Now she could no longer do so: afraid of driving Harlow, who already hated her stepfather, even further away and closer to Powell, Mother Jean ejected Bello from Beverly Glen. He sought a $250,000 "property settlement" but settled for $22,000—all that remained of Harlow's earnings—and a release from the $22,500 chattel mortgage he had taken during her salary strike. To help Harlow with the debt, Mayer obtained a bank loan for her, made M-G-M its guarantor, and deducted weekly sums from her salary.

On September 26, 1935, Mother Jean appeared in divorce court to charge Bello with mental cruelty. "The man truly acted as though he were a maniac," she testified. "He said he operated some mines, but I never saw any of his money." The hearing took fifteen minutes. Bello was not present.

For the first time in her life, Harlow had control of her finances, and with Powell's support she made plans for her future, buying annuities and drafting a "Last Will and Testament" with her mother as sole beneficiary. Powell also urged Harlow to sell Beverly Glen but Mother Jean refused to move. Torn between the mother she worshipped and the man she adored, Harlow took a typically passive approach to avoid confrontation.

Her career also had problems, though superficially it seemed fine. Spurred by *Time*'s cover story and other rave reviews, *China Seas* made $2.9 million, Harlow's highest grosser to date. But despite her "first-rate" performance in it, she could not keep playing characters "in defiance of the Legion of Decency," and although no one noticed, she had worn a wig once again. Censorship had turned both Harlow's heroines and her hair into anachronisms from a prior, permissive era, and Irving Thalberg knew it. To change with the times, Harlow needed a new look and image; with typical foresight, Thalberg transformed them together. The "Platinum Blonde" was past. A new shade would shape Harlow's future.

Part Five

Brownette

Chapter Sixteen

At M-G-M, remaking a star was serious business. After years spent promoting her as brazen and provocative, Howard Strickling planted stories revealing the "real" Harlow ("She's Not What You Think!" proclaimed *Film Pictorial*) as shy and refined, and for a more conservative style to match her new image, British designer Dolly Tree replaced the brilliant but flamboyant Gilbert Adrian as her M-G-M *couturier*. Meanwhile studio hairdresser Edith Hubner and makeup artist Violet Denoyer experimented on Harlow herself. "They tried everything," remembered George Hurrell. "They even put her in a black wig." Finally still photographer Ted Allan solved the problem. "The first requisite was that I present her as more of a lady," he recalls. "I insisted her hair be toned down" to a "halfway brown" tint which Strickling dubbed "brownette." A shoulder-length wig was handmade for Harlow, whose damaged hair was dyed the same color.

At her first brownette sitting, Harlow "threw a fishnet over her shoulders, then suggested it would show up better if there was bare skin beneath it," Ted Allan continues. "I went back to the camera to adjust things, and when I looked up, she was walking around with [the fishnet] wrapped around her and nothing underneath. It didn't bother her at all." Like Hurrell, Allan witnessed Harlow's uninhibited nature, though by now it seemed less natural than necessary. "I realized then that she needed something personal, that feeling of being liked. It made her feel secure." So did a bottle of gin, which Harlow brought with her. "She could fall into poses like nobody's business," Allan discovered, "and after a couple of drinks, she'd get in the mood and enjoy it." In the past she had not needed liquor to do so.

Her transformation thrilled Harlow. "I've always hated my hair," she admitted, "not only because it limited me as an actress, but because it limited me as a person. It made me look hard and spectacular; I had to live up to that platinum personality." As a brownette, she appeared softer and prettier, with a personality more suited to her actual self. "No woman," she promised, "will ever be afraid of me again."

For her brownette debut, Irving Thalberg produced *Riffraff,* a comedy-drama of a cocky tuna fisherman (Spencer Tracy) and the wisecracking cannery worker who humbles him. Four years earlier Tracy had branded and beaten Harlow in *Goldie,* but now she was an M-G-M star and he was an alcoholic new arrival whose latest bender delayed *Riffraff* for ten days. A consummate professional who curtailed her drinking during shooting, Harlow resented his behavior, and when it persisted, she walked off the set. Makeup artist Layne Britton followed. "What's wrong, Baby?" he asked.

"Tracy's gassed," Harlow answered, "and I'm not going to work 'til he gets straightened out." Her ultimatum was so uncharacteristic that Tracy stayed sober for the rest of *Riffraff*, and though they fought constantly in the film, their offscreen warmth was obvious. "When I shot them together and he drew her close, there was a tenderness expressed that was very touching," said Hurrell. In his private diary, Tracy called Harlow a "grand girl." His other phrase for her: "a square shooter if ever there was one."

Structurally, *Riffraff* resembled *Hold Your Man*: after a lively start, its tone turned solemn and its characters self-sacrificing. The consequences of censorship and Harlow's new image were also apparent, as a comparison with her former film shows. In *Hold Your Man*, Harlow's virginity is ancient history; in *Riffraff*, she guards it with gusto. *Hold Your Man* sends its heroine to reform school, unwed and "in trouble"; *Riffraff* puts her in prison, pregnant but married. Such details not only sanitized the latter film's story, but deprived it of drama. Still, quality was secondary to a more pressing concern: would audiences accept the "Platinum Blonde" without her trademark tresses?

The answer was unanimous. "Not even a brunette rinse can dim the platinum potency of her allure," the New York *Times* announced. "Maybe it's the 'brownette' hair that works the charm, or maybe it's a more experienced little Harlow," patronized Louella Parsons, "but something has inspired her, because she gives her most sincere and convincing performance." Assuring exhibitors that "Harlow has the rare opportunity to be pure and hot at the same time," *Variety* assessed *Riffraff*: "It ain't art, but it's box-office." A $1.05 million gross confirmed it. Harlow's hair did not affect her appeal.

Taking no risks, M-G-M rushed her into *Wife vs. Secretary*, an all-star, "super-special" production whose title was its plot. Clark Gable played a publisher, Myrna Loy his spouse, and Harlow the stenographer who arouses her suspicion. "After all, she is an uncommonly good-looking girl," observes Loy of Harlow, "and people aren't willing to believe that looks go with brains." Harlow has both, yet Loy assumes the worst and charges Gable with it. "If you leave him now, you're never going to get him back," Harlow warns her. "If he turns to me, I won't turn away." Loy feigns indifference. "You're a fool," murmurs Harlow, "for which I am grateful." Stunned by her honesty, Loy realizes her error and reconciles with Gable. An ennobled Harlow returns to her own suitor.

To elevate such material from melodrama, Harlow decided "to try a different approach," stated *Wife vs. Secretary* director Clarence Brown. "Before we began, she came to me and said, 'You tell me what to do and I'll do it.' " Brown urged Harlow to be herself, with extraordinary results: for the first time on film, she played a character with subtlety, dignity, depth, and class. Unlike her *Red-Headed Woman*, who took dictation as foreplay and made men her career, Harlow's heroine in *Wife vs. Secretary* was hindered by her sexuality, which subverted her skills and trivialized her talents. This was the "real" Harlow, and despite its soppy story, *Wife vs. Secretary* remains unique for that reason.

Given her breakthrough, it was ironic that other women in *Wife vs. Secretary* saw only Harlow's beauty. "My God, I've never seen such skin," marveled Myrna Loy of her costar's "creamy complexion," which supporting actress Gloria Holden compared to "pink ivory. It had a *luminosity* to it."

Her on-screen suitor saw more. "She was just wonderful," stammers James Stewart, an M-G-M newcomer at the time. "I don't know what 'glamour' means, but she had it." Harlow's photographic memory also "amazed" him. "She could look at a page of dialogue and just *do* it, with every word exactly as written."

A trio of stars and a surefire title ensured *Wife vs. Secretary*'s success, so its $2.1 million gross caused less comment than Harlow's unprecedented performance. "Unquestionably the picture will mark a brand new career for Harlow," claimed the *Hollywood Reporter*. "Playing with repression and great charm, her secretary is among the finest things she has ever given us." *Variety* lauded Gable and Loy "but it is Harlow who profits most. She clicks in every scene without going spectacular. She shows she really can act something beside the vamp roles with which she has been chiefly identified." If *Riffraff* had introduced her new hair, then *Wife vs. Secretary* inaugurated her new image. Harlow turned both into triumphs.

On December 11, 1935, during shooting on *Wife vs. Secretary*, Harlow collapsed on the set. Rather than rely on Christian Science, Mother Jean contacted Dr. Leland Chapman, a prominent internist whose patients included Walt Disney and George S. Patton. "They don't make doctors like Dad anymore," says his son, Richard Chapman, and with his tailored brown suits, physician's black bag, constant house calls, and soothing bedside manner, Dr. Chapman does evoke a figure from a bygone era. Sixty years later his initial diagnosis of Harlow has been lost—newspapers called it "fatigue caused by overwork"—but its consequence is certain: she developed a crush on her forty-two-year-old, unmarried doctor and made excuses to meet him. "She'd call from the studio and tell Dad she didn't feel well, when in fact she felt fine," Richard Chapman continues. "She just wanted to see him.

"Dad was not a good-looking man, but he was brilliant. He carried himself well, and I suppose he represented stability for her." Though strictly professional, Dr. Chapman's demeanor fed Harlow's dream of a home and family, which she craved more than money or fame. "I'm *home-conscious*," she confessed, "if there's a phrase like that." Whatever her phrasing, Harlow's home-consciousness caused yet another schism between her public image and private self. "She always played such sluts on the screen," explained M-G-M diva Jeanette MacDonald, "and at heart was a young, naive, nice girl who just wanted to be somebody's wife."

"Having to be a sex symbol was the worst," agreed Rosalind Russell, whom Harlow taught to hemstitch on the set of *China Seas*. "She wanted to be a housewife."

"She was *meant* to be a housewife," Virginia Conway concurs. "All she wanted was a family. She loved children."

The feeling was mutual. "From a child's perspective, she was a very warm, loving person," remembers Juanita Quigley, Harlow's screen niece in *Riffraff*. "I loved her immediately," adds actress Edith Fellows. "When we met, she gave me a big hug, and even though I was a child, she didn't talk down to me. She was so warm and affectionate." M-G-M magazine editor Kay Mulvey watched Harlow teach her six-year-old son, Dick Mulvey, to put raw eggs in his mud pies "because they stuck together better." She also bought him a pony.

"She was absolutely *mad* about Patrick, my younger son," Virginia Conway continues. Spotting the five-year-old on her set, Harlow "rushed up from behind" and held him close. "Take my picture with Pat!" she told a photographer. Afterward the boy turned and touched Harlow's breast. "What's this?" he wondered.

"The whole set went into hysterics," says Virginia Conway, and though her anecdote is amusing, it also suggests why Harlow wanted children: to them, her anatomy was an afterthought, not a preoccupation. While adults recognized her beauty, children responded to the woman within. "Kids have an instinct about people," explains Edith Fellows, "which was why I loved her, and not her mother. I just *knew*."

So did Millicent Siegel, the four-year-old daughter of mobster Benjamin Siegel. He had been nicknamed "Bugsy" for his hairtrigger temper but was only called "Ben" to his face, and his crimes included bookmaking, bootlegging, drug smuggling, hijacking, rape, robbery, and murder—all by age twenty-one. Subsequently he and Meyer Lansky formed "the Bug and Meyer mob," a gang of contract killers serving New York and New Jersey. There Siegel befriended Longy Zwillman, and when the two traveled to Los Angeles in 1933, actor George Raft took Siegel to the *Bombshell* set and Bello introduced him to Harlow.

Two years later Siegel moved west to consolidate mob-controlled gambling in California. Eager to curry favor, Bello became a frequent visitor to Siegel's Holmby Hills estate, and before his divorce from Mother Jean, he often brought Harlow along. She went to see Millicent, who recalls Harlow as "very blonde, very pretty, very sweet, and very loving. I responded to her warmth." While Bello ingratiated himself with Siegel—"he was just a gopher for my father," sneers his daughter today—Harlow played mother to Millicent, "giving me baths and fussing over me a great deal." Soon she requested another role. "She wanted to be my godmother, so my parents let her. It wasn't a formal ceremony; she just decided she was going to be my godmother, so that's what she became."

To commemorate the occasion, Harlow's new goddaughter received a signed photograph of her as a brownette. MILLICENT DEAREST, its inscription read, DO YOU LIKE AUNTIE JEAN'S NEW HAIR? LOVE TO A SWEET BABY, JH 1935. Though the thought was Harlow's, the handwriting was Mother Jean's. "She was just the opposite of Auntie Jean," remembers Millicent. "She didn't fuss over me, and Auntie Jean did.

"Her mother was all over her. 'Baby' this, 'Baby' that ... 'Baby, don't get dirty,' 'Baby, don't eat that' ... I don't know how she stood it."

Godmotherhood was Harlow's rehearsal for her own home and family, yet by March 14, 1936, the day her divorce from Hal Rosson became final, each seemed less likely than ever. After almost two years together, she and Powell remained unmarried, and although the *Hollywood Reporter* considered their wedding "a foregone conclusion," Harlow denied even an engagement. "I will never marry while I'm working in pictures," she stated. "I don't think you can divide your attention between marriage and work and make a success of either. Both are full-time jobs."

Pressured further by Louella Parsons, Harlow told the truth. "Poppy feels we shouldn't get married."

"How do you feel?" asked Parsons.

"I love him," said Harlow. "He's the only man I'd want to settle down with and raise a family. But I suppose he's right. Marriage hasn't panned out for either of us in the past, and perhaps two movie people with careers shouldn't marry."

It was a crushing prospect. "She was in love with him, and she desperately wanted to get married," confirms Virginia Conway. "She would show up at the studio when she wasn't working and sit on his set, just to be with him. She did his sewing and mending. She knitted him sweaters." Her total devotion disturbed Dorothy Manners, who felt Harlow behaved "like a little puppet" around Powell. "She was so in love with him that she wasn't terribly interesting, if you know what I mean. She became very servile." Rather than attend *Riffraff*'s preview, Harlow stayed home to run lines with Powell, and six months later, at his insistence and against Mother Jean's wishes, she sold Beverly Glen for $125,000 and leased a small house at 512 North Palm Drive in Beverly Hills for $300 a month. It was a wise move, and Mother Jean blamed Powell for it. "I never felt Bill loved the Baby with the wholehearted intensity, the unselfishness, and the adoring worship she gave him," she sniped later.

Jealous of anyone beloved by her Baby, Mother Jean extended her enmity to Aunt Jetty and her son, Don

Roberson, whom Harlow considered her surrogate family. "Harlean called last night," wrote Aunt Jetty at the time, "and wanted me to go with Don and spend the day at the studio. She said she must see me, but I told her I did not think it best as it would only make trouble for us. She said she would phone me when she found time and could talk. Poor girl; I suppose something's wrong . . .

"She always wants to see me, but it always makes trouble as [Mother] Jean is such a tiger about her coming to me. But I sent her a letter by Don this morning . . ." Discovering the document, Mother Jean barred Aunt Jetty and Don Roberson from Palm Drive. Her edict forced Harlow to sneak from the studio to their home, where she cooked meals, kept house, and complained sporadically of "a pain in my side."

That spring she began *Suzy*, a contrived World War I caper with Cary Grant. "They got along wonderfully," says Virgil Apger, although Grant disliked the script (written by, among others, Dorothy Parker) and at first refused to do it. As an American chorine stranded in Europe, Harlow wore a honey-blonde wig and sang "Did I Remember?" dubbed by Eadie Adams. Shooting went smoothly until late April, when *Suzy* shut down due to its star's current ailment: "a cold." Mother Jean summoned Dr. Chapman, and when he arrived, Harlow greeted him at the door. She was nude.

In her case, it was characteristic. "Once I delivered a script to her," remembers Arthur Landau's son, "and there she was, lying on a chaise by the swimming pool, absolutely naked." While he "stood there gaping," Harlow "never blinked an eye. It was as though she was fully dressed. She wasn't embarrassed a bit." Neither was Dr. Chapman, whose fondness for Harlow upset Marcella Arthur, his bride-to-be. "Mother was very emotional, and she was jealous of Jean Harlow," reveals Richard Chapman. "She made Dad swear not to see her anymore." Honoring his future wife's wishes, Dr. Chapman "went to Harlow's mother and said, 'I'm sorry, I can't attend to her any longer.'" Harlow recovered—or so it seemed—without his care, and on May 2, a day after she returned to *Suzy*, Dr. Chapman married Marcella Arthur.

The next time he saw Harlow was the last week of her life.

Chapter Seventeen

As always, Harlow marked Mother's Day with reverence. Her 1936 paean, scribbled in pencil:

Mother:

Somehow words are futile . . . God who expresses all through us expressed His whole beauty of life when He made you. To say that I am grateful to you is so utterly empty. I can only say this—all my life I will forever be thankful to God for you.

me

Sentiments like these made it clear that, after two years together, Powell had not freed Harlow from her mother. "The grip she had on that girl was unbelievable," Myrna Loy lamented, and that month Harlow made it official. At a Superior Court hearing on May 27, "Harlean Carpenter McGrew Bern Rosson" changed her legal name to "Jean Harlow," eroding her identity even further. Small wonder she still signed her letters "me." Harlow did not have her own name.

Two days later "Mrs. Jean Carpenter," her latest alias and another former name of her mother, was admitted to Good Samaritan Hospital. Accompanied by "Mrs. Webb" (Mother Jean) and Dr. Harold Barnard, the mystery patient listed her profession as "Actress," left her "Religious Denomination" blank, and requested Room 826, the same suite Harlow had occupied during her appendectomy. According to Good Samaritan records, she had "entered the hospital to rest." Actually, she was there for an abortion.

Harlow was discharged after three days. "Accomplished purpose," claimed Dr. Barnard cryptically, and with Good Samaritan's tight security, the public never learned of her hospitalization. Neither did Powell, whose reluctance to marry Harlow had necessitated the procedure. The child was his, and although Harlow wanted it desperately, she was forced to abort once again.

Depressed and disillusioned, she drowned her sorrows with Don Roberson. "Mrs. Graves calling," Harlow would inform her cousin by phone, then buy a bottle of Graves gin (hence her code name), pick him up in her Cadillac, drive to a secluded spot, and drink. By the end of such binges Harlow would be "weepy and nostalgic," crying for Chuck McGrew and imagining her life as his wife, not a star.

In the past Mother Jean had monitored such behavior, but now she was busy with her own beau, Henry "Heinie" Brand. Termed "a *different* brand of Brand" by his disapproving family, he was four years Mother Jean's junior and lacked Bello's looks and manner. "I was shocked when I heard she was Heinie's girlfriend," says his sister-in-law,

Sybil Brand, "because he was *not* the sort of man I thought she'd go for. Mrs. Bello was an elegant lady, and Heinie was *gruff.*" An avid outdoorsman, Brand fished off Catalina Island, and as their relationship developed, Mother Jean accompanied him. Her absence gave Harlow a small degree of freedom. She was too forlorn to care.

At the depths of personal despair, Harlow reached a professional peak. Despite snide reviews—"with padded horns of dialogue and venerable plot whiskers ... *Suzy* must have been born under the sign of Capricorn," scorned the New York *Times*—her latest release was a surprise sensation, with an extended run and a $1.8 million gross, triple its $614,000 cost. As a gesture of gratitude, Mayer gave Harlow a $5,000 bonus and top billing in *Libeled Lady,* a screwball comedy with Powell, Tracy, and Loy that began shooting in July. A month later director Jack Conway took Powell and Loy on location, so Harlow visited her mother and Heinie Brand on Catalina Island, returned home by speedboat, and suffered second-degree burns. "She was never supposed to go in the sun, and she got *really* burnt," recalls Virginia Conway. Barbara Brown found Harlow in bed and "in agony. Her face was so red." Forbidden from seeing Dr. Chapman, she settled for Dr. Sidney Burnap, who had removed her appendix three years earlier. Dr. Burnap confined Harlow to bed, and since she could not appear before a camera, *Libeled Lady* halted production. "I've got pneumonia," Harlow announced on a live radio interview. It was her fourth malady in nine months.

Given her real-life plight, *Libeled Lady*'s plot—as a favor to Tracy, Harlow weds Powell against her will—was unwittingly cruel. "Trying to marry *me* off to that . . . that *baboon!*" she bristles, and though their enforced marriage was funny on film, its off-camera correlative had no such humor. Throughout shooting "there were rumors that the Baby and Bill were going to get married," says script supervisor Carl Roup, but Powell would not propose. That Harlow also played a frustrated fiancée in *Libeled Lady* added to the irony, and in spite of the film's comic antics, her portrayal has genuine poignance. "If you don't want to marry me, just say so," she implores Tracy moments before marrying Powell. Forty-five years later, New York *Times* critic Vincent Canby called it "one of the dearest moments in all of American filmmaking."

After her wholesome heroines in *Wife vs. Secretary* and *Suzy, Libeled Lady* let Harlow be brazen, go braless, and throw tantrums once again. "We are pathetically grateful to Metro for restoring Miss Harlow to her proper metier," rejoiced the New York *Times*. "Few actresses," *Variety* asserted, "would have the courage to tackle a role such as Harlow has." An instant classic, *Libeled Lady* earned $2.7 million and an Academy Award nomination for Best Picture. Her latest success certified Harlow as M-G-M's most popular female star.

On September 14, two weeks after *Libeled Lady* finished shooting, thirty-seven-year-old Irving Thalberg died in his sleep. For the first time in history, M-G-M shut down for a funeral.

Four days later Powell and Loy went on location to San Francisco for *After the Thin Man*, a sequel to their prior success. Harlow was not in the film but went along anyway. "I'm here to chaperone Miss Loy," she teased reporters, then returned to reading a new novel entitled *Gone with the Wind.*

At the St. Francis Hotel, the threesome learned a suite had been held for Powell and Loy, whom the management presumed were married. "Well, of course, it was hysterical," Loy remembered. "Here was Jean, but we couldn't be obvious about the situation with the press on our heels." Unsure how to handle the matter, Loy looked to Harlow. "I didn't know what to do, but Jean was marvelous. 'There's nothing for you to do,' she said. 'We'll just have to put Bill downstairs.' " Though he "complained bitterly," the two women shared a suite.

"That mix-up brought me one of my most treasured friendships," Loy continued. "You'd have thought Jean and I were in boarding school, we had so much fun. We'd stay up half the night talking and sipping gin, sometimes laughing, sometimes discussing more serious things." Listening to Harlow, Loy "realized how deeply she loved Bill, a total childlike love, full of the exuberance and wonder that characterized her." The catch: "She wanted marriage, but he was afraid to marry her." Harlow hoped Powell's fear would subside.

To fill Harlow's days while Powell "worked terribly hard on that San Francisco location," Loy introduced her to Jeanne Pope, a local socialite and close friend. "The first time I went up to her hotel suite," reminisces Pope today, "she was wearing a very fancy cocktail suit and an *enormous* corsage of orchids. We sat and talked for a few minutes, then she excused herself. A few minutes later she returned in a simple dress with no orchids, which I thought was very perceptive on her part." For the rest of her stay Harlow "palled around" with Pope, who thought her "dear and quiet—and much too sensitive for the life she was leading."

Its penalty was apparent. "Her face was always puffy for a few hours in the morning," Pope noticed, "and at lunch she ate nothing but spinach. It was a bit distressing." Myrna Loy agreed: Harlow looked heavier, "tired easily, and in the morning her usually snow-white skin sometimes seemed slate-gray. I sensed she was a sick girl." At a cocktail party Loy prodded Pope's husband, Dr. Saxton Pope, to study Harlow. " 'Take a good look at this girl,' I told him. 'See what you can find out about her health.' " Pretending to admire Harlow's bracelets, Dr. Pope clasped her wrist and checked her pulse. It was "very irregular."

"He wanted to give her a thorough examination," wrote Loy, "so I made her promise she'd come back there for a proper checkup. I even arranged for an appointment at the medical center, but she never made up her mind to do it."

Her swollen face, slate-gray skin, frequent fatigue, and abnormal pulse did not deter Harlow from drinking. "She used to take a glass of gin and say, 'Here goes another baked potato!' " reveals Jeanne Pope. "She didn't want to give up Bill Powell, or those 'baked potatoes' . . ."

Their stagnant relationship made Harlow drink harder, and by the time she returned to Hollywood, the effect of the alcohol was evident. "She was pale," Ted Allan discovered, "and she didn't have her usual verve." At a sitting that winter, Allan watched Harlow consume "an entire bottle of gin by herself. I had one sip."

Just before Christmas, Powell bought Harlow an 85-carat star sapphire ring. "It was big, but it wasn't gem quality," states her jeweler, John Gershgorn. "Powell didn't know about quality, and he didn't care. He was a tightwad." Myrna Loy thought the ring "really was *too* big, but Jean was thrilled. This meant so much to her." Since she "proudly displayed" it on her right (i.e., wrong) hand, reporters asked Harlow if her engagement was official. "It is as far as I'm concerned!" she replied.

Powell was noncommittal. "I knew she'd like it," he shrugged. "It's so vulgar."

The dig destroyed Harlow. "It was almost like he was *trying* to hurt her," says Dorothy Manners, "and he did, very deeply. Bill was the only man she'd ever really loved, and he made her feel inferior. He would make cracks about her being dumb, which she was *not*."

"I liked Bill, but he put her down," Jeanne Pope concurs. "She was so glamorous, and it was his way of keeping her in place." Anita Loos blamed Powell's behavior on Carole Lombard, whose "incredible glamour . . . reduced his ego practically to the situation of a Paul Bern" during their marriage. As a result, "Bill needed some Little Miss Nobody to regain his polarity."

He admitted as much. "I learned my lesson when I was 'Mr. Carole Lombard,'" Powell contended. "You don't marry someone half of America wants to sleep with." Coming from Harlow's male counterpart, it was the height of hypocrisy.

In a further sign of his insensitivity, Powell likened Lombard to Harlow though their similarity was superficial. Both were curvaceous blondes and beloved comediennes, but as even Hal Rosson had realized, "Lombard was an entirely different type of individual," a canny careerist with intense inner drive. Harlow was her opposite. "Carole Lombard seems like a real movie star to me," she once said. "I've always felt more like an outsider who got an unbelievable break in Hollywood." Her honesty did not prevent Powell from treating Harlow like Lombard and assuming she could take it.

He was wrong. "Harlow wasn't Lombard," maintains M-G-M drama coach Lillian Burns. "She couldn't fight him. Lombard could fight *anybody*. She had confidence, and I don't think Harlow ever believed in herself." On-screen both could act tough, but in Harlow's case, it was only an act; "inside," observed actor George O'Brien, "she was as soft as a grape." Had Powell discerned this, he might not have hurt Harlow's feelings and downplayed her devotion. When he did, "she didn't stand a chance."

After the holidays Harlow began *The Man in Possession,* a dull farce already filmed by M-G-M five years earlier. Refurbished for her and heartthrob Robert Taylor as *Personal Property,* the project was assigned to director W. S. Van Dyke, known as "One-Take Woody" for his fast shooting style. Harlow played a penniless widow yet wore her star sapphire ring anyway, and at Van Dyke's grueling pace, *Personal Property* completed production in just twenty-two days. The following week its stars and Paramount actress Marsha Hunt departed for Washington, D.C., at President Roosevelt's invitation. Naturally Mother Jean went along.

Arriving in the capital on January 29, 1937, Harlow attended twenty-two functions in two days, including a White House luncheon with Eleanor Roosevelt; a machine-gun demonstration by J. Edgar Hoover (whose files linked Harlow to Longy Zwillman and Bugsy Siegel); a charity ball for FDR's fifty-fifth birthday; and a private audience with the President himself. "We went up to his office," recalls Marsha Hunt. "She was *terrified*." Harlow called it "the highlight of my whole life," though the trip itself exhausted her. "She had a very bad cold and was really quite unwell," Hunt continues. "But she made all the stops, went to each event, and smiled bravely." By the time their return train reached Chicago, both Harlow and her mother were so "seriously ill" with influenza that nurses were necessary.

Mother Jean recovered swiftly. Harlow did not, and in retakes of *Personal Property*, her body looked bloated and her eyes appeared glazed. "I could tell she wasn't well," confirmed George Hurrell. "She looked heavier, and she faded fast." In prior photographs Harlow's figure had been flawless. Now Hurrell retouched her jawline, arms, hips, and ankles.

On March 3, her twenty-sixth birthday, M-G-M slated Harlow and Powell for *The World's Our Oyster*. The following evening they joined Gable and Lombard, Hollywood's other high-profile couple, at the Academy Awards, where Powell and Lombard were nominated for *My Man Godfrey* and *Libeled Lady* competed for the year's Best Picture. None won, but *The Great Ziegfeld*, a $2 million musical with Powell in the title role, took the top prize. He and Harlow were at the height of their careers, and though their offscreen relationship seemed just as successful, in truth "it was at a dead end," Dorothy Manners divulges. "She couldn't take any more of the way Bill was treating her." Summoned to Palm Drive, Manners found Harlow "beside herself. Pacing up and down, up and down. *Very* distressed about Bill. 'This is so one-sided,' she said. 'I'm the one who does all the giving.' "

"Baby, *all* men do that," consoled Manners.

"Maybe," Harlow muttered, "but I can't stand it anymore. He's driving me crazy. He's breaking my heart."

Her listener believed it. "She looked like hell," Manners remembers. "Her face was puffy, she was extremely unhappy, and she was alone. You would never have known it was Jean Harlow."

"She was a sad girl, driven by her mother, madly in love with a man who wouldn't marry her, and . . . drinking too much," wrote Rosalind Russell. "I went into a lot of bars to try and get her out." On one rescue mission, Russell noticed Harlow's polar bear rug. "What happened to his teeth?" she wondered.

"I kicked 'em in," said Harlow. She also named Barbara Brown and Blanche Williams as "the only people who never get on my nerves."

Brown was baffled. "I never saw her get angry at *anyone*," she says, which was both Harlow's paradox and her problem. On the surface, she was sweet and easygoing, but beneath lurked latent hostility—and by now, after a lifetime of repression, this side was equally strong. To express it, Harlow bolstered her courage with liquor, then confronted the root of her rage: Mother Jean, who had slave-driven her to stardom, sabotaged her marriages, squandered her money, and sacrificed her happiness. "The more she drank, the more she hated her mother," said eyewitness Blanche Williams. "She became very verbally abusive." On film, Harlow's fury was funny. Offscreen, her tantrums were terrifying.

Unable to acknowledge her anger consciously, Harlow would awaken from a binge with no memory of her behavior. "When she sobered up, she'd be her meek self again," Williams discovered. Ever the dutiful daughter, Harlow even scolded Elaine St. Johns "when she thought I had been rude to my mother. She was very kindly about it, but she would not brook any disrespect." According to St. Johns, Harlow's doctrine was simple. "No matter what your mother did or what you *thought* your mother did, she was your *mother*, and you maintained a certain attitude toward her."

St. Johns adored Harlow but felt "she had a fixation. I think Mother Jean reiterated how much she'd done for her, and the Baby believed it." Liquor replaced this fantasy with reality: in the guise of maternal devotion, Mother Jean had exploited Harlow mercilessly. All she wanted was a home and family. Instead she was a film star, which was her mother's wish, not her own.

Harlow's Jekyll-Hyde transformations "were extremely frightening to Mother Jean," observed Blanche Williams. "She wanted to get the Baby off booze." Ashamed of her daughter's alcoholism, Mother Jean claimed "the Baby wasn't supposed to drink because she'd had polio as a child." This was absurd, but without Powell to oppose her, Mother Jean manipulated Harlow once more. A letter to Arthur Landau conveys her calculation:

Pops darling,

The situation here is as I would like it. I see the tiniest let-up. It is SO slight that I think the person herself has not recognized it: in fact, I know she has not but you know I know that little fellow so well that I can see things that she is entirely unconscious of. She would certainly deny it if it were mentioned to her and feel absolutely honest in her denial, but it will gradually work out as we hope, with no great break. I am not worrying about it now.

Mother

Of more immediate worry was Harlow's latest ailment, a painful toothache which led her to Dr. Leroy Buckmiller. "He was a good Mormon and an excellent dentist," says fellow patient Barbara Brown. "We thought the world of him."

Now a nonagenarian, Dr. Buckmiller describes ensuing events. "She needed her wisdom teeth removed. I recommended extracting one at a time, but the mother insisted on having them all done at once. She felt it was too much for her daughter to go to the hospital four times.

"I felt it was too much for her *not* to. She was under a great deal of strain, and one extraction at a time was enough. I thought it was all she could take." Ignoring this, Mother Jean asked Dr. Emil Tholen, a plastic surgeon, and Dr. Julian Dow, an ophthalmologist, to perform the procedure. Neither practiced dentistry, nor were they informed of Harlow's poor health.

"It just amazed me," sighs Dr. Buckmiller. "I'd been her dentist for years, yet she didn't take my advice. She had confidence in me, but as you know, the control came from other sources . . ."

On March 23, Mother Jean accompanied Harlow to

Good Samaritan Hospital, where she occupied the same room as she had for her appendectomy and abortion. The next morning Dr. Tholen, Dr. Dow, and Dr. John Dunlop, a hospital anesthesiologist, began what should have been routine surgery.

Instead disaster struck. "After three teeth, she went out on the table," Dr. Buckmiller was told. "They lost a heartbeat, so they stopped the operation."

"It was very serious," says Barbara Brown. "She almost died."

This was headline news, yet besides a brief mention ("Those four wisdom teeth which put Jean Harlow in the hospital have brought about a much more serious condition than anyone suspected," the New York *American* disclosed), Harlow's brush with death went unreported. Even Louis B. Mayer assumed she had postoperative complications. Had he known otherwise, her eighteen-day hospitalization would have caused more concern.

Harlow and Powell's estrangement prompted Mayer to shelve *The World's Our Oyster* and switch her to *Saratoga*, a racetrack romance devised for Joan Crawford. Harlow was a last-minute substitution. For the fourth time in fifteen months, her health delayed shooting.

Harlow left Good Samaritan on April 10. "After this experience I never want to *hear* of wisdom teeth," Mother Jean wrote Arthur Landau in her daughter's name. "I have looked like a 'double-exposure' of Harlow for so long that when I am normal [I] probably will feel sorry for the old sunken face." Confined to Palm Drive so her mother could supervise her convalescence, Harlow rose early, sneaked across the street, and cooked breakfast in bed for Dr. Harold Barnard and his wife, who knew "she did it just to get away from Mother Jean for a while."

Without Powell or Aunt Jetty, she had nowhere else to go.

Chapter Eighteen

That spring she found a new suitor: Donald Friede, whose colorful past resembled a picaresque novel. Born in New York but schooled in France, Switzerland, Germany, Japan, China, Sweden, and prerevolutionary Russia, where his father had the first Ford dealership, then expelled from Harvard, Yale, and Princeton, Friede had heeded the advice of his Freudian analyst, abandoned a business career, and bought into Boni & Liveright, an eminent publisher in need of quick cash. In his first year alone, Friede published T. S. Eliot, Sigmund Freud, and Eugene O'Neill; first works by William Faulkner and Ernest Hemingway; *Gentlemen Prefer Blondes*; and *An American Tragedy*, for which he was charged with obscenity and defended by Clarence Darrow. It was 1925. Friede was twenty-four.

One decade and three marriages later, Friede moved to Hollywood to sell film rights to fiction by Pearl S. Buck, John Dos Passos, Theodore Dreiser, Somerset Maugham, H. G. Wells, and, rumor had it, Harlow, for whom he was hawking *Today Is Tonight*. Actually, M-G-M already owned her novel, and Friede's interest was not as an agent. "He was in love with her," confirmed Friede's fifth wife, culinary author M. F. K. Fisher. "He said she was more beautiful physically and personally than any p.r. work could show." Both Fisher and Friede's widow, sixth wife Eleanor Friede, believed he proposed to Harlow: "They planned to marry, I'm sure."

Even so, she pined for Powell. "In the face of Hollywood's mounting suspicions, Jean Harlow assures me that things are the same as ever between her and Bill Powell," wrote columnist Harrison Carroll. "Recently, she has been seeing a good deal of Donald Friede, 'but that is nothing for people who have been going together for three years,' explained Jean. 'I'm giving you the lowdown. Bill and I are the same as ever.'"

This was wishful thinking, and despite Friede's discretion "we all knew what was going on," says Phyllis Cerf. At the Andalusian, an elegant apartment court where Friede lived, Cerf glimpsed Harlow "coming and going" and actress Anne Shirley accidentally met her in his home. "I was in awe," she admits. "She was dressed casually, but to me she was a goddess." Warm and gracious, Harlow urged Shirley and her fiancé, actor John Payne, to play Friede's phonograph while they swam in the pool. "Aren't you lucky," she added. "You can swim and have fun, and I have to get my hair done."

Shirley pitied Harlow. "It was poignant. She envied us 'young people,' and she was only twenty-six herself."

She looked years older. "I've been worn out since that trip to Washington," Harlow told Louella Parsons, who saw her at Jim's Beauty Studio and was shocked by her appearance. Once the possessor of "pink ivory" skin and a perfect figure, her complexion was chalky and "her body looked bloated," remarks Lillian Burns. "I talked to her on the set of *Saratoga*, and even through her makeup she didn't look well. She was perspiring a great deal, and it wasn't that hot."

Rather than run a current portrait of Harlow on its May 3, 1937, cover, *Life* magazine chose a photograph taken two years earlier. The contrast was alarming, and Mother Jean knew it. "Baby, you must take care of yourself," Dorothy Manners heard her command. "You must look well before the camera." Instead Harlow drank during shooting, suffering severe morning headaches and missing several 6 A.M. calls. "Baby, why don't you tell us when you're going to be late so we can *all* sleep longer?" Jack Conway chided.

"You're lucky I'm here," snapped Harlow. Both her tardiness and tone were atypical.

While she toiled on *Saratoga*, Mother Jean returned to Catalina Island with Heinie Brand. DEAREST HEART, she wired Harlow on her favorite holiday. THIS IS MOTHER'S DAY AND I HAD TO TELL YOU AGAIN THAT OF ALL THE MOTHERS I AM THE MOST FORTUNATE. NEVER WAS THERE A BABY SO TENDER, SO PRECIOUS, SO WONDERFUL AS MY BABY. EACH AND EVERY YEAR I REALIZE MORE HOW BLEST [*sic*] I AM TO HAVE YOU. MY HEART IS SO FILLED WITH GRATITUDE FOR JUST YOU, MY BABY. I LOVE YOU. MOTHER. This year, for the first time, she received no reply.

On the third anniversary of Harlow and Powell's first date, a cake with three candles arrived at Palm Drive. A card accompanied it: "To my three-year-old, from her

Daddy." Touched and thrilled, Harlow fed the cake to *Saratoga*'s crew, informed Louella Parsons of Powell's gesture, and returned his star sapphire ring to her right-hand finger. A reconciliation seemed imminent, yet after three years and no wedding, Harlow had lost hope. "I'm constantly trying to be what Bill wants me to," she confided, "but I know we'll never be married." Her disillusionment fueled her drinking, which Friede deemed an "escape . . . and a not particularly effective one."

On Sunday, May 23, Harlow and Friede made a rare public appearance; in spite of the balmy weather, she wore a fur coat. Two days later she filmed a scene with Gable in which he worries about her health, then shared a cottage cheese salad with Barbara Brown in her dressing room. "Do you mind if we don't talk?" asked Harlow. "I don't feel very well."

Brown was stunned. "In all the years I'd known her, it was the only time I ever heard her say that." Afterward she watched Harlow drain her mouth, fighting infection from her botched operation. Clearly she had not recovered, and on Thursday, May 27, *Saratoga* crew member George Sidney noticed Harlow lying down in her dressing room. "Toothache," she told him. "I had my wisdom teeth removed." Sidney wondered why, after more than two months, she was still in such pain. Harlow "shrugged apathetically."

That afternoon she and Gable posed for Clarence Sinclair Bull, creator of "Harlow's halo" from a small surgeon's lamp. "I've never seen her so beautiful, so full of life," said Bull. In fact she was neither, and by Saturday morning, May 29, her illness was obvious to Maureen

O'Sullivan, who rode to work with Harlow in Mother Jean's chauffeured car. "She looked pale and fragile," states O'Sullivan, "and that ring from Bill Powell seemed too heavy for her hand." Harlow confessed that she "wasn't feeling well" but blamed her condition on menstrual cramps.

At the studio, her condition "shocked" *Saratoga* assistant director Tom Andre. "She was so bloated," he said later. "It was obviously fluid retention." Before shooting began, Harlow had a wardrobe fitting with Ted Tetrick. "We were in a tiny portable dressing room," he recalls. "I felt her head, and it was dripping."

"You'd better get her to a hospital," Tetrick warned Jack Conway, who summoned a studio nurse. "She said the Baby should quit, but she didn't." To keep *Saratoga* on schedule, Harlow insisted on completing a scene with supporting actor Walter Pidgeon.

After a rehearsal, she took script supervisor Carl Roup aside. "Please ask Walter to hold me very lightly," Harlow whispered. "My stomach is just killing me." Roup complied, but by now it made no difference. "Just before lunch, she suddenly doubled up in my arms and said, 'I have a terrible pain,' " Pidgeon remembered. "I called to Jack Conway, 'Baby's got a pain.' He told her to go have lunch in her dressing room and rest."

"I never saw her again."

For the rest of her life, Mother Jean would maintain that she brought Harlow home from the studio. Actually, she was on Catalina Island at the time, so her critically ill daughter changed into street clothes and stopped by the set of *Double Wedding*, Powell's latest production. "He was sitting in a chair reading a script," recalled director Richard Thorpe, "when she came by and said, 'Daddy, I don't feel good. I'm going home.'

" 'OK, honey,' Powell replied. 'I'll be over as soon as I can.' "

"He didn't seem particularly worried," adds Virgil Apger, who also overheard the exchange. "But she must have been feeling very bad, because she didn't last much longer."

Six decades later, it is time to learn why.

Part Six

Powell sobs at siren's deathbed

 EVENING NEWS

LOS ANGELES, CALIFORNIA, MONDAY, JUNE 7, 1937

HARLOW DEAD!

EXTRA

HERALD Express

MONDAY, JUNE 7, 1937

JEAN HARLOW IS DEAD; STAR SUCCUMBS IN COMA

Lansing General Strike Called Off After Day of Terror

Los Angeles Examiner

JEAN HARLOW'S DEATH STUNS FILM WORLD; RITES TOMORROW

General Walkout CONCESSIONS   Death Dims Radiance   LEAVES MILLION

"She Never Will"

Chapter Nineteen

When she stopped by his set and said, "I'm going home," Harlow meant Powell's mansion, where she stayed that weekend while he worked on *Double Wedding*. Feverish, chilled, nauseous, and congested, she neither ate nor drank, and when she showed no improvement by Sunday evening, May 30, Powell called Mother Jean on Catalina Island. "He waited because no one thought her illness was serious," explained Kay Mulvey, and given Harlow's symptoms, this appeared true. She had the flu. No doctor was necessary.

Mother Jean disagreed, so on Monday, May 31, she cut short her trip and sent for Dr. Ernest Fishbaugh, the senior partner of Harlow's crush, Dr. Chapman. Six weeks earlier Dr. Fishbaugh had hospitalized grandmother Ella Harlow during her visit to Hollywood; now, on Memorial Day, he examined Harlow at Palm Drive, noted her "severe cold" and "stomach ailment," took blood and urine samples, and assigned Good Samaritan Hospital nurses

Catherine Lemond and Grace Temple to the case. From his first house call, she had round-the-clock care.

The following morning—Tuesday, June 1—Harlow called Jack Conway at home. "Jack, I'm so sick," she cried. "I can't come to work." Conway assured her that *Saratoga* would continue on schedule, but Harlow knew better. "She was hysterical," recalls Virginia Conway, "because she knew they'd have to shoot around her, and a professional hates to do that."

Since her health had already delayed *Wife vs. Secretary*, *Suzy*, *Libeled Lady*, and *Saratoga*, Harlow's latest absence caused little concern. That day she made different news: in exchange for Tyrone Power, whom Mayer wanted for *Madame X*, M-G-M would loan Harlow to Twentieth Century-Fox for *In Old Chicago*. The swap confirmed her status, and with Norma Shearer's career foundering without Thalberg and both Joan Crawford and Greta Garbo branded "box-office poison," Harlow had no competition. Five years and thirteen films after her arrival at the studio, she was M-G-M's top female star. After *In Old Chicago*, she would appear in *The Best Dressed Woman in Paris*, a solo star vehicle; *The Shopworn Angel*, purchased for her from Paramount; *Spring Tide* with Robert Taylor; *Tell It to the Marines* with Spencer Tracy; and *The World's Our Oyster*, again in preparation for her and Powell. More than any memory, M-G-M's big plans for Harlow show its faith in her bright future.

That she would not survive seemed inconceivable. "We knew she was sick," concedes production manager J. J. Cohn. "We *didn't* know she was dying."

On Wednesday, June 2, Harlow complained of intense

abdominal pain, then vomited and grew "delirious." Terming her "too weak to be moved," Dr. Fishbaugh ordered "special medical equipment" from Good Samaritan, transforming Palm Drive into "virtually a hospital" with nurses Lemond, Temple, and Adah Wilson, who had tended Harlow after Paul Bern's death, on duty. Mother Jean was also present, and when her incoherent daughter finally fell asleep, she informed Louella Parsons of Dr. Fishbaugh's diagnosis: cholecystitis, a gallbladder inflammation and "critical condition." Fearing publicity in Parsons' column, Dr. Fishbaugh denied it. "Miss Harlow," he commented, "just has a cold."

Legend contends that news of Harlow's sickness was suppressed until her death. Actually, the first published reports appeared on Thursday, June 3, 1937, while the world's attention was elsewhere: that day Edward VIII married American divorcée Wallis Simpson, for whom he had abdicated his throne. Though their wedding made headlines, Harlow was also a front-page story. JEAN HARLOW SERIOUSLY ILL, announced the Los Angeles *Times*. CINEMA STAR STRICKEN ON STUDIO SET, elaborated Louella Parsons, whose column praised Harlow's "gallant fight against an attack of cholecystitis, with her physician awaiting developments to see if she can avoid complications."

That afternoon Harlow sat up in bed, ate a light meal, and started *Gone with the Wind* for the second time. HARLOW PAST ILLNESS CRISIS, proclaimed the Los Angeles *Herald*. "This baby of mine is much improved," rejoiced Mother Jean. "Her doctor says she is out of danger." Despite this prognosis, Harlow's symptoms persisted, and although she was drowsy, she could not seem to sleep. To "bolster her strength" and prevent dehydration, Dr. Fish-baugh administered an intravenous dextrose injection, and when Mother Jean "expressed deep concern" about her daughter's relapse, he assured her that Harlow had "virtually recovered." Consequently "executives at Metro-Goldwyn-Mayer said they looked forward to her return tomorrow [Friday, June 4] or Monday to resume work on *Saratoga*."

Instead she remained bedridden, leaving friends and coworkers confused and suspicious. Attempts to reach Harlow had been foiled by her mother, who fielded calls and discouraged visits. While some sympathized—"I didn't presume she'd want to see me," says Barbara Brown, "and I didn't want to intrude"—others were less understanding. Aunt Jetty was "deeply hurt," Donald Friede felt "bitterly angry," and Carmelita Geraghty Wilson, at whose wedding Harlow had been matron of honor, drove straight to Palm Drive and demanded entrance. Mother Jean refused. Wilson was adamant. "She insisted that she see the Baby," remembers actress Patsy Ruth Miller, "and after she did, she called me and said Jean looked just awful." Apprised of this, Carey Wilson warned Jack Conway, who telephoned Harlow's home from the *Saratoga* set. "Mrs. Bello," he begged, "you must get the Baby to a hospital."

Mother Jean was immovable. "We are Christian Scientists," she told Conway. *"We are Christian Scientists."*

Here began the Hollywood myth that Harlow's mother, a "devout" Christian Scientist, denied her a doctor and hastened her death. In fact, a licensed physician and three private nurses attended her all week, providing blood and urine tests, dextrose injections, and sulfa drugs. Mother Jean may have preached Christian Science, but Dr. Fishbaugh—like Dr. Lipman, Dr. Barnard, Dr. Kennicott, Dr. Burnap, Dr. Chapman, Dr. Buckmiller, Dr. Tholen, Dr. Dow, and Dr. Dunlop before him—practiced medicine, and Harlow was his patient at her mother's behest. And though Barbara Brown assumes that, sometime that week, Christian Science practitioner Genevieve Smith was asked to treat Harlow, Mother Jean turned to Dr. Fishbaugh first. She did not get fanatical, hysterical, or mystical. She did not kill her daughter.

So why did Mother Jean cite Christian Science and create this misconception? For the same reason she reinterpreted her religion: control. In a hospital, Mother Jean would have to consign her daughter to strangers; at home, she could supervise the situation and hide Harlow's alcoholism, which she secretly blamed for her present problems. Assuming sobriety would both restore her daughter's health and end her drunken rages, Mother Jean hatched a plan: after Dr. Fishbaugh cured Harlow's cholecystitis, she would "dry out" her daughter right there at Palm Drive. Tragically, she picked the worst time to do so. Harlow was dying. Liquor was the least of her problems.

Not only her mother mistook Harlow's current ailment for her chronic alcoholism. "Probably drunk again," Clark Gable told Anita Loos, who thought his assertion "a pretty stupid joke because the Baby was not given to drinking on the job." Actually, Gable's banter expressed his affection for Harlow, and after Mother Jean's alarming conversation with Jack Conway, he and *Saratoga* producer Bernie Hyman rushed to Palm Drive. There they beheld a "shocking" sight: Harlow's body had ballooned to twice its size. Bending forward to greet her, Gable smelled urine on her breath. "It was like kissing a dead person, a rotting person," he said later. "It was a terrible thing to walk into."

Mother Jean knew it. "The Baby is suffering such pain," she informed Louella Parsons. "This is more serious than anyone realizes." Alerted by Gable and Hyman, Louis B. Mayer and Howard Strickling arrived at Palm Drive to offer the services of Dr. Edward B. Jones, Mayer's personal physician. Five years earlier Dr. Jones had exposed Harlow's lack of "domestic relations" with Paul Bern; as a result, an unforgiving Mother Jean "didn't want to have anything to do with him." Rather than offend Mayer, she again used Christian Science as an excuse.

It was not a wise move. "Mr. Mayer was furious," remembers M-G-M receptionist Gladys Searles. "He came back to the office, stood by my desk, and said, 'This is nothing but legalized murder.'"

What followed was stranger than fiction: dissatisfied with Dr. Fishbaugh and in search of a second opinion, Mother Jean contacted Dr. Chapman, who had promised his "insanely jealous" wife not to treat Harlow. To complicate matters further, Marcella Chapman had heard about Harlow's 1936 abortion, confronted her husband, and accused him of fathering the child. Clearly she was deluded, but Dr. Chapman adored her. A month earlier they had celebrated their first anniversary. He could not see Harlow now.

Mother Jean was beside herself. "You've got to help the Baby," she begged. "She's not getting better." Dr. Chapman expressed confidence in his colleague. "*The*

Baby is dying," declared Harlow's mother. "*This doctor is killing her.*"

Torn between personal and professional duties, Dr. Chapman received a call from nurse Wilson. "Doctor, I hope I'm not overstepping my bounds," she began, "but I really believe you are needed here. You should come over."

Dr. Chapman went to Palm Drive.

When he saw Harlow, he burst into tears. "It was too late," he said later. "There was nothing left." Studying her test results, Dr. Chapman noted Harlow's high blood urea and diagnosed acute nephritis, a technical term for kidney failure. "Fishbaugh had misdiagnosed her," he discovered. "He said she had cholecystitis." Harlow needed diuretics, not dextrose injections; by prescribing the latter, Dr. Fishbaugh "gave her fluids, which was the worst thing for her."

This put Dr. Chapman in a delicate position. "Fishbaugh was a good doctor," he maintained to his son. "But you've got to remember, everybody makes mistakes—and in this case, it happened with a very famous patient." For the rest of his life Dr. Chapman protected his senior partner, whose misdiagnosis of Harlow was never made public. And though Dr. Fishbaugh remained her doctor of record, Dr. Chapman took charge of her case.

On Saturday, June 5, word spread that Harlow was back at M-G-M shooting *Saratoga*. In truth, she had contracted uremia, a toxic consequence of kidney failure. Unable to urinate through the usual channel, she excreted waste in her breath, as Gable had smelled, and her sweat. Blanche Williams saw Harlow "in intense, horrible pain." The stench was unbearable.

"There wasn't anything I could do to save her," sighed Dr. Chapman, and although he meant it medically—in the days before antibiotics, dialysis, or transplants, acute nephritis was grisly and fatal—he also sensed Harlow's emotional surrender. "She didn't *want* to be saved," Dr. Chapman continued. "She had no will to live whatsoever." Never a fighter, Harlow faced death with the same passivity which characterized her life. Considering its circumstances, her attitude was understandable: after forty-two movies, three marriages, two abortions, scandal, alcoholism, gonorrhea, and heartbreak, Harlow had lived too hard for a twenty-six-year-old. At least acute nephritis would take her off the treadmill.

"Poor little soul," says nurse Temple today. "I don't think she knew how sick she was, and I don't think she cared. She was so unhappy."

Acute nephritis at Harlow's age implied her kidneys had been failing for years. Since she alternated doctors so often, no complete medical history existed, leading Dr. Chapman to question Mother Jean directly. She maintained that her daughter's condition was due to "polio as a child." Discounting this, Dr. Chapman asked about other childhood ailments. Her mother recalled Harlow's bout with scarlet fever, which she had caught at Camp Chaton-ka in the summer of 1926. Braving quarantine, Mother Jean had been responsible for her recovery, or so she thought until Dr. Chapman's correction. In a cruel twist of fate, fifteen-year-old Harlean Carpenter's scarlet fever had been followed by glomerulonephritis, a post-streptococcal kidney infection that had induced high blood pressure (hence Harlow's grinding headaches, which she mistook for hangovers), hypertension, and nephritis. Her kidneys had degenerated steadily ever since.

Because a kidney can operate on 10 percent of its total function, not even Harlow was aware that hers were failing. Others saw signs—her "puffy" face, "slate-gray" skin, and "bloated" body were textbook clues of kidney disease—but could not determine their cause. By faulting her drinking, Mother Jean missed the point: though it did not affect her nephritis, liquor lowered Harlow's resistance to autoimmune diseases like influenza, which she had caught while in Washington and which robbed her ravaged kidneys of what little function was left. Today Mother Jean could donate a kidney (and relish the drama) for transplantation; at the time, no such procedure was possible. Nephritis doomed Harlow long before fame.

Throughout the week Mother Jean portrayed Powell as "a very faithful and wonderful visitor" to her daughter's bedside. Actually, he was busy with *Double Wedding* and actress Bernadine Hayes, whom he dated while Harlow lay dying. Powell paid his first visit on Sunday, June 6. "I thought she looked wan," he admitted, "but that was all."

Harlow squinted. "You look fuzzy," she said.

Powell raised his hand. "How many fingers?" he teased. Harlow shook her head. Uremia had blurred her vision.

"Her kidneys were completely gone," realized Dr. Chapman. While he called an ambulance, a half-conscious Harlow reminded Blanche Williams to pack *Gone with the Wind*, which she planned to finish "before I get back." SHE NEVER WILL, wrote nurse Wilson. Williams destroyed the note.

At 6:30 P.M., "Miss Jean Harlow" was admitted to Good Samaritan Hospital and taken to Room 826, the same room she stayed in for her appendectomy, abortion, and dental surgery. Her nephritic swelling was "very much a shock" to Dr. Harold Barnard, whose "hand could not span her [formerly] tiny wrist—and her face looked like Fatty Arbuckle."

Placed in an oxygen tent, Harlow passed an agonizing night despite two blood transfusions and the presence of her mother, her maid, her doctors, and hospital nurses Mona Campbell, Miriam Godshall, and Nora Uren. Powell was not present.

By dawn on Monday morning—June 7, 1937—Harlow had retained so much fluid that her skull began to swell. To relieve the pressure, Dr. Chapman considered drilling holes in her temples but feared brain leakage. Besides, she was too weak for neurosurgery. Her "cerebral edema" could not be counteracted.

JEAN HARLOW DYING, declared an early edition of the New York *Sun*. Informed of this, Mother Jean summoned both Marino Bello and Heinie Brand (introduced to the press as "an old friend of the family") to a hospital room across the hall, where they waited with Jack and Virginia Conway. Finally, on his way to work that morning, Powell appeared with actor Warner Baxter.

However selfish Powell had been in the past, the sight of Harlow dying devastated him. "When Bill came out of her room, his face was *purple* from crying," recalls Virginia Conway. "It was *out of shape*."

"You'd better come now," Powell whispered. Jack Conway crossed the hall without his wife. "Thank God I

235

didn't take you in there," he said later. "They'd shaved her head, and she looked like a bag of bones. I never would have recognized her."

Since Mother Jean had not asked Aunt Jetty to the hospital, Dr. Chapman did so himself. "I wouldn't have been allowed in her room if not for him," Aunt Jetty revealed later. "He took me in and opened the [oxygen] tent. Just my hand went in to grasp hers. She said, 'I love you,' and in all her horrible suffering *winked* at me."

Aunt Jetty held Harlow's hand. "Harlean, please," she pleaded. "Try to get better."

"I don't want to," sighed Harlow. Nearing hysteria, her relative left the room. "Where is Aunt Jetty?" she heard Harlow murmur. "Hope she didn't run out on me . . ."

These were her last words. At 9 A.M. she grew incoherent, then slipped into a coma. Dr. Fishbaugh called the Los Angeles Fire Department, which sent Captain Warren Blake and "inhalator squad" members Ralph Beal and William Thomas to Good Samaritan. The men placed a mask on Harlow's face and pumped four tanks of oxygen into her fluid-filled lungs. Powell entered, tried to speak, but ran sobbing from the room. Mother Jean stayed by her daughter's bedside, "shaking her lightly" and trying to rouse her. "I talked to her for two hours and thirty-seven minutes," she boasted, "and never stopped talking. I said over and over and over again, 'Mother loves you, darling. You know that, don't you? Mother loves you. Mother needs you. You know me. You know I'm here. You recognize me, don't you, Baby?' "

Jean Harlow did not, and at 11:38 that morning, she shuddered once and died.

Chapter Twenty

*H*er funeral was a spectacle. Held on June 9 at Forest Lawn Memorial Park, a Glendale cemetery that *Time* termed "the Valhalla of the cinema business," the ceremony attracted an all-star cast—Clark Gable, Carole Lombard, Spencer Tracy, Myrna Loy, Norma Shearer, Wallace Beery, Lionel Barrymore, Warner Baxter, Ronald Colman, the Marx brothers, and Robert Montgomery—floral tributes worth $15,000, a mob of morbid onlookers, and the tightest security in industry history. "It was the first big Hollywood funeral," explains honorary pallbearer J. J. Cohn. "Thalberg wasn't a public figure and Valentino had died in New York, so it was quite a scene."

Inside the nondenominational Wee Kirk o' the Heather chapel, celebrity mourners mingled with, among others, Louis B. Mayer, Marino Bello, Heinie Brand, Mont and Maude Carpenter, Aunt Jetty and Don Roberson, Hal Rosson, Donald Friede, Jack and Virginia Conway, Carey and Carmelita Wilson, and the group Harlow called "my gang": Barbara Brown, Blanche Williams, Violet Denoyer, and M-G-M hairdresser Peggy McDonald, who helped Pierce Brothers morticians prepare Harlow's body. She wore a full wig, a pink silk negligee from *Saratoga*, and white sandals. "She looked beautiful," says Barbara Brown, "but I felt so bad I fainted." Front-page stories pronounced her "hysterical."

Before her funeral, Harlow's casket was opened to family members and special friends, then closed and covered with 1,500 lilies of the valley and 500 gardenias supplied by her studio. A prostrate Bill Powell arrived with his mother and M-G-M publicist Otis Wiles. "He was crying and shaking, and he almost passed out," recounts publicist Teet Carle. "A complete breakdown."

Coworkers shared Powell's sorrow. "The day the Baby died, there wasn't one sound in the M-G-M commissary for three hours," recalled screenwriter Harry Ruskin. "Not one goddamn sound."

"The whole studio seemed to be in mourning," remembers Mickey Rooney. "It wasn't a star passing away. It wasn't a legend. It wasn't 'Jean Harlow.' It was one of our *family*." Beside exotic roses from Howard Hughes and exquisite larkspur from Sophie Tucker lay modest bouquets from gaffers, grips, prop boys, and script girls. Even *Saratoga*'s extras sent flowers.

At 9 A.M., Hollywood studios observed a minute of silence as Harlow's funeral service began. Jeanette MacDonald sang "Indian Love Call." Christian Science practitioner Genevieve Smith read from the Twenty-ninth Psalm, recited the Lord's Prayer, and delivered a thirty-eight-second eulogy. "Her outstanding attributes were love and courage," said Smith through tears. The service ended with

Nelson Eddy's rendition of "Ah, Sweet Mystery of Life" a mere twenty-three minutes later.

"I've been to every big Hollywood funeral," declares Virginia Conway, "but I've never heard such demonstrations of grief as I did that day." There was an exception. "I was sitting next to Mother Jean," Conway continues. "Her chin was slightly lifted, and she had a smile on her face— and *not one tear* in her eye."

Harlow's life was over, but her legend had just begun. Medically naive and accustomed to cover-ups, the Hollywood community swapped outrageous rumors about her fatal ailment. Word had it that Harlow died of cancer, heart disease, menstrual problems, a miscarriage, polio, peroxide poisoning (which "seeped into her brain and killed her," claimed Cary Grant "with great assurance"), a septic abortion, sunburn, and/or syphilis. On one point all agreed: her mother had withheld treatment until it was too late. "I hold that woman responsible for Jean's death," wrote Myrna Loy. "She killed the one she loved most," says Marcella Rabwin.

Mother Jean was more concerned with Harlow's corpse. At first she chose cremation, then decided a lasting monument should be erected. Skip Harlow offered a spot in the family's Kansas plot, but Mother Jean sought a local, loftier marker. In a ploy to obtain it, she issued a surprise statement. "I believe it is only fair to disclose," Mother Jean announced, "that as a shrine for the Baby, Bill Powell bought the room where she will lie forever." Located in Forest Lawn's lavish "Sanctuary of Benediction" mausoleum, Harlow's "shrine" was a 9×10-foot, marble-lined mortuary chamber near Marie Dressler, who had died of cancer in 1934, and "next-door" to Irving Thalberg. Cost with deluxe coffin: $30,000.

A "dumbstruck" Powell could hardly protest. "The poor slob didn't know what hit him," said Dr. Chapman. "By the time he got the bill for building that mausoleum, he almost had a heart attack." With characteristic cunning, Mother Jean not only made Powell buy Harlow's last resting place, but her own: the Sanctuary of Benediction chamber contained two other spaces, one of which she reserved for herself.

Chiseled in marble, the inscription on Harlow's crypt read simply OUR BABY. Only in death did Mother Jean share her.

Based on her income from her seven-year career, news reports estimated Harlow's worth at $1 million. Internal Revenue Service records reveal otherwise. At the time of her death, Harlow owed $76,000 in back taxes and debts. Since her assets totaled only $24,000—the equivalent of just six weeks' salary—her estate was technically insolvent, which prompted reports that Harlow died broke. In fact, she had followed Powell's advice and planned for her future, purchasing retirement annuities and putting her money in joint tenancy with Mother Jean. The result: since Bello's ouster as her business manager, Harlow had amassed $105,000 in nontaxable benefits which neither the IRS nor her mother, who demanded the entire sum at once, could touch. As sole beneficiary, Mother Jean would receive $305 a month for life. To supplement it, Louis B. Mayer signed her to a seven-year, $137-a-week contract as an M-G-M "reader" and "talent scout."

GREAT DEMAND FOR HARLOW FILMS, headlined the

Hollywood Reporter on the day of her funeral. "Exhibitors are anxious to play her pictures and distributors are being deluged with telegrams demanding prints for immediate bookings." Released three months earlier, *Personal Property* returned to theaters and earned $1.8 million, an enormous profit on its $299,000 cost. Howard Hughes reissued *Hell's Angels*, Universal revived *The Iron Man*, and Columbia capitalized on *Platinum Blonde*. Denied the Legion of Decency's approval, Warner Brothers abandoned plans to rerelease *The Public Enemy*.

The fate of *Saratoga* was uncertain. "In accordance with our policy, it was written for two distinct personalities," Louis B. Mayer stated publicly. "Therefore production will be indefinitely delayed until we can rewrite the story to fit another feminine personality." Privately he feared a $500,000 loss and asked Carole Lombard to assume the role as written. She declined. Jean Arthur, Virginia Bruce, and Gladys George were also considered.

Harlow's fans had other ideas. "The public went wild," Virginia Conway recalls. "They wanted to see her to the very end." Deluged with pleas to show *Saratoga* even in unfinished form, George Sidney was given "the gruesome task of finding a new Jean Harlow" for her few unshot scenes. Sidney tested starlets Virginia Grey and Rita Johnson, hairdresser Peggy McDonald, double Jean Phillips, and dancer Mary Dees. Because of her similar build and coloring, Dees was hired as Harlow's body double. Radio actress Paula Winslowe would supply her voice.

Saratoga resumed shooting in mid-June. "It was awful," says Bill Edmondson. "Nobody wanted to do it." Her sudden fame gave Dees "a grim thrill" that soon turned sour. Today she refuses to discuss *Saratoga.*

Winslowe is more forthcoming. "You saw her, and you heard me," she explains, though the film's use of Dees—whether in long shot, with her back to the camera, behind binoculars, or wearing a wide-brimmed hat—is "laughably obvious" and contains little dialogue. Other scenes intended for *Saratoga* heroine "Carol Clayton" ascribe her absence to "a slight headache" or being "busy with guests," clumsy excuses preferable to Harlow herself. Pale, puffy, and spent, her nephritic symptoms seem shockingly apparent.

So does *Saratoga*'s sloppiness. In one sequence, Harlow's wig varies from "master" to "two-shot"; in another, she has an uncontrolled coughing fit. Worse yet, her character's health is the film's running gag, with Clark Gable duping Walter Pidgeon about her condition:

"You know, Carol's not her old self at all."

"Has she seen a doctor?"

"No. No, she hasn't . . ."

Margaret Booth assembled *Saratoga*'s "before" and "after" footage. "It wasn't hard to edit," she comments, "but it was emotionally painful." Afraid that filmgoers would feel likewise, M-G-M held a sneak preview in Glendale on July 13. Each scene with Harlow brought cheers and applause.

Saratoga was released ten days later. Ignoring what *Variety* dubbed its "peculiarly delicate problem," most reviewers hailed Harlow's final performance as her finest. Only the New York *Times* thought she "was patently not her tempestuous self," the New York *Herald Tribune* described her as "looking ill much of the time," and future Nobel Prize winner Graham Greene condemned *Saratoga* as "tough and conscienceless." Greene's review ended with an epitaph: "She toted a breast," he wrote of Harlow, "like a man totes a gun."

Despite a sweltering summer and stiff competition, *Saratoga* set "all-time house records" and grossed $3.3 million, more than any movie that year. Harlow's last film was hardly her best, but it was her most successful.

Powell could barely continue *Double Wedding*. "He was so devastated, we laid off for five weeks," Virgil Apger discloses. Once an alter ego of his suave *Thin Man* hero, "poor Powell looked frighteningly old."

He sounded it, too. "I hardly recognized his voice," recalled George Hurrell. "The underlying, mocking tone was gone, and he sounded strained and wounded." Now an M-G-M makeup artist, Don Roberson saw Powell "sobbing his heart out" at Harlow's dressing-room door. To Myrna Loy he contemplated suicide.

"She was a sad little girl, and I helped make her happy," Powell insisted, and although his grief was genuine, many knew what motivated it: guilt. "He blamed himself for Jean's death," Loy revealed. "He had loved her but hadn't married her and taken her away from her mother." Powell assumed Harlow's fate was preventable. Again he had failed her.

Shortly thereafter, the guilt-ridden actor disappeared from the screen. M-G-M cited Harlow's death and "adhesions." Doctors diagnosed rectal cancer.

Two years and two operations later, Powell recovered

miraculously and returned to work. "He was a different man," discovered Virginia Conway. "He had matured." At forty-seven, Powell was finally ready for commitment, so on January 6, 1940, he wed Diana Lewis, a twenty-one-year-old starlet he had known for three weeks. Unlike Harlow, his bride was no bombshell. "Her nickname was 'Mousie,'" remarks Elaine St. Johns, "which says it all."

"Mousie" Powell heard little about Harlow. "Bill never discussed her," she states today. "It was a closed chapter."

Mother Jean was an open book. "Poor soul, I pity her," Aunt Jetty wrote. "Her *world* is gone, and remorse is eating her life away." Shunned by the film industry, Mother Jean lost fifty pounds, moved to the San Fernando Valley, and decorated her home as a shrine to her daughter. "There were photographs all over the walls," Kay Mulvey remembered, "with flowers under them. Her mother stored most of Jean's clothes, but she would go to the warehouse all the time, just to touch them." Unwilling to acknowledge her daughter's death, Mother Jean claimed Harlow "went away." To contact her, she consulted psychics.

In 1944 Mother Jean married Heinie Brand in Tecate, Mexico. Divorced two years later, she opened an antiques shop in Palm Desert, then rented a tiny apartment on Beverly Glen Boulevard, the same street on which she had lived in her former mansion. Since Aunt Jetty had died in 1941, Ella Harlow in 1942, and Skip Harlow in 1947, few were aware of her existence.

Mother Jean did not remind them. "She wouldn't go out," recalls Herb Read, who interviewed her at home. "She got very heavy, and when I visited her, she was too embarrassed to stand up." Still a nominal Christian Scientist, she summoned Dr. Chapman on the slightest pretext. "Dad never charged her," says Richard Chapman, "and she was a *demanding* patient. He went out there weekly, and all she ever talked about was 'my Baby.' "

On June 7, 1958, the twenty-first anniversary of her daughter's death, Mother Jean entered Good Samaritan Hospital. As usual, she seized control. "If there isn't a dress suitable for me in my casket, then buy a soft gray shroud," her handwritten will instructed. "Just call Forest Lawn and have them take my body, to be put in a crypt with my blessed Baby." Four days later she died of a heart attack. She was sixty-nine.

Mother Jean was not mourned and her tomb is unmarked. In a way, this seems fitting. "To the world we were two people, but really we are one," she declared after Harlow's death. "My life began when her life began, and was completed when she went away."

On July 17, 1946, a twenty-year-old photographer's model met *Hell's Angels* star Ben Lyon at Twentieth Century-Fox. Now a studio talent scout, Lyon scheduled a screen test. "I got a cold chill," said its cameraman, Leon Shamroy. "She got sex on a piece of film like Jean Harlow." Weeping with gratitude, the would-be bombshell signed a seven-year, $75-a-week contract and changed her name from Norma Jeane Dougherty to Marilyn Monroe.

Her fixation with Harlow had started in childhood. "I used to look at movie magazines and cut out the pictures of Jean Harlow," Monroe confessed. "That's what I wanted to be someday—a Jean Harlow." Like her idol, Monroe

TIME

The Weekly Newsmagazine

Volume XXVI

JEAN HARLOW
Fine feathers make fine fans.
(See CINEMA)

Number 8

The August 19, 1935, cover of *Time*. Its caption: "JEAN HARLOW: Fine feathers make fine fans." (copyright Time Warner Inc.; used by permission)

Hemstitching with Rosalind Russell on the *China Seas* set. (Ed Baker Collection)

A "brownette" rinse changed Harlow's image—and saved her scalp. (Photofest)

Harlow and her "gang" on location for *Suzy*. *Top*, Barbara Brown and Violet Denoyer; *bottom*, Edith Hubner and Blanche Williams.

(courtesy of Barbara Brown)

(courtesy of Virginia Conway)

After this 1936 photo was taken, five-year-old Patrick Conway turned and touched Harlow's breast. "What's this?" he wondered.

At a Hollywood party with Rouben Mamoulian, Marlene Dietrich, and Josef von Sternberg. Harlow's wig hides her damaged hair. (Ed Baker Collection)

Harlow arrives in San Francisco with Powell and Loy. Her puffy face betrays her failing health. Note her first edition of *Gone with the Wind*. (Ed Baker Collection)

Invited to Washington
for FDR's birthday,
Harlow meets
J. Edgar Hoover. . .

. . . and the First Lady.

Performing live on
Lux Radio Theater.
An extremely rare
photograph, for an
obvious reason.

In *Personal Property*
with Robert Taylor,
Harlow wore Powell's
star sapphire "engagement"
ring on her right (i.e.,
wrong) hand. (Ed Baker
Collection)

At Harlow's last sitting
with George Hurrell, she
still wore Powell's ring
but had lost hope of
marrying him.
(courtesy of George Hurrell)

May 23: Harlow and Donald Friede
at her final public appearance.

May 8, 1937: Harlow models a pink
silk negligee designed by Dolly Tree.
A month later she would be buried in
it. (Ed Baker Collection)

May 29: An outtake from *Saratoga* with
Walter Pidgeon and a visibly bloated
Harlow. She left the set early and never
returned. (Ed Baker Collection)

Dr. Leland Chapman and wife Marcella, who forbade him to treat Harlow until it was too late. (courtesy of Richard Chapman)

512 North Palm Drive in Beverly Hills, as Harlow lay dying. (Ed Baker Collection)

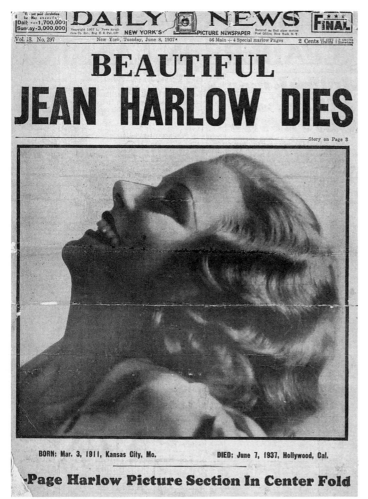

DAILY ● NEWS FINAL

Daily ---1,700,000
Sunday -3,000,000

Copyright 1937 L. News Synd.
Date Co. Inc., Reg. U.S. Pat. Off.

NEW YORK'S

PICTURE NEWSPAPER

Entered as 2nd class matter
Post Office, New York, N.Y.

Vol. 18. No. 297

New York, Tuesday, June 8, 1937*

56 Main ÷ 4 Special Harlow Pages

2 Cents

BEAUTIFUL
JEAN HARLOW DIES

Story on Page 3

BORN: Mar. 3, 1911, Kansas City, Mo.   DIED: June 7, 1937, Hollywood, Cal.

-Page Harlow Picture Section In Center Fold

Blanche Williams and Adah Wilson leave Good Samaritan Hospital after Harlow's "horrible" death.
(Ed Baker Collection)

"The day the Baby died, there wasn't one sound in the M-G-M commissary for three hours. Not one goddamn sound."
(Culver Pictures)

. . . Don Roberson with
Mont and Maude Carpenter . . .

At the funeral:
Clark Gable and Carole Lombard . . .

. . . and Mother Jean, escorted by Powell
and Carey Wilson.

. . . a sobbing Powell with his
mother and Otis Wiles . . .

After Harlow's death,
Mother Jean commissioned
a life-sized oil painting of
her Baby entitled
Farewell to Earth.
Both the portrait and
Harlow's star sapphire
ring have since
disappeared.

bleached her hair (hiring Pearl Porterfield, Harlow's "bleach and dye specialist," to do so), flaunted her body, and brought wit and pathos to her "dumb blonde" persona. Harlow was her role model. "She and Marilyn were quite different," commented George Cukor, "but they had this in common: they were both extremely attractive, and they both had the knack of concealing what they knew. The comedy seemed quite natural, yet they knew exactly what they were doing."

"Monroe was smart," says Joseph Newman, "but Harlow was smarter." She was also not a narcissist. Narcissism would prove Monroe's undoing: as her career progressed, so did her neuroses. Asked about Monroe's constant delays during *The Misfits*, her final film, costar Clark Gable stated that "in the old days of Jean Harlow, a star would be fired for being late all the time." Harlow's successor lacked her self-discipline.

Given their similarities, it was inevitable that Monroe portray Harlow in a "biopic" of her life. "She should be done humanly," Monroe stipulated as Ben Hecht, Adela Rogers St. Johns, and Sidney Skolsky drafted separate treatments of *The Jean Harlow Story*. In a special *Life* feature, Monroe posed as Harlow for photographer Richard Avedon.

The Jean Harlow Story stalled when Monroe read its script. "I hope they don't do that to me after I'm gone," she told her agent and refused the role. Still interested in playing Harlow, she agreed to see Skolsky on August 5, 1962. Early that day her death was announced.

Two years later Arthur Landau and novelist Irving Shulman collaborated on *Harlow: An Intimate Biography*.

A scurrilous bestseller, *Harlow* portrayed Harlow as a profane, promiscuous wretch whose kidneys were damaged by a wedding-night beating from Paul Bern. "Sonofabitching little fairy!" she shrieks. "You've got no right to be alive!" Bern begs for forgiveness and dons a dildo. Humiliated further, his suicide follows.

Harlow charged Mother Jean with murder. A crazed Christian Scientist, she ignores Landau's pleas (in truth he was not present) and bars doctors from Palm Drive. A sample exchange between agent and parent:

"Mama [*sic*] Jean, your Baby's sick."

"She's not! She's just pretending, to make a fool of me. I hate her!"

Critics hated *Harlow*. "A standard by which to measure shoddiness," scorned *Newsweek*. "Sordidly vivisective," sneered the New York *Times*. Loyal friends were also infuriated. "I've never read anything like it in my entire life," fumed Maureen O'Sullivan to Shulman. "You should have written it as fiction." Dr. Chapman called the book "a blatant lie." Debating Shulman on live television, seventy-year-old Adela Rogers St. Johns leaped over a table and hit him with her purse. "I meant to kill him," she muttered. "He never talked to a living soul who knew Jean Harlow."

"The line between biographical fiction and fictional biography is very fine indeed," equivocated Shulman, who soon regretted his sloppy research. Presumed dead, eighty-seven-year-old Mont Carpenter sued for $3 million. "That book broke his heart," Herb Read reveals. "I tried to help, but his lawyers settled for a puny sum. They were afraid he would die before he could get the money." A $100,000 movie sale was made to Paramount, whose *Harlow* starred

Carroll Baker and featured Angela Lansbury as "Mama" Jean and Peter Lawford as Paul Bern. Also released in 1965, a rival version in "Electronovision" cast Carol Lynley as Harlow, Ginger Rogers (a last-minute replacement for Judy Garland) as "Mama" Jean, and Hurd Hatfield as Bern. Both films flopped. Landau died a year later.

Subsequent books have been hatchet jobs or hagiographies, with Harlow a slut or a saint. In *Hollywood Babylon*, author Kenneth Anger misidentifies a pigtailed platinum blonde posing nude as Harlow. In *Deadly Illusions*, ex-M-G-M story editor Samuel Marx cites circumstantial evidence, not conclusive proof, that Dorothy Millette murdered Paul Bern.

Her films have fared better. While other studios let their holdings decompose into dust, M-G-M preserved its movies on acetate (safety) film stock, storing them in a Kansas salt mine 650 feet underground. Always popular in repertory cinemas and television airings, classics like *Red-Headed Woman*, *Red Dust*, *Bombshell*, *Dinner at Eight*, and a "colorized" *China Seas* are currently available on videocassette through media tycoon Ted Turner, whose company acquired the M-G-M film library in 1986. Discovered in John Wayne's private collection, a print of *Hell's Angels* with its two-color Technicolor sequence—the only such footage ever shot of Harlow—was restored by the UCLA Film & Television Archive in 1988. A year later *Hell's Angels* received a second "world premiere" at the Smithsonian National Air & Space Museum, six decades after its debut.

Today Harlow embodies Hollywood's "golden age," yet remains a distinct aberration. She was born into upper-class comfort and sent to a fancy finishing school, so even her early life resembled no rags-to-riches, fan magazine myth. As if by fate, film stardom found *her*, and Harlow accepted it as she did everything else: with complete, profound passivity. She lived to please others despite professional imprisonment by her public image and personal manipulation by, among others, Marino Bello, Paul Bern, William Powell, and her mother. Known worldwide but a stranger to herself, Harlow passed through life like a phantom. "Jean was a figment of M-G-M's imagination," Virginia Conway contends. "They created her, and she tried to accommodate the studio. The tragedy of her life is that she had to be someone she wasn't." This is indeed tragic but somewhat too simple. Harlow "had to be someone she wasn't" because she never knew who she was.

"I wasn't born an actress, you know," Harlow admitted. "Events made me one." Lacking experience or training, she literally learned on the job, mutating from wooden sexpot to sublime comic in record time. "I'm lucky, and I know it," she told a New York *Times* reporter on the *Saratoga* set. "I'm not a great actress, and I never thought I was. But I happen to have something the public likes."

"Most actresses outgrow their public; they think of them as morons. But ever since I clicked, I've worked with one realization: that in me, whether I could define it or not, was something the public wanted." We still do, and although Barbara Brown believes "she would be dumbfounded if she knew people remembered her," the films of Jean Harlow are hard to forget. And so, in the end, is she.

Postscript

David *"Thor" Arnold*, summer beau of Harlean Carpenter at Camp Cha-ton-ka, married actress Betty Grable's sister. He died in 1984.

A year after his affair with Harlow, boxer *Max Baer* became the heavyweight champion of the world. Remarried in 1935, he made a half-dozen more films before his death in 1959. His son, Max Baer, Jr., gained fame as "Jethro" in *The Beverly Hillbillies.*

Marino Bello accompanied *Benjamin "Bugsy" Siegel* on a treasure hunt in 1938. "Siegel let him bring his nurse," states fellow passenger Richard Gully. "She was young, attractive, and blonde—and before we got to Cocos Island, Bello married her." Divorced by nurse Evelyn Husby, he wed fourth wife Violette Hartman, promoted "oil conversion prospects" in Oklahoma, and died in 1953, six years after Siegel was gunned down in his Beverly Hills home.

At the time of his 1969 murder by Charles Manson "family" members, hairdresser Jay Sebring rented the Easton Drive home once owned by *Paul Bern.* Today this "haunted house" is private property.

Bern's boyhood pal *Edward L. Bernays* turned 101 in 1992. His brother *Henry Bern* died in 1971. So did *Heinie Brand.*

Still living in the same Hollywood home where she met Harlean Carpenter in 1925, *Barbara Brown* cherishes her memories and her granddaughter, Harlean.

Mont Carpenter died in 1974 at age ninety-six. His widow, *Maude Carpenter*, survived him by eleven years.

After Harlow's death, *Dr. Leland Chapman* dissolved his partnership with Dr. Ernest Fishbaugh to establish his own practice. His "insanely jealous" wife, *Marcella Chapman*, was diagnosed as a paranoid schizophrenic and committed suicide in 1959. At the time of his own death in 1977, eighty-three-year-old Dr. Chapman still made house calls.

Donald Friede died in 1965. His sixth wife and widow, Eleanor Friede, is an editor-publisher. His fifth wife, culinary author M. F. K. Fisher, died in 1992.

The grotesque decline of *Howard Hughes* has been widely documented. Less well known is his 1976 cause of death: chronic kidney failure.

Still at work when he succumbed to cancer in 1992, *George Hurrell* photographed Natalie Cole for *Unforgettable* and Warren Beatty in *Bugsy*. His portraits of Harlow are avidly collected. Present worth of a signed print: $15,000.

After a twenty-seven-year reign, M-G-M monarch *Louis B. Mayer* was deposed by Loew's in 1951. He died of leukemia six years later. *M-G-M* itself has been conquered, plundered, divided, and divested. At present its library is owned by Turner Entertainment, its lot by Sony, its lab by Technicolor, and its logo by Kirk Kerkorian. What remains is controlled by French bank Crédit Lyonnais.

Chuck McGrew's second marriage to socialite Marion Webb lasted two years. His third wife, rocket scientist Margaret Wood, encouraged him to become a technical writer. The couple had two children. McGrew died in 1971.

After Dorothy Millette jumped off the *Delta King* (now a floating hotel in Old Sacramento), ex-husband *Lowell Mellett* became an administrative assistant to President Roosevelt, then the Bureau of Motion Pictures chief of the Office of War Information. He died in 1960.

Married to "Mousie" for forty-four years, *William Powell* died in 1984 at age ninety-one. His ashes were scattered in Palm Springs. The third space in Harlow's crypt is unoccupied.

Fired by Howard Hughes for his liberal politics, former Caddo Company publicity director *Lincoln Quarberg*, the man who pronounced Harlow the "Platinum Blonde," died in obscurity in 1979.

Hal Roach celebrated his one hundredth birthday in 1992 and died later that year. *Don Roberson* applied makeup to Munchkins on *The Wizard of Oz*, then became Clark Gable's favorite makeup artist and close friend. He died in 1982.

The remarkable career of *Hal Rosson* continued with classics like *The Wizard of Oz*, *The Asphalt Jungle*, and *Singin' in the Rain*. Divorced from third wife Yvonne Crellin, he retired in 1967 and died in 1988 at age ninety-three.

Irene Mayer Selznick died in 1990. *Genevieve Smith* died in 1956. *Blanche Williams* worked for Rosalind Russell, Hedy Lamarr, and, briefly, Zsa Zsa Gabor before her death in 1984.

On trial for income-tax evasion in 1956, *Longy Zwill-man* attempted to bribe two jurors but was caught by the FBI. Three years later he tossed an electric cord over a rafter in his twenty-room New Jersey mansion, wrapped it around his neck, and strangled himself.

Filmography

Titles are listed in order of production. All films contain dialogue unless otherwise noted.

HONOR BOUND (Fox, seven reels, silent, b&w)
production: 1928
release: April 29, 1928

Director: Alfred E. Green. Adaptation: Philip Klein. Scenario: C. Graham Baker. Titles: William Kernell. Photography: Joseph August. Editor: J. Edwin Robbins.

Cast: George O'Brien, Estelle Taylor, Leila Hyams, Tom Santschi, Frank Cooley, Sam De Grasse, Al Hart, Harry Gripp, George Irving, Jean Harlow (unbilled extra).

MORAN OF THE MARINES (Paramount, seven reels, silent, b&w)
production: July 16–August 28, 1928
release: October 13, 1928

Director: Frank Strayer. Scenario: Sam Mintz, Ray Harris. Story: Linton Wells. Screenplay: Agnes Brand Leahy. Titles: George Marion. Photography: Edward Cronjager. Editor: Otto Lovering.

Cast: Richard Dix, Ruth Elder, Roscoe Karns, Brooks Benedict, Jean Harlow (unbilled extra).

CHASING HUSBANDS (Hal Roach Studios, two reels, silent, b&w)
production: September 4–14, 1928
copyright: December 6, 1928

Director: James Parrott. Story: Leo McCarey. Titles: H. M. Walker. Photography: Art Lloyd. Editor: Richard Currier.

Cast: Charley Chase, Edgar Kennedy, Kalla Pasha, Gertrude Astor, Iris Adrian, Clara Guiol, Ann Lewis, Ami Ingraham, Eunice Hamilton, Ruby McCoy, Jean Harlow.

FUGITIVES (Fox, six reels, synchronized musical score, b&w)
production: fall, 1928
release: January 27, 1929

Director: William Beaudine. Scenario: John Stone, from the book *Exiles* by Richard Harding Davis. Titles: Malcolm Stuart Boylan. Photography: Chester Lyons.

Cast: Madge Bellamy, Don Terry, Arthur Stone, Earle Foxe, Matthew Betz, Lumsden Hare, Jean Harlow (unbilled extra).

WHY BE GOOD? (First National, eight reels, musical score, b&w)
production: fall, 1928
release: February 28, 1929

Director: William A. Seiter. Story-Scenario: Carey Wilson. Titles: Paul Perez. Photography: Sidney Hickox. Editor: Terry Morse.

Cast: Colleen Moore, Neil Hamilton, John Sainpolis, Edward Martindel, Eddie Clayton, Lincoln Stedman, Jean Harlow (unbilled extra).

THE UNKISSED MAN (Hal Roach Studios, two reels, silent, b&w)
production: December 3–8, 1928
copyright: May 20, 1929

Director: Hal Roach. Story: Leo McCarey. Titles: H. M. Walker. Photography: John McBurnie. Editor: Richard Currier.

Cast: Bryant Washburn, Marion Byron, Eddie Dunn, Jean Harlow.

WHY IS A PLUMBER? (Hal Roach Studios, two reels, silent, b&w)
production: December 13–18, 1928
copyright: March 11, 1929

Director: Hal Roach. Story: Leo McCarey. Titles: H. M. Walker. Photography: John McBurnie. Editor: Richard Currier.

Cast: Edgar Kennedy, Jean Harlow, Albert Conti, Eddie Dunn, Gertrude Sutton.

LIBERTY (Hal Roach Studios, two reels, silent & limited sound versions, b&w)
production: December 19–24, 1928
release: January 26, 1929

Director: Leo McCarey. Story: Leo McCarey. Titles: H. M. Walker. Photography: George Stevens. Editor: Richard Currier and William Terhune.

Cast: Laurel & Hardy, James Finlayson, Tom Kennedy, "Harlean Carpenter" (Jean Harlow).

THUNDERING TOUPEES (Hal Roach Studios, two reels, silent, b&w)
production: December 20–26, 1928
copyright: June 27, 1929

Director: Hal Roach. Story: Leo McCarey. Titles: H. M. Walker. Photography: John McBurnie. Editor: Richard Currier.

Cast: Edgar Kennedy, Vivien Oakland, Jean Harlow, Eddie Dunn, Mickey Daniels.

CLOSE HARMONY (Paramount, 66 minutes, b&w)
production: December 22, 1928–January 14, 1929
release: April 12, 1929

Director: John Cromwell, Edward Sutherland. Story: Elsie Janis, Gene Markey. Adaptation: Percy Heath. Dialogue: John V. A. Weaver, Percy Heath. Photography: J. Roy Hunt. Editor: Tay Malarkey.

Cast: Charles "Buddy" Rogers, Nancy Carroll, Harry Green, Jack Oakie, Richard "Skeets" Gallagher, Jean Harlow (unbilled extra).

DOUBLE WHOOPEE (Hal Roach Studios, two reels, silent, b&w)
production: February 5–9, 1929
release: May 18, 1929

Director: Lewis R. Foster. Story: Leo McCarey. Titles: H. M. Walker. Photography: George Stevens, Jack Roach. Editor: Richard Currier.

Cast: Laurel & Hardy, Charles Hall, Jean Harlow, Rolfe Sedan.

BACON GRABBERS (Hal Roach Studios, two reels, musical score and sound effects, b&w)
production: February 18–27, 1929
release: October 19, 1929

Director: Lewis R. Foster. Story: Leo McCarey. Titles: H. M. Walker. Photography: George Stevens, Jack Roach. Editor: Richard Currier.

Cast: Laurel & Hardy, Edgar Kennedy, Charles Hall, Jean Harlow.

MASQUERADE (Fox, 65 minutes, b&w)
production: 1929
release: July 14, 1929

Director: Russell J. Birdwell. Dialogue-Scenario: Frederick Hazlitt Brennan, Malcolm Stuart Boylan, from the novel by Louis Vance. Photography: Charles Clarke, Don Anderson. Editor: Ralph Dietrich.

Cast: Alan Birmingham, Leila Hyams, Arnold Lucy, Clyde Cook, J. Farrell MacDonald, George Pierce, Rita Le Roy, Jean Harlow (unbilled extra).

THIS THING CALLED LOVE (Pathé, 72 minutes, b&w with Technicolor sequence)
production: 1929
release: December 13, 1929

Director: Paul L. Stein, under the supervision of Ralph Block. Adaptation-Dialogue: Horace Jackson, from the play by Edwin Burke. Photography: Norbert Brodine. Editor: Doane Harrison.

Cast: Edmund Lowe, Constance Bennett, Roscoe Karns, ZaSu Pitts, Carmelita Geraghty, Stuart Erwin, Ruth Taylor, Jean Harlow (unbilled extra).

CITY LIGHTS (United Artists, 87 minutes, silent with synchronized musical score and sound effects, b&w)
production: December 31, 1927–January 22, 1931
release: February 7, 1931

Director-writer: Charles Chaplin. Photography: Roland H. Totheroh. Cameramen: Gordon Pollock, Mark Marlatt.

Cast: Charles Chaplin, Virginia Cherrill, Harry Myers, Allan Garcia, Hank Mann, Jean Harlow (unbilled extra).

[*NOTE:* Jean Harlow is visible in still photographs from *City Lights*, but not in the film itself.]

NEW YORK NIGHTS (United Artists, 81 minutes, b&w)
production: 1929
release: December 28, 1929

Director: Lewis Milestone. Adaptation: Jules Furthman, from the play by Hugh Stanislaws Stange. Photography: Ray June. Editor: Hal C. Kern.

Cast: Norma Talmadge, Gilbert Roland, John Wray, Lilyan Tashman, Mary Doran, Roscoe Karns, Jean Harlow (unbilled extra).

THE LOVE PARADE (Paramount, 112 minutes, b&w)
production: June 17–July 31, 1929
release: November 19, 1929

Director: Ernst Lubitsch. Dialogue director: Perry Ivins. Libretto: Guy Bolton. Story: Ernest Vajda. Photography: Victor Milner. Editor: Merrill White.

Cast: Maurice Chevalier, Jeanette MacDonald, Lupino Lane, Lillian Roth, Eugene Pallette, Ben Turpin, Jean Harlow (unbilled extra).

THE SATURDAY NIGHT KID (Paramount, 62 minutes, b&w)
production: July 27–August 19, 1929
release: October 25, 1929

Director: Edward Sutherland. Screenplay: Ethel Doherty. Dialogue: Lloyd Corrigan, Edward E. Paramore, Jr. Titles: Joseph L. Mankiewicz. Adaptation: Lloyd Corrigan. Story: George Abbott, John V. A. Weaver. Camera: Harry Fischbeck. Editor: Jane Loring.

Cast: Clara Bow, James Hall, Jean Arthur, Charles Sellon, Ethel Wales, Frank Ross, Edna May Oliver, Hyman Meyer, Eddie Dunn, Leone Lane, Jean Harlow.

WEAK BUT WILLING (Al Christie Comedies, two reels, b&w)
production: September 1929
release: December 14, 1929

Director: William Watson. Story: Will King.

Cast: Will King, Billy Bevan, Dot Farley, Jean Harlow (unbilled extra).

HELL'S ANGELS (United Artists, 125 minutes, b&w with Technicolor sequence)
production: fall, 1927–spring, 1929 (silent version)
            October–December 1929 (sound version)
release: May 27, 1930 (Hollywood premiere)
            August 15, 1930 (New York premiere)
            November 15, 1930 (general release)

Director: Howard Hughes. Dialogue staged by: James Whale. Story: Marshall Neilan and Joseph Moncure March. Adaptation and continuity: Howard Estabrook and Harry Behn. Dialogue: Joseph Moncure March. Photography: Antonio Gaudio, Harry Perry, Harry Zech, E. Burton Steene, Dewey Wrigley, Elmer Dyer. Editor: Frank Lawrence, Douglass Biggs.

Cast: Ben Lyon, James Hall, Jean Harlow, John Darrow, Lucien Prival, Frank Clarke, Roy Wilson, Douglas Gilmore, Jane Winton.

THE SECRET SIX (M-G-M, 83 minutes, b&w)
production: December 1930
release: April 25, 1931

Director: George Hill. Story and dialogue: Frances Marion. Photography: Harold Wenstrom. Editor: Blanche Sewell.

Cast: Wallace Beery, Lewis Stone, John Mack Brown, Jean Harlow, Marjorie Rambeau, Paul Hurst, Clark Gable, Ralph Bellamy, John Miljan.

THE IRON MAN (Universal, 73 minutes, b&w)
production: January 19–February 20, 1931
release: April 15, 1931

Director: Tod Browning. Screenplay: Francis Edward Faragoh, from the novel by W. R. Burnett. Photography: Percy Hilburn. Editor: Milton Carruth.

Cast: Lew Ayres, Robert Armstrong, Jean Harlow, John Miljan, Eddie Dillon, Mike Donlin, Mary Doran, Ned Sparks.

[*NOTE:* In a 1951 remake of *The Iron Man* by Universal, Jean Harlow's role of "Rose Mason" was played by Evelyn Keyes.]

THE PUBLIC ENEMY (Warner Brothers, 83 minutes, b&w)
production: January–February 1931
release: April 23, 1931

Director: William A. Wellman. Screen adaptation: Harvey Thew, from a story by Kubec Glasmon and John Bright. Photography: Dev Jennings. Editor: Edward M. McDermott.

Cast: James Cagney, Jean Harlow, Edward Woods, Joan Blondell, Donald Cook, Leslie Fenton, Beryl Mercer, Mae Clarke.

SCARFACE (United Artists, 93 minutes, b&w)
production: April–June 1931
release: May 19, 1932

Director: Howard Hawks. Screen story: Ben Hecht, from the book
by Armitage Trail. Continuity and dialogue: Seton I. Miller, John
Lee Mahin, and W. R. Burnett. Photography: Lee Garmes and
L. W. O'Connell. Editor: Edward Curtiss.

Cast: Paul Muni, Ann Dvorak, Karen Morley, Osgood Perkins, C.
Henry Gordon, George Raft, Boris Karloff, Jean Harlow (unbilled
cameo appearance).

GOLDIE (Fox, 68 minutes, b&w)
production: May 1931
release: June 28, 1931

Director: Benjamin Stoloff. Writer: Gene Towne and Paul Perez.
Photography: Ernest Palmer. Editor: Alex Troffey.

Cast: Spencer Tracy, Warren Hymer, Jean Harlow, Lina Basquette,
Maria Alba, Eddie Kane, George Raft (unbilled "bit" player).

[*NOTE: Goldie* was a remake of *A Girl in Every Port* (Fox, 1928).]

PLATINUM BLONDE (Columbia, 88 minutes, b&w)
production: August–September 1931
release: October 31, 1931
Director: Frank Capra. Adaptation: Jo Swerling, from a story by
Harry E. Chandler and Douglas W. Churchill. Continuity: Dorothy
Howell. Dialogue: Robert Riskin. Photography: Joseph Walker.
Editor: Gene Milford.

Cast: Loretta Young, Robert Williams, Jean Harlow, Louise Closser
Hale, Donald Dillaway, Reginald Owen, Walter Catlett.

THREE WISE GIRLS (Columbia, 68 minutes, b&w)
production: October 1931
release: February 9, 1932

Director: William Beaudine. Adaptation: Agnes C. Johnson, from a
story by Wilson Collison. Dialogue: Robert Riskin. Photography: Ted
Tetzlaff. Editor: Jack Dennis.

Cast: Jean Harlow, Mae Clarke, Walter Byron, Marie Prevost, Andy
Devine, Natalie Moorhead, Jameson Thomas, Lucy Beaumont.

THE BEAST OF THE CITY (M-G-M, 87 minutes, b&w)
production: November 1931
release: February 13, 1932

Director: Charles Brabin. Screenplay: John Lee Mahin, Ben Hecht (uncredited), from a story by W. R. Burnett. Photography: Barney McGill. Editor: Ralph Dawson.

Cast: Walter Huston, Jean Harlow, Wallace Ford, Jean Hersholt, Dorothy Peterson, Tully Marshall, John Miljan, Emmett Corrigan, J. Carroll Naish, Mickey Rooney, Julie Haydon.

RED-HEADED WOMAN (M-G-M, 74 minutes, b&w)
production: April–May 1932
release: June 25, 1932

Director: Jack Conway. Screenplay: Anita Loos, from the novel by Katharine Brush. Photography: Harold Rosson. Editor: Blanche Sewell.

Cast: Jean Harlow, Chester Morris, Lewis Stone, Leila Hyams, Una Merkel, Henry Stephenson, May Robson, Charles Boyer, Harvey Clark.

RED DUST (M-G-M, 83 minutes, b&w)
production: August 23–October 1, 1932
release: October 22, 1932

Director: Victor Fleming. Screenplay: John Lee Mahin, Donald Ogden Stewart (uncredited), from the play by Wilson Collison. Photography: Harold Rosson. Editor: Blanche Sewell.

Cast: Clark Gable, Jean Harlow, Gene Raymond, Mary Astor, Donald Crisp, Tully Marshall, Forrester Harvey, Willie Fung.

[*NOTE: Red Dust*'s story and setting were used in *Congo Maisie* (M-G-M, 1940) starring Ann Southern and John Carroll. The film was officially remade as *Mogambo* (M-G-M, 1953) with Clark Gable reprising his original role, Ava Gardner in Jean Harlow's, and Grace Kelly in Mary Astor's.]

DINNER AT EIGHT (M-G-M, 113 minutes, b&w)
production: March–April 1933
release: August 29, 1933 (Hollywood premiere)
        January 12, 1934 (general release)

Director: George Cukor. Screenplay: Frances Marion and Herman J. Mankiewicz, from the play by George S. Kaufman and Edna Ferber. Additional dialogue: Donald Ogden Stewart. Art director: Hobe Erwin and Fred Hope. Photography: William Daniels. Editor: Ben Lewis.

Cast: Marie Dressler, John Barrymore, Wallace Beery, Jean Harlow, Lionel Barrymore, Lee Tracy, Edmund Lowe, Billie Burke, Madge Evans, Jean Hersholt, Karen Morley, Louise Closser Hale, Phillips Holmes, May Robson, Grant Mitchell, Hilda Vaughn, Edward Woods.

[*NOTE:* In a 1989 remake of *Dinner at Eight* by Turner Network Television, Jean Harlow's role of "Kitty Packard" was played by Ellen Greene.]

HOLD YOUR MAN (M-G-M, 89 minutes, b&w)
production: April 16–May 1933
release: July 7, 1933

Director: Sam Wood. Screenplay: Anita Loos and Howard Emmett Rogers, from a story by Anita Loos. Photography: Harold Rosson. Editor: Frank Sullivan.

Cast: Jean Harlow, Clark Gable, Stuart Erwin, Dorothy Burgess, Muriel Kirkland, Garry Owen, Barbara Barondess, Paul Hurst, Elizabeth Patterson.

BOMBSHELL (M-G-M, 91 minutes, b&w)
production: August–September 1933
release: October 13, 1933

Director: Victor Fleming. Screenplay: Jules Furthman and John Lee Mahin from a play by Caroline Francke and Mack Crane. Photography: Chester Lyons and Harold Rosson. Editor: Margaret Booth.

Cast: Jean Harlow, Lee Tracy, Frank Morgan, Franchot Tone, Pat O'Brien, Una Merkel, Ted Healy, Ivan Lebedeff, Isabel Jewell, Louise Beavers, Leonard Carey, Mary Forbes, C. Aubrey Smith, June Brewster.

THE GIRL FROM MISSOURI (M-G-M, 75 minutes, b&w)
production: April–June 1934
release: August 3, 1934

Director: Jack Conway. Writer: Anita Loos and John Emerson. Photography: Ray June, Harold Rosson (uncredited). Editor: Tom Held.

Cast: Jean Harlow, Lionel Barrymore, Franchot Tone, Lewis Stone, Patsy Kelly, Alan Mowbray, Clara Blandick, Hale Hamilton, Nat Kolker, Nat Pendleton, Lane Chandler.

RECKLESS (M-G-M, 96 minutes, b&w)
production: December 6, 1934–February 23, 1935
release: April 19, 1935

Director: Victor Fleming. Screenplay: P. J. Wolfson, from a story by Oliver Jeffries [David O. Selznick]. Music and lyrics: Jerome Kern, Oscar Hammerstein II, Con Conrad, Herbert Magidson, Jack King, Edwin Knopf, Harold Adamson. Photography: George Folsey. Editor: Margaret Booth.

Cast: Jean Harlow, William Powell, Franchot Tone, May Robson, Ted Healy, Nat Pendleton, Robert Light, Rosalind Russell, Henry Stephenson, Mickey Rooney, Allan Jones, Nina Mae McKinney.

[*NOTE:* Virginia Verrill dubbed Jean Harlow's songs in *Reckless*, and Betty Halsey doubled her dances.]

CHINA SEAS (M-G-M, 90 minutes, b&w)
production: March–May 1935
release: August 16, 1935

Director: Tay Garnett. Screenplay: Jules Furthman and James Keven McGuinness, John Lee Mahin (uncredited), from the novel by Crosbie Garstin. Photography: Ray June. Editor: William Levanway.

Cast: Clark Gable, Jean Harlow, Wallace Beery, Lewis Stone, Rosalind Russell, Dudley Digges, C. Aubrey Smith, Robert Benchley, William Henry, Lillian Bond, Donald Meek, Carol Ann Beery, Akim Tamiroff, Hattie McDaniel.

RIFFRAFF (M-G-M, 89 minutes, b&w)
production: August–October 1935
release: January 3, 1936

Director: J. Walter Ruben. Screenplay: Frances Marion, from a story by Frances Marion, H. W. Hanemann, and Anita Loos. Photography: Ray June. Editor: Frank Sullivan.

Cast: Jean Harlow, Spencer Tracy, Una Merkel, Joseph Calleia, Victor Kilian, Mickey Rooney, J. Farrell MacDonald, Roger Imhoff, Juanita Quigley, Paul Hurst, Dorothy Appleby, Judith Wood.

WIFE VS. SECRETARY (M-G-M, 88 minutes, b&w)
production: November 26, 1935–January 13, 1936
release: February 28, 1936

Director: Clarence Brown. Screenplay: Norman Krasna, Alice Duer Miller, John Lee Mahin, from a story by Faith Baldwin. Photography: Ray June. Editor: Frank E. Hull.

Cast: Clark Gable, Jean Harlow, Myrna Loy, May Robson, George Barbier, James Stewart, Hobart Cavanaugh, Gilbert Emery, Margaret Irving, Gloria Holden, Tom Dugan.

SUZY (M-G-M, 99 minutes, b&w)
production: April–May 1936
release: July 20, 1936

Director: George Fitzmaurice. Screenplay: Dorothy Parker, Alan Campbell, Horace Jackson, Lenore Coffee, from the novel by Herbert Gorman. Photography: Ray June. Editor: George Boemler.

Cast: Jean Harlow, Franchot Tone, Cary Grant, Lewis Stone, Benita Hume, Reginald Mason, Inez Courtney, Robert Livingston, Una O'Connor.

[*NOTE:* Eadie Adams dubbed Jean Harlow's songs in *Suzy*.]

LIBELED LADY (M-G-M, 98 minutes, b&w)
production: July 13–September 1, 1936
release: October 9, 1936

Director: Jack Conway. Screenplay: Maurice Watkins, Howard Emmett Rogers, George Oppenheimer, from a story by Wallace Sullivan. Photography: Norbert Brodine. Editor: Frederick Y. Smith.

Cast: Jean Harlow, William Powell, Myrna Loy, Spencer Tracy, Walter Connolly, Charley Grapewin, Cora Witherspoon, E. E. Clive, Lauri Beatty, William Benedict, Hattie McDaniel.

[*NOTE:* In *Easy to Wed*, a 1946 remake of *Libeled Lady* by M-G-M, Jean Harlow's role of "Gladys Benton" was played by Lucille Ball.]

PERSONAL PROPERTY (M-G-M, 84 minutes, b&w)
production: December 1936–January 21, 1937
release: March 19, 1937

Director: W. S. Van Dyke II. Screenplay: Hugh Mills and Ernest Vajda, from the play *Man in Possession* by H. M. Harwood. Photography: William Daniels. Editor: Ben Lewis.

Cast: Jean Harlow, Robert Taylor, Reginald Owen, Una O'Connor, Henrietta Crosman, E. E. Clive, Cora Witherspoon, Marla Shelton.

[*NOTE: Personal Property* was a remake of *The Man in Possession* (M-G-M, 1931), in which Irene Purcell played Jean Harlow's role.]

SARATOGA (M-G-M, 94 minutes, b&w)
production: April 22–June 22, 1937
release: July 23, 1937

Director: Jack Conway. Writer: Anita Loos and Robert Hopkins. Photography: Ray June. Editor: Elmo Vernon, Margaret Booth (uncredited).

Cast: Clark Gable, Jean Harlow, Lionel Barrymore, Frank Morgan, Walter Pidgeon, Una Merkel, Cliff Edwards, George Zucco, Jonathan Hale, Hattie McDaniel, Frankie Darro, Margaret Hamilton.

[*NOTE:* After Jean Harlow's death, *Saratoga* was completed with Mary Dees as her body double and Paula Winslowe as her voice double.]

Radio Appearances

All programs were broadcast live from Hollywood unless otherwise noted.

Hell's Angels premiere, Grauman's Chinese Theatre (NBC)
    broadcast date: May 27, 1930
    program: Jean Harlow (escorted by Paul Bern) greets radio
        audience

WDAF, Kansas City, Missouri (NBC affiliate)
    broadcast date: November 20, 1930
    program: Landon Laird interviews Jean Harlow

Lucky Strike Dance Orchestra (NBC)
    broadcast date: December 1, 1931
    program: Jean Harlow makes a guest appearance

Lucky Strike Dance Orchestra (NBC)
    broadcast date: December 17, 1931
    program: Jean Harlow makes a guest appearance

Grand Hotel premiere, Grauman's Chinese Theatre (NBC)
    broadcast date: April 29, 1932
    masters of ceremonies: Conrad Nagel, Will Rogers
    program: Jean Harlow (escorted by Paul Bern) greets radio
        audience

California Melodies (CBS)
    broadcast date: July 11, 1933
    program: Jean Harlow makes a guest appearance

Dinner at Eight premiere, Grauman's Chinese Theatre (CBS)
    broadcast date: August 29, 1933
    masters of ceremonies: Pete Smith, Bill Henry
    program: Jean Harlow greets radio audience

Queen Christina premiere, Grauman's Chinese Theatre (CBS)
    broadcast date: February 9, 1934
    master of ceremonies: Charles Irwin
    program: Jean Harlow (escorted by Harold Rosson) greets radio
             audience

Hollywood on the Air (NBC)
    broadcast date: c. 1933–34
    host: Jimmie Fidler
    program: Jean Harlow makes a guest appearance

Hollywood Hotel (CBS)
    broadcast date: October 19, 1934
    hosts: Louella Parsons and Dick Powell
    program: Louella Parsons interviews Jean Harlow

Hollywood Hotel (CBS)
    broadcast date: August 9, 1935
    hosts: Louella Parsons and Dick Powell
    program: Jean Harlow, Clark Gable, and Rosalind Russell
             perform scenes from *China Seas*

Elza Schallert Reviews (NBC)
    broadcast date: August 28, 1936
    program: Elza Schallert interviews Jean Harlow

Lux Radio Theater (CBS)
    broadcast date: December 14, 1936
    host: Cecil B. De Mille
    program: Jean Harlow, Robert Taylor, Claude Rains, and
             C. Henry Gordon perform *Madame Sans-Gêne*

Franklin D. Roosevelt's Birthday Ball, Washington, D.C. (CBS, NBC)
    broadcast date: January 30, 1937
    program: Jean Harlow, Robert Taylor, Marsha Hunt, and
                Eleanor Roosevelt attend President Roosevelt's
                birthday festivities at the Wardman Park Hotel

Interviews

Morris Abrams, Jack Ackerman, Iris Adrian, Elizabeth Allan, Ted Allan, Elois Andre, Virgil Apger, David Peter Arnold, Jean Arthur, Lew Ayres, Max Baer, Jr., Charlotte Baiano, Solly Baiano, William Bakewell, Vince Barbie, Betty Barker, William Barnard, Binnie Barnes, Barbara Barondess, Lina Basquette, Tony Beacon, William Beaudine, Jr., John Beckman, Madge Bellamy, Ralph Bellamy, Evelyn Husby Bello, William Benedict, Joan Bennett, Helen Berguson, Betsy Bern, Edward L. Bernays, Margaret Booth, Osmond Borradaile, Ruth Brand, Sybil Brand, John Bright, Layne Britton, Jeanette Brooks, Phyllis Brooks, Barbara Brown, Mrs. Clarence Brown, Henrietta Bucker, Leroy Buckmiller, Naneen Burnap, Irene Burns, Lillian Burns, Ernest Byfield, Jr., Kitty Byfield, Teet Carle, Mary Carlisle, George Cartlich, Jr., Phyllis Cerf, Richard Chapman, Virginia Cherrill, Marguerite Churchill, Mae Clarke, Ruth Clifford, J. J. Cohn, Cora Sue Collins, Marvel Condaffer, Virginia Conway, Jackie Cooper, Lucinda Costa, Virginia Cox, Constance Cummings, Adeline Cummins, Helen Davis, E. Clarke Deacon, Elinor Deamer, Diane Dearborn, Agnes DeMille, Cecilia De Mille, Richard de Mille, Michael Desosa, John Detlie, Johnny Downs, Judith Donelan, Mary Doran, Dean Dorn, Gordon Douglas, Frances Drake, Dorothy Dunbar, Mary Duncan, Buddy Ebsen, Bill Edmondson, Harry Edwards, George Eppich, Edith Fellows, Ernestine Fishbaugh, M. F. K. Fisher, Susan Fleming, Milo Frank, Eleanor Friede, Harry Friedenberg, Chip Gaither, Harold Garrison, Jr., Anita Garvin, John Gershgorn, Leatrice Gilbert, Gene Goldman, Kenneth Grossman, Albert Hackett, Betty Halsey, Jane Hammack, Irene Harrison, Skip Hathaway, Julie Haydon, John

Michael Hayes, Lenore Heidorn, Katharine Hepburn, Dorothy Hesketh, Gloria Holden, Thelma Hope, Leonora Hornblow, Jean Howard, Marsha Hunt, George Hurrell, Arthur Jacobson, Allan Jones, Barbara Jones, J. Lorenz Jones, Philip Jones, Maxine Jones, Jane Kennicott, Richard Landau, Burton Lane, June Lang, Betty Lasky, Jane Latshaw, Eddie Lawrence, Fred Lee, Jada Leland, Arthur Levine, Prince Johannes von Liechtenstein, Robert Light, Robert Longnecker, Mary Anita Loos, William Ludwig, Earl Luick, Ida Lupino, James Lydon, Marcel Machu, Dorothy Mackaill, Joseph L. Mankiewicz, David Manners, Dorothy Manners, Joan Marsh, David Marx, Samuel Marx, Liz Massey, Dominic McBride, Joel McCrea, Marcia McDaniel, Roddy McDowall, Margo McGrew, Robert McGrew, Anne Mellett, Tess Michaels, Dorothy Milford, Patsy Ruth Miller, Madrine Molen, Karen Morley, Movita, Eleanor Newell, Joseph Newman, Robert Orth, Carol Ortner, Maureen O'Sullivan, Alfred Pagano, Eugene Pagano, Anita Page, Virginia Parsons, Gilbert Perkins, Fred Phillips, Jeanne Pope, Harold Porterfield, Diana Powell, James Pratt, Aileen Pringle, Alston Purvis, Juanita Quigley, Marcella Rabwin, Luise Rainer, Esther Ralston, Maurice Rapf, Gene Raymond, Herb Read, Gottfried Reinhardt, Frances Rich, Allen Rivkin, Hal Roach, Dianne Roberson, Charles "Buddy" Rogers, Gilbert Roland, Cesar Romero, Frank Ross, Helene Rosson, Carl Roup, Rosalie Roy, Al St. Hillaire, Elaine St. Johns, Chester Schaeffer, Charles Schram, Gladys Searles, Roy Seawright, Irene Mayer Selznick, Willard Sheldon, Marla Shelton, Anne Shirley, Irving Shulman, George Sidney, Millicent Siegel, Penny Singleton, Estelle Skolsky, Jacqueline Smith, Ralph Soto-Hall, John Steinbach, K. T. Stevens, James Stewart, Andrew L. Stone, Paula Stone, Ann Straus, Gloria Stuart, Etta Sugarman, Lyle Talbot, Wilson Tait, Grace Temple, Robert Terry, Ted Tetrick, Ted Tetzlaff, Muriel Tholen, Richard Thorpe, Loie Tilton, Emily Torchia, Claire Trevor, William Tuttle, Virginia Verrill, Gretchen Williams, Hortense Williams, Paula Winslowe, Judith Wood, Gabrielle Woods, Wallace Worsley, Jr., Robert Wright.

Archives

United States

Arizona
Clerk of the Superior Court, Phoenix
Clerk of the Superior Court, Yuma
Coconino County Sheriff's Office, Flagstaff
    Criminal Investigations Dept. (Sgt. Osegueda)
Page Public Library, Page (Marilyn Jaques)

Arkansas
University of Arkansas, Fayetteville
    Alumni Association
    Pi Beta Phi chapter

California
Academy of Motion Picture Arts & Sciences, Beverly Hills
    Motion Picture Study Center (Sam Gill, Howard Prouty)
Alameda County Coroner's Bureau, Oakland
American Film Institute, Los Angeles
    Louis B. Mayer Library (Rod Merl)
Berkeley Vital Records Department
Beverly Hills Public Library
Bison Archives, Beverly Hills (Marc Wanamaker)
Board of Registered Nursing, Sacramento (Jacque Kelly)
Bureau of Medical Quality Assurance, Sacramento

Cal-Poly, San Luis Obispo
    Special Collections, Kennedy Library (Nancy Loe)
California Nurses Association (Angela Lacey)
California State Bar Association, San Francisco
California State Library, Sacramento (Sybil Zemitis)
Catalina Island Museum Society
Chicago Title Company, Rosemead (Isaura Duran)
Church of the Latter Day Saints, Los Angeles
    Family History Center
Culver City Historical Society (Maryann Schwartz)
Culver City Public Library (Josie Zoretich)
Directors Guild of America, Los Angeles (Selise Eiseman, Derek
        Rowlett)
Film Preservation Associates, Sun Valley (David Shepard, Nick
        Lovrovich)
Forest Lawn Memorial Park (Vicki Little)
Good Samaritan Hospital, Los Angeles (Dr. Robert Rand)
Hearst Castle, San Simeon
Inglewood Cemetery, Inglewood (Sandra Sambiano)
Institute of the American Musical, Los Angeles (Miles Krueger)
KUSC, Los Angeles (Leslie Yngojo-Bowes)
Los Angeles City Archives (Hynda Rudd, Robert Freeman)
Los Angeles County Archives (Gabrielle Carey)
Los Angeles County Coroner's Office (Elvira Sanchez)
Los Angeles County Fire Department
    Pension Office (Mary Washington)
Los Angeles County Medical Association
Los Angeles County Records Center (Don Cameron)
Los Angeles County Registrar Recorder
    Real Estate Records Division
    Vital Records Division
Los Angeles Police Department
    Pension Records (Mary Washington)
    Records & Investigation (Joe Bonino)
Los Angeles Public Library
    History Department
Los Angeles *Times*
    Public Information Service
Makeup Artists & Hairstylists Local #706, North Hollywood
        (Howard Smit)
Maritime Museum, San Francisco
    J. Porter Shaw Library

Maritime Museum, San Pedro (Bill Oleson)
Mark Hopkins Hotel, San Francisco
Max Factor Museum, Hollywood
Mitchell, Silberberg & Knupp, Los Angeles
Motion Picture and Television Archive, Los Angeles (Sid Avery)
Motion Picture Country Home, Woodland Hills (Deborah Hyde)
Motion Picture Industry Pension Plan, Studio City (Marie Capriota)
Motion Picture Mothers, Encino (Audrey Gillespie)
Orange County Clerk's Office, Santa Ana
Orange County Recorder's Office, Santa Ana
Pacific Pioneer Broadcasters (Martin Halperin, Ron Wolf)
Paramount Pictures, Hollywood (Michael Schlesinger)
Pierce Brothers Mortuary, Los Angeles
Riverside County Recorder's Office
Rosicrucian Order, AMORC, San Jose
Sacramento Board of Registered Nurses
Sacramento County Clerk's Office (Christine Lewis)
Sacramento County Coroner's Office (Bob Bowers, Susan Criedman)
Sacramento County Department of Parks and Community Services
    (Charlene Gilbert)
Sacramento County Deputy Public Administrator's Office
    (Ramona Munes)
Sacramento County Recorder's Office
Sacramento History Center
San Bernardino County Vital Records Division
San Francisco Department of Health
San Francisco Public Library (Gardner Haskell)
San Joaquin County Recorder's Office
San Luis Obispo County Recorder's Office
Santa Ana Public Library
Sonoma County Public Health Department, Santa Rosa
University of California, Berkeley
  Special Collections, Bancroft Library (Dr. Bonnie Hardwick)
  University of California, Los Angeles
  Film Archives (Robert Gitt)
University of Southern California
  American Literature Special Collections (Victoria Steel)
  Cinema-Television Library
    Special Collections (Ned Comstock)
    Warner Brothers Collection (Leith Adams, Stuart Ng)
  Special Collections (Dace Taube)
  KUSC (Leslie Yngojo-Bowes)

Variety, Los Angeles (Woody Wilson)
Yolo County Coroner's Office, Woodland (Patsy Brookshire)

Colorado
Colorado Department of Health, Denver

Connecticut
Department of Vital Records, Hartford
Greenwich Historical Society (William Finch)
Greenwich Public Library (Richard Hart)

Delaware
Division of Historical and Cultural Affairs, Dover

District of Columbia
American Association of Retired Persons
Department of Vital Records
Federal Bureau of Investigation
   Freedom of Information Act Office
Library of Congress
   Motion Picture, Broadcasting, and Recorded Sound Division
      (Karen C. Lund)
Marine Corps Headquarters
National Archives
   Civil War Pension Records
   Ship Passenger Arrival Records
   Suitland Reference Center
United States Department of State (Margaret Roman)

Florida
Dade County Public Library, Miami
Florida Board of Nursing, Jacksonville
Marriage License Bureau, Miami (Carolyn McKenzie)
Office of Vital Statistics, Jacksonville

Georgia
Department of Vital Records, Atlanta

Illinois
American Dental Association, Chicago (Aletha Kowitz)

American Medical Association, Chicago (Fred W. Hunter)
Bloomington Historical Society, Bloomington (Greg Koos)
Bloomington Public Library, Bloomington (Sandra Beye)
Chicago Historical Society
Chicago Public Library
Christian County Clerk's Office, Taylorville
Circuit Court Clerk, Waukegan
Highland Park Library, Highland Park
Lake Forest Academy, Lake Forest (Kim Ziebell)
Museum of Broadcast Communications, Chicago
National Archives, Chicago (Kelly Green)
Newberry Library, Chicago
   Special Collections (Diana Haskell)
St. Luke's Hospital Nursing School, Chicago (Stuart Campbell)
Shelby County Clerk's Office, Shelbyville
Trabert & Hoeffer, Chicago (Donald Levinson)

Indiana
Dubois County Health Department, Jasper (Doretha Mundy)
Indiana State Library, Indianapolis (Charles G. Hill)
Marion County Circuit Court Clerk, Indianapolis
Marion County Historical Society, Indianapolis (Lynne Conant)
Marion County Records Division, Indianapolis (Keith Beaven)
Marion County Vital Records Division, Indianapolis (Julia Bishop)

Iowa
Iowa State Vital Statistics, Des Moines
Marshalltown Court Recorder, Marshalltown

Kansas
Kansas State Bureau of Vital Statistics, Topeka
Kansas State Historical Society, Topeka
Leavenworth Federal Penitentiary, Leavenworth
Memorial Park Cemetery, Kansas City
Wyandotte County Court House, Kansas City
Wyandotte County Probate Department, Kansas City

Maryland
Department of Health & Human Services, Baltimore
   Social Security Administration
Suitland Reference Branch, Suitland
   Office of War Information Records

Massachusetts
Boston Historical Society (Philip Bergen)
Boston University
  Mugar Memorial Library
    Special Collections (Dr. Howard Gotlieb, Margaret Goostray)
First Church of Christ, Scientist, Boston (David K. Nartonis)
John Hancock Mutual Life Insurance Company, Boston
New England Historical Genealogical Society, Boston
Registry of Vital Records and Statistics, Boston
Town Clerk Department, Orleans
Town Clerk's Office, Lenox

Michigan
Office of State Registrar and Center for Health Statistics, Lansing

Missouri
Clay County Archives, Liberty
Miss Barstow's School, Kansas City (Nancy Wright)
Jackson County Court House, Kansas City
Jackson County Records Department, Kansas City
Kansas City Public Library (Sara Hallier)
Missouri Bureau of Vital Records, Jefferson City
Missouri State Archives, Jefferson City (Mary A. Beck, Michael
    O'Malley)
National Personnel Records Center, St. Louis
Notre Dame de Sion School of Kansas City (Sheila Weiford)
Ozark Memorial Park, Joplin
Unity Village Heritage Room, Kansas City (Judy Helman)
WDAF-AM, Kansas City (Don Crawley)

Nebraska
Bureau of Vital Statistics, Lincoln

Nevada
Summa Corporation, Las Vegas (Vernon C. Olson)
Washoe County Clerk's Office, Reno

New Jersey
Essex County Jail, Newark (Sgt. Bassett)
National Archives, Bayonne

Newark Public Library (Simone Galik)
New Jersey State Archives, Trenton
New Jersey State Department of Health, Trenton
Riviera Hotel, Newark
Newark Sheriff's Office (Sgt. Carey)

New York
Algonquin Hotel, Manhattan (Lucille Scola)
American Academy of Dramatic Arts, Manhattan (Meg McSweeney)
Bettmann/UPI, Manhattan
Bureau of Vital Records, Manhattan
City Clerk's Office, Bronx
City Clerk's Office, Brooklyn
City Clerk's Office, Glens Falls
City Clerk's Office, Queens
City Clerk's Office, Queensbury
Columbia University, Manhattan
   Oral History Research Office, Butler Library
County Clerk's Office, Manhattan (Bruce Abrams)
Culver Pictures, Manhattan (Peter Tomlinson)
Fashion Institute of Technology, Manhattan (Harold Koda, Fred
      Dennis)
Franklin D. Roosevelt Library, Hyde Park (Raymond Teichman)
Globe Photos, Manhattan
Killiam Shows, Manhattan (Bruce Lawton)
Kino International, Manhattan (Jessica Rosner)
Kobal Collection, Manhattan (Bob Cosenza)
Marriage License Bureau, Brooklyn
Mount Zion Cemetery, Queens
Municipal Archives, Manhattan
Museum of Modern Art, Manhattan
   Film Stills Archive (Mary Corliss)
Museum of Television and Radio, Manhattan
National Kidney Foundation, Manhattan
New York Bar Association, Manhattan
New-York Historical Society, Manhattan
New York Life Insurance Company, Manhattan (Bob Haggerty)
New York Public Library, Lincoln Center, Manhattan
   Theater Collection (Dr. Rod Blaidell, Dorothy Swerdlove)
New York State Board of Nursing, Albany
New York State Education Department, Albany (W. A. Evans)

New York State Health Department, Albany
   Genealogy Department, Vital Records
New York State Library, Albany
   Cultural Education Center (Melinda Yates)
Office of the Chief Medical Examiner, Manhattan (Tony Alago)
Rochester General Hospital
   School of Practical Nursing
Rochester Public Library
Sotheby's, Manhattan (Tom Cashin)
Wide World Photos, Manhattan (Don Bowden)

North Carolina
Duke University, Durham
   William R. Perkins Library (Natalie M. Houston)

Ohio
Department of Vital Statistics, Columbus
Franklin County Probate Court, Columbus
Hancock County Public Library, Findlay (Dianne Wood)
Lucas County Court House, Toledo
Ohio Historical Society, Columbus
Ohio University Library, Athens
   Special Collections (George W. Bain)
Toledo Department of Health

Oklahoma
Oklahoma State University, Stillwater (Leonard J. Leff)
Oklahoma State Vital Records, Oklahoma City

Oregon
Medford Public Library (Shyla Hungerford)
Oregon State Vital Statistics, Portland
Rogue Valley Manor, Medford (Pat Seggelink)

Pennsylvania
State Board of Nursing, Harrisburg (Cathy Rhoades)
Vital Records, New Castle

Rhode Island
Division of Vital Records, Providence

Tennessee
Department of Health, Nashville
Memphis State University Libraries, Memphis
    Radio Program History Collection
University of Tennessee, Knoxville
    Special Collections (Nick Wyman)

Texas
National Museum of Communications, Irving (Bill Bragg)
Southern Methodist University, Dallas
    Oral History Program (Ronald L. Davis)
Stamford Public Library, Stamford
University of Texas, Austin
    Harry Ransom Humanities Research Center (Charles Bell)

Utah
Brigham Young University, Provo
    Arts & Communications Archive (James V. D'Arc)

Virginia
Edgar Allan Poe Foundation, Richmond (Dr. Bruce English)

Washington
Center for Health Statistics, Olympia
King County Auditor's Office, Seattle
King County Clerk's Office, Seattle
Longview Public Library, Longview (Susan Maxey)
Pierce County Marriage License Department, Tacoma
Pierce County Superior Court Clerk's Office, Tacoma

Wyoming
University of Wyoming, Laramie
    American Heritage Center (Rick Ewig)

International

Canada
Division of Vital Statistics, Victoria, B.C.
Nanaimo General Hospital, Nanaimo, B.C.

Office of the Registrar General, Thunder Bay, Ontario
Registered Nurses Association of British Columbia, Vancouver
(Claire Kermacks)
Royal Jubilee Hospital, Victoria, B.C. (Shirley Anderson)
Toronto Historical Board, Toronto, Ontario (Joan E. Crosbie)

Czechoslovakia
Ceskoslovensky Filmovy Ustav-Filmovy Archiv, Prague (Vladimir
Opela, Ewa Kacerova)

England
Burke's Peerage, London (Katy Heywood-Lonsdale)
Kobal Collection, London

Italy
Cineteca Italiana, Milan
Ufficio Dello Stato Civile, Trieste

Mexico
Oficina de Registros, Tecate, Baja California

Newspapers and Periodicals

American Cinematographer, Architectural Digest, Chicago *American,* Chicago *Daily News, Christian Science Monitor, Coast, Film Daily, Films in Review,* Findlay (Ohio) *Republican Courier, Fortune, High Fidelity,* Hollywood *Citizen News, Hollywood Magazine, Hollywood Reporter, Hollywood Studio Magazine,* Kansas City *Kansan,* Kansas City *Post,* Kansas City *Star,* Kansas City *Times, Le Petit Parisien, Liberty, Life, Look,* Los Angeles *Citizen News,* Los Angeles *Evening News,* Los Angeles *Examiner,* Los Angeles *Herald,* Los Angeles *Post Record,* Los Angeles *Times, Modern Romances, Motion Picture, Motion Picture Almanac, Motion Picture Exhibitors Herald, Motion Picture News, Movie Classic, New Movie Magazine,* New York *American,* New York *Daily Mirror,* New York *Daily News,* New York *Evening Journal,* New York *Herald Tribune,* New York *Journal-American,* New York *Sun,* New York *Times, New Yorker, Newsweek, Night and Day,* Page (Arizona) *Chronicle, Photoplay, Picturegoer, Playboy,* Sacramento *Bee,* San Francisco *Call,* San Francisco *Chronicle,* San Francisco *Examiner, Saturday Evening Post, Screen Book, Screen Guide, Screenland, Screenplay, Silver Screen, Time, Vanity Fair, Variety* (daily/weekly), Washington *Daily News,* Washington *Post, West.*

Bibliography

American Film Institute, *Index of Feature Films: 1921–1930.*

Astor, Mary, *A Life on Film*. Delacorte, 1967.

Bakewell, William, *Hollywood Be Thy Name*. Scarecrow Press, 1991.

Bankhead, Tallulah, *Tallulah*. Harper & Bros., 1952.

Bartlett, Donald L., and Steele, James B., *Empire: The Life, Legend, and Madness of Howard Hughes*. Norton, 1979.

Behlmer, Rudy (editor), *Memo from David O. Selznick*. Grove, 1972.

Berg, A. Scott, *Goldwyn*. Knopf, 1989.

Berman, Louis, M.D., *The Glands Regulating Personality*. Macmillan, 1928.

Brush, Katharine, *Red-Headed Woman*. Grosset & Dunlap, 1931.

Bull, Clarence Sinclair, with Raymond Lee, *The Faces of Hollywood*. A. S. Barnes, 1968.

Cameron, Stewart, *Kidney Disease*. Oxford University Press, 1986.

Coffee, Lenore, *Storyline*. Cassell & Co. Ltd., 1973.

Davies, Marion, *The Times We Had*. Bobbs-Merrill, 1975.

Drew, William M., *Speaking of Silents: First Ladies of the Screen*. Vestal Press, 1989.

Eddy, Mary Baker, *Science and Health with Key to the Scriptures*. First Church of Christ, Scientist, 1971.

Fahey, David, and Rich, Linda, *Masters of Starlight: Photographers in Hollywood*. Ballantine Books, 1987.

Fairbanks, Douglas, Jr., *The Salad Days*. Doubleday, 1988.

Finch, Christopher, & Rosenkrantz, Linda, *Gone Hollywood: The Movie Colony in the Golden Age*. Doubleday, 1979.

Fountain, Leatrice Gilbert, with John R. Maxim, *Dark Star: The Untold Story of the Meteoric Rise and Fall of the Legendary John Gilbert*. St. Martin's, 1985.

Fox, Roy, *Hollywood Mayfair, and All That Jazz*. Leslie Frewin, 1975.

Friede, Donald, *The Mechanical Angel*. Knopf, 1948.

Gabler, Neal, *An Empire of Their Own: How the Jews Invented Hollywood*. Crown, 1988.

Granlund, Nils Thor, with Sid Feder and Ralph Hancock, *Blondes, Brunettes, and Bullets*. McKay, 1957.

Harlow, Jean, *Today Is Tonight*. Dell, 1965.

Haver, Ronald, *David O. Selznick's Hollywood*. Bonanza Books, 1980.

Hay, Peter, *M-G-M: When the Lion Roars*. Turner Publishing, 1991.

Head, Edith, and Calistro, Paddy, *Edith Head's Hollywood*. E. P. Dutton, 1983.

Hurrell, George (text by Whitney Stine), *50 Years of Photographing Hollywood: The Hurrell Style*. Greenwich House, 1983.

Kael, Pauline, *5001 Nights at the Movies*. Holt, Rinehart & Winston, 1982.

Kaufman, George S., and Ferber, Edna, *Dinner at Eight*. Samuel French, 1931.

Knight, R. P., *Discourse on the Worship of Priapus*. Dilettanti Society, 1786.

Kobal, John, *The Art of the Great Hollywood Portrait Photographers*. Knopf, 1980.

————, *People Will Talk*. Knopf, 1985.

Kotsilibas-Davis, James, and Loy, Myrna, *Myrna Loy: Being and Becoming*. Knopf, 1987.

Loos, Anita, *Kiss Hollywood Good-by*. Viking, 1974.

MacLean, Barbara Barondess, *One Life Is Not Enough*. Hippocrene, 1986.

Marion, Frances, *Off with Their Heads!* Macmillan, 1972.

McBride, Joseph, *Frank Capra: The Catastrophe of Success*. Simon & Schuster, 1992.

McGilligan, Pat, *Backstory: Interviews with Screenwriters of Hollywood's Golden Age*. University of California Press, 1986.

McGilligan, Patrick, *George Cukor: A Double Life*. St. Martin's, 1991.

Moore, Colleen, *Silent Star*. Doubleday, 1968.

Nemilov, A. (translated by Stephanie Ofental), *The Biological Tragedy of Woman*. Covici, Friede, 1932.

Newquist, Roy, *Conversations with Joan Crawford*. Citadel, 1980.

Norman, Barry, *The Hollywood Greats*. Franklin Watts, 1980.

Pepper, Terence, and Kobal, John, *The Man Who Shot Garbo: The Hollywood Photographs of Clarence Sinclair Bull*. Simon & Schuster, 1989.

Richman, Harry, and Gehman, Richard, *A Hell of a Life*. Duell, Sloan & Pierce, 1966.

Russell, Rosalind, and Chase, Chris, *Life Is a Banquet*. Random House, 1977.

St. Johns, Adela Rogers, *Love, Laughter and Tears: My Hollywood Story*. Doubleday, 1978.

Schatz, Thomas, *The Genius of the System*. Pantheon, 1988.

Scott, Evelyn F., *Hollywood When Silents Were Golden*. McGraw-Hill, 1972.

Selznick, Irene Mayer, *A Private View*. Knopf, 1983.

Server, Lee, *Screenwriter*. Main Street Press, 1987.

Skolsky, Sidney, *Don't Get Me Wrong—I Love Hollywood*. Putnam, 1975.

Skretvedt, Randy, *Laurel & Hardy: The Magic Behind the Movies*. Moonstone Press, 1987.

Slide, Anthony, *Nitrate Won't Wait: Film Preservation in the United States*. McFarland & Co., 1992.

Spoto, Donald, *Marilyn Monroe: The Biography*. HarperCollins, 1993.

Stenn, David, *Clara Bow: Runnin' Wild*. Doubleday, 1988.

Stuart, Mark A., *Gangster #2: Longy Zwillman, the Man Who Invented Organized Crime*. Lyle Stuart, 1985.

Thomson, David, *Showman: The Life of David O. Selznick*. Knopf, 1992.

Tornabene, Lyn, *Long Live the King: A Biography of Clark Gable*. Putnam's, 1976.

Walker, Alexander (authorized by Metro-Goldwyn-Mayer), *Joan Crawford: The Ultimate Star*. Harper & Row, 1983.

Walker, Joseph, and Walker, Juanita, *The Light on Her Face*. ASC Press, 1984.

Wiley, Mason, and Bona, Damien, *Inside Oscar*. Ballantine Books, 1986.

Young, Jordan, *Reel Characters*. Moonstone Press, 1975.

Acknowledgments

Woolsey Ackerman, Karen Aderman, Richard Adkins, Mary Ann Anderson, Patricia Angelin, Army Archerd, Sandy Arcieri, Ed Baker, David L. Baldwin, Jodi Balsam, Richard Bann, Diana Barton, Chris Basinger, Anne Bayliss, Joseph Blotner, Patricia Boaz, Wes Bond, David Bradley, Larry Buchanan, Brian Bundy, Larry Burnett, David Burnham, H. Keith Burns, Bill Cappello, Esmee Chandlee, Bill Chapman, George Christy, Maria Ciaccia, David Columbia, Don Conway, Bob Courtney, George Cowap, Kirk Crivello, Donna Crowe, Crit Davis, David Del Valle, George Eels, Michael Eisenhower, Dale Eunson, Joan Evans, William K. Everson, Penelope March Fantacci, Kay Fidler, Bill Forbriger, Gene Fowler, Jr., Milo Frank, David Frankel, Dr. Sheldon Glabman, Kathie Greenacre, Sydney Guilaroff, Richard Gully, Pat Hackett, Joan B. Harris, Jay Hickerson, Carolyn Talbot Hoagland, Carole Hughes, Deborah Irmas, Nancy Kapitanoff, Bruce Kellner, Chris Kershaw, Don Koll, James Kotsilibas-Davis, Irv Kupcinet, Pat Silver-Lasky, Fred L. Lee, Dr. Jan Leestma, Christine Longfellow, Arthur Lubin, Patrick Lucas, Ivor McCray, Jr., Kevin MacKelvie, Doug Major, Leonard Maltin, Howard Mandelbaum, Judith Markham, Dr. Richard Marohn, Doug Milne, Jon Mirsalis, Ron Mita, Scott Moyers, Darcy O'Brien, William V. Ochs, Jr., Stuart Oderman, Marvin Paige, Wayne Parks, William Pettite, G. Thomas Poe, Alston Purvis, Cannon Quigley, Lawrence J. Quirk, Louise Roberg, Mark Rogister, Bill Schaefer, Ursula Scott-Larsen, Stephanie Segal, Daniel Selznick, L. Jeffrey Selznick, Richard Settle, Stephen Shearer, Barbara Siegel, Kenneth Silverman, Randy Skretvedt, Robert Slatzer, Sarah Stenn, Harvey Stewart, Lisa Stewart, Linda Teeple, Beverly

Thomas, Frank Thompson, Jane Thompson, Laurie Thompson, Pascal Franchot Tone, Emily Torchia, Bruce Torrence, Tom Toth, Bruce Tracy, Susan Tracy, Roi Uselton, Mark A. Vieira, Delmar Watson, Bob Weide, William Wellman, Jr., Selden West, Douglas Whitney, Lois Williams, Charles Williamson, Mark Willoughby, Geraldine Winerman, Michael Yakaitis, Dianne Young, Joe Yranski.

Notes

"To DS" denotes interview with author. Interviews by others are credited accordingly. All sources are attributed.

Prologue

"shaking her lightly": "Battle for Life Told by Fireman," Los Angeles *Examiner*, June 8, 1937.   p. 1

"keep on fighting": Los Angeles *Examiner*, June 7, 1937.   p. 1

"virtually recovered": "Jean Harlow Conquers Flu," Los Angeles *Times*, June 4, 1937.   p. 1

"inhalator squad": Captain Warren Blake, Ralph Beal, and William Thomas of the Los Angeles Fire Department (see Chapter Nineteen).   p. 1

"I guess we won't need this": "Star Collapses in Beverly Hills Home; Dies Later," Bedford [Pennsylvania] *Gazette*, June 8, 1937.   p. 2

"a cold": "Jean Harlow Improves as Crisis Passes," Hollywood *Citizen News*, June 3, 1937; Los Angeles *Examiner*, June 4, 1937; "Jean Harlow Gains Slowly," New York *Herald Tribune*, June 5, 1937.   p. 2

"a regular girl": "The One Star Who Has No Enemies,"   p. 2
Screen Book, July 1934.

"no vanity whatsoever": Anita Loos Oral History, Columbia   p. 2
University.

"the worst actress": Kansas City *Times*, June 9, 1937.   p. 2

"she played comedy": Statement by George Cukor [August   p. 2
1964], Academy of Motion Picture Arts & Sciences
(AMPAS).

"I'm handicapped": "Jean Harlow Answers Your Questions,"   p. 3
Motion Picture, July 1933.

"my gang": Statement by Jean Bello [c. 1955], AMPAS.   p. 3

"I could be a better hooker": Lee Server, *Screenwriter*; Allen   p. 3
Rivkin to DS; Ronald Haver, *David O. Selznick's Hollywood*.

Part One: Harlean

Chapter One

"She was the prettiest woman": Hortense Williams to DS.   p. 7

"Strangers would follow her": Henrietta Bucker to DS.   p. 7

cutting remark . . . slap in the face: Hortense Williams to DS.   p. 7

affair with a railroad conductor: Ibid. His name is unknown.   p. 8

"handsome and dignified": Barbara Brown to DS.   p. 8

"Mont Carpenter was a gentleman": Hortense Williams to   p. 8
DS.

"Skip Harlow was the head": Virginia Cox to DS.   p. 8

October 1, 1908: Mont Clair Carpenter/Jean Poe Harlow   p. 9
marriage certificate; "Gossip of Society," Kansas City *Star*,
October 2, 1908; Kansas City *Post*, October 4, 1908.

3344 Olive Street: Kansas City, Missouri. Skip Harlow's   p. 9
home at 930 Orville Avenue was in Kansas City, Kansas.

"From the moment I knew," etc.: "Is Jean Harlow Dead?   p. 9
Her Mother Says No!" *Modern Romances*, March and April
1938.

March 3, 1911: Harlean Carpenter birth certificate.   p. 9

"Shirley Jean": "The Authentic Story of My Life by Jean   p. 10
Harlow," *New Movie Magazine*, September 1934.

"There is nothing else in my life": "Is Jean Harlow   p. 10
Dead? . . ."

Harlean Harlow Carpenter: The middle name appears on   p. 10
Harlean's birth announcement, but not her birth certificate.

Chapter Two

4409 Robert Gillham Road: Kansas City, Missouri.   p. 11

Red Gables: Bonner Springs, Kansas.   p. 11

"I have seen him come home": Hortense Williams to DS.   p. 11

"All through my childhood": Los Angeles *Examiner*, June 8,   p. 11
1937.

"Every morning when I wake up": Hortense Williams to DS.   p. 12

Dr. Herbert Lipman: "The Authentic Story of My Life by   p. 12
Jean Harlow," *New Movie Magazine*, September 1934.

"spinal meningitis": "Jean Harlow Answers Your   p. 12
Questions," *Motion Picture*, July 1933.

"a social climber": Gene Goldman (son of Virginia Cartlich)   p. 13
to DS.

"She was always *all mine*": "Is Jean Harlow Dead? Her   p. 13
Mother Says No!" *Modern Romances*, March and April 1938.

Dearest dearest Mother: Note from Harlean Carpenter to Jean Carpenter, [March 3, 1919]. p. 13

Miss Barstow's School: A 1921 story ("An Elf's Adventures") and 1922 poem ("The Mother's Song") by Harlean Carpenter appeared in *The Weather-cock*, a school publication. p. 13

1312 East 79th Street: Kansas City, Missouri. p. 13

granted a divorce: *Jean H. Carpenter v. Mont C. Carpenter*, Jackson County [Missouri] Circuit Court, September 29, 1922. p. 14

"After the divorce": Hortense Williams to DS. p. 14

"She went to Hollywood": Ibid. p. 14

crush on . . . Buck Jones: Maxine Jones (daughter) to DS; Los Angeles *Examiner*, June 9, 1937. p. 15

single room . . . Sunset Boulevard mansion: Barbara Brown to DS. The address is unknown. p. 15

"Little Miss Harlean Carpenter": Irene Mayer Selznick, *A Private View*. p. 15

"They all just walked": Evelyn F. Scott, *Hollywood When Silents Were Golden*. p. 16

"My first recollection of Harlean": Virginia Parsons to DS. p. 16

"so many conquests": Cecil B. De Mille on *Lux Radio Theater* (CBS), December 14, 1936. p. 16

"Baby Jeritza": Irene Mayer Selznick to DS. At the time, Maria Jeritza (1887–1982) sang at the Metropolitan Opera in New York. p. 16

"She was blonde": Scott, *Hollywood When Silents Were Golden*. p. 16

"Mrs. Carpenter was large and blonde": Virginia Parsons to DS. p. 16

"adored": Carol Ortner (daughter of Marjorie Kendal) to DS.   p. 17

"a very handsome Continental gentleman": Irene Mayer   p. 17
Selznick to DS.

"Harlean sought refuge": Carol Ortner to DS.   p. 17

"My father": Barbara Brown to DS.   p. 17

1302 North La Brea Avenue: Los Angeles directory, 1925.   p. 17

"were so homesick": "The Authentic Story of My Life by   p. 17
Jean Harlow."

"She dropped out without notice": Selznick, *A Private View*.   p. 17

Chapter Three

"Mother was so lonely": "The Authentic Story of My Life by   p. 18
Jean Harlow," *New Movie Magazine*, September 1934.

"That camp," etc.: Ibid.   p. 18

"There's nothing worse": Fred L. Lee (son of Jean Moore) to   p. 18
DS.

"One afternoon," etc.: David Thornton Arnold to Fred L.   p. 18
Lee.

Born illegitimate: Marino Bello birth certificate, November   p. 20
11, 1883. "*Illegitimo*" is marked upon it.

cane . . . concealed a sword: Harold Rosson Oral History by   p. 20
Bill Gleason, American Film Institute (AFI).

"He was a tall, dominating figure": Joan Marsh to DS.   p. 20

"He was an extremely *exotic* person": Madge Bellamy to DS.   p. 20

he married Mildred Maas: Marino Bello/Mildred Maas   p. 20
marriage certificate, August 15, 1914.

he immigrated to Chicago: Marino and Mildred Bello arrived   p. 20
at Ellis Island on October 5, 1919, aboard the *Presidente
Wilson.*

Sherman Hotel owner Ernest Byfield: Ernest Byfield, Jr., to   p. 20
DS.

Bello was a naturalized citizen: U.S. Immigration and   p. 20
Naturalization Service records, December 14, 1925.

"and that was the beginning": "The Authentic Story of My   p. 21
Life by Jean Harlow."

"She didn't take him seriously": Barbara Brown to DS.   p. 21

"She wasn't in love": Marcella Rabwin to DS.   p. 21

"money-grubbing S.O.B.": Elaine St. Johns to DS.   p. 21

"He *detested* him": Hortense Williams to DS.   p. 21

"Mother took a room": "The Authentic Story of My Life by   p. 22
Jean Harlow." The Highland Park Hotel stood at 504
Central Avenue; Bello lived at 280 Central Avenue.

"Even at that age": Jada Leland to DS.   p. 22

Chapter Four

tragedy struck: Roscoe and Enyd McGrew drowned on June   p. 24
6, 1923, en route to Twin Pine Island in Trout Lake,
Wisconsin.

"Chuck was a terrific guy": Jada Leland to DS.   p. 24

"fell completely in love": Margo McGrew to DS.   p. 24

"was the best-looking boy": Louella O. Parsons, "Jean   p. 24
Harlow's Life Story" (memorial magazine), 1937.

"They really related": Margo McGrew to DS.   p. 24

"marry him for the millions": Jada Leland to DS. Eugene   p. 25
Byfield was killed while playing polo in 1930. He never
married.

a friend to spy: Rod Adams. "He was my hero," Harlean   p. 25
recalled. ("The Authentic Story of My Life by Jean Harlow,"
New Movie Magazine, September 1934.)

"repeatedly struck and beaten her": *Mildred Bello v. Marino*   p. 25
Bello, Lake County [Illinois] Circuit Court, December 16,
1926.

January 18, 1927: Marino Bello/Jean Carpenter marriage   p. 25
certificate.

"She didn't like school": Jada Leland to DS.   p. 25

Chuck told Alfred Forrest: Ibid.   p. 25

"telling him what a lovely person Harlean was": Ibid.   p. 25

the "St. Louis Blues" blared: Parsons, "Jean Harlow's Life   p. 26
Story."

September 21, 1927: Charles F. McGrew 2nd/Harlean   p. 26
Carpenter marriage certificate.

received $200,000: *Harlean Carpenter McGrew v. Charles F.*   p. 26
McGrew II, Los Angeles County [California] Superior Court,
September 28, 1929.

"He had a problem": Margo McGrew to DS.   p. 26

Chuck stayed drunk: *McGrew v. McGrew*.   p. 26

January 1928: Ibid.   p. 26

618 North Linden Drive: Ibid.   p. 26

"They loved the outdoors": Robert McGrew to DS.   p. 27

"a very intelligent, deeply sensitive girl": Ibid.   p. 27

"Aunt Jetty": Hortense Williams (niece) to DS; Henrietta   p. 27
Bucker (granddaughter) to DS; Virginia Cox (grandniece) to
DS.

"bridge party": Rosalie Roy to DS.   p. 27

"I can truly say": Ibid.   p. 27

"and since she had no car": "The Authentic Story of My Life   p. 27
by Jean Harlow."

"was fascinated by the place": Ibid.   p. 27

"noticed me as I stood there": Ibid.   p. 27

"They wagered": Ibid.   p. 28

applied as "Jean Harlow": Her mother maintained that   p. 28
Harlean asked to do so. This may be, since Mother Jean's
maiden name was more appropriate than "Harlean
McGrew."

"a few days later": "The Authentic Story of My Life by Jean   p. 28
Harlow."

extra work in *Honor Bound*: Though Harlow never   p. 29
mentioned this film by name, Mother Jean disclosed later
that her daughter's first extra work was for director Alfred E.
Green, whose sole release in 1928 was *Honor Bound*. ("Is
Jean Harlow Dead? Her Mother Says No!" *Modern
Romances*, March and April 1938.)

"She had a perfect figure": Iris Adrian to DS.   p. 29

"Look": William M. Drew, *Speaking of Silents*.   p. 29

"She was *different*": Hal Roach to DS.   p. 30

"He said Mother Jean": Margo McGrew to DS.   p. 30

December 26, 1928 . . . contract: Hal Roach Studios records,   p. 30
Special Collections, University of Southern California (USC).

accompanied Chuck: *McGrew v. McGrew*.   p. 30

"We talked about Kansas City": Charles "Buddy" Rogers to DS. p. 30

"There was something special": Nancy Carroll to Douglas Whitney. p. 31

"We weren't told": Randy Skretvedt, *Laurel & Hardy: The Magic Behind the Movies*. p. 31

"underdressed": Hal Roach to Kevin Brownlow. p. 31

Edwin Bower Hesser: Hollywood actresses who posed seminude for Hesser include Clara Bow, Bessie Love, Norma Shearer, Gloria Swanson, Norma Talmadge, and Anna May Wong. p. 32

"She said her husband": Hal Roach to DS. p. 32

"I wanted the child": Kansas City *Times*, June 9, 1937. p. 32

June 11, 1929: *McGrew v. McGrew*. p. 33

"He said her mother": Margo McGrew to DS. p. 33

"Chuck went away": "Is Jean Harlow Dead? . . ." p. 33

Chapter Five

City Lights: Harlow appears in a still from *City Lights* but not in the film itself. Apparently the scene was reshot without her. p. 34

"Did I notice her?": Gilbert Roland to DS. p. 34

"She was lovely": Joel McCrea to DS. p. 34

"I can truthfully say": Roy Fox, *Hollywood, Mayfair, and All That Jazz*. p. 34

Chuck refused to support them: *McGrew v. McGrew*. p. 35

Skip Harlow . . . despised it: "The Authentic Story of My Life   p. 35
by Jean Harlow," *New Movie Magazine*, September 1934.

"I turned to motion pictures": " 'I Shall Marry Again,' Says   p. 35
Jean Harlow," *Motion Picture*, April 1933.

"This was not": Evelyn F. Scott, *Hollywood When Silents*   p. 35
Were Golden.

"Extra Girl Gets Her First Close-Up": *Hollywood Reporter*,   p. 35
September 30, 1935.

admitted was autobiographical: Jean Harlow on *Elza*   p. 35
Schallert Reviews (NBC), August 28, 1936.

"When she walked onto the set": Arthur Jacobson to DS;   p. 36
David Stenn, *Clara Bow: Runnin' Wild*.

"Tell 'em t'take her off": Ibid.   p. 36

"I always wondered": Ibid.   p. 36

"made" Harlean: David Marx to DS.   p. 36

"She was simply fascinated": Edith Head & Paddy Calistro,   p. 36
Edith Head's Hollywood.

"See if ya can help her out": Teet Carle to DS.   p. 36

Arthur Landau . . . advanced her $500: Letter from Arthur   p. 37
Landau to Irving Shulman, July 24, 1962.

"a country hick": Osmond Borradaile to DS.   p. 37

"feared embarrassment": Rupert Hughes, "Howard Hughes,   p. 38
Record Breaker," *Liberty*, February 6, 1937.

"Gee, kid": David Marx to DS.   p. 38

"Jimmy told Hughes": Ibid.   p. 38

"She had almost albino blonde hair": Letter from Joseph   p. 38
Moncure March to *Look*, March 23, 1954.

"Well?": Jean Bello to Herb Read.   p. 39

"He hired me": Ibid.   p. 39

Part Two: Platinum Blonde

Chapter Six

five-year contract: Caddo Company and "Harlean Carpenter   p. 43
McGrew, known professionally as Jean Harlow" agreement,
October 24, 1929.

"a nineteen-year-old": "Chicago Society Girl with Caddo,"   p. 43
Los Angeles *Examiner*, October 29, 1929.

Dear Mr. Hughes: Letter from Jean Bello (as/for Jean   p. 44
Harlow) to Howard Hughes, [1929].

sold today: As recently as 1992, a "historical document"   p. 44
dealer in Beverly Hills offered inauthentic autographs for
$4,000 apiece.

"insecure": Ridgeway Callow Oral History by Rudy Behlmer,   p. 44
AMPAS.

"a pig": Gregory Mank, "Jean Harlow," *Films in Review*,   p. 44
December 1978.

"nervous and tense": "Jean Harlow Answers Your   p. 44
Questions," *Motion Picture*, July 1933.

"Harlow was quite aware," etc.: Letter from Joseph Moncure   p. 44
March to *Look*, March 23, 1954.

"the corniest line": Jesse Lasky, Jr., *Whatever Happened to* p. 45
Hollywood? Funk & Wagnalls, 1975.

"It was impossible": Ridgeway Callow Oral History.   p. 45

two-color Technicolor: See Chapter Twenty.   p. 45

"It was practically unbearable": Ridgeway Callow Oral   p. 45
History.

"Klieg eyes": "The Story Jean Harlow Has Never Told,"   p. 46
Screen Book, [date unknown].

Paul Bern: "He took me to my first Hollywood party,"   p. 46
Harlow recalled. "Irene [Mayer] Selznick, whom I had
known in school, had invited me to her house and Paul acted
as my escort." (Los Angeles *Examiner*, June 26, 1932.)

premiere of *Hell's Angels: Variety*, May 28, 1930, and June 4,   p. 46
1930.

"Thank you": *Hell's Angels* premiere footage, May 27, 1930.   p. 46
Paul Bern, Mother Jean, and Marino Bello are visible behind
Harlow.

"How I got through": Louella O. Parsons, "Jean Harlow's   p. 47
Life Story" (Memorial magazine), 1937.

"While she is the center": New York *Times*, August 16, 1930.   p. 47

"Jean Harlow": Pauline Kael, *5001 Nights at the Movies*.   p. 47

"It doesn't make much difference": *Variety*, June 4, 1930.   p. 47

"like a bitch in heat": Adela Rogers St. Johns, *Love,*   p. 48
Laughter, and Tears: My Hollywood Story.

"Harlow hated herself": Arthur Landau notes, [1962],   p. 48
AMPAS.

"She was disgusted": Kansas City *Times*, June 9, 1937.   p. 48

"lay off": Margo McGrew to DS.   p. 48

"spent an hour with Harlean": Letter from Jetty Chadsey to   p. 48
Joe Boylan, [c. December 1930].

"Her eyes shot *fire*": Ibid. The conversation is recorded here.   p. 49

"I know interstate service": Harlean Carpenter McGrew,   p. 49

Jean Carpenter Bello, and Marino Bello affidavits, *McGrew v. McGrew*, July 16, 1930.

he never saw Harlow: Margo McGrew to DS.   p. 50

Mother Jean decided: Jada Leland to DS.   p. 50

"objectionable photographic poses": Los Angeles *Examiner*,   p. 50
August 4, 1930. *McGrew v. McGrew* (July 25, 1930) cites the
photographs without submitting them to the court.

Harlow . . . denied their existence: "I simply wish to deny his p. 50
charge that I ever posed for indecent pictures," she said.
"Such pictures absolutely do not exist. They were never
taken." (Kansas City *Times*, August 14, 1930.)

New York and Seattle premieres: Harlow promoted *Hell's*   p. 50
Angels in New York on August 15, 1930, and in Seattle on
July 20, 1930.

$150 a week: Letter from Caddo Company to Jean Harlow,   p. 50
July 16, 1930.

"got letters from all over": Barbara Brown to DS.   p. 50

"I get about fifty letters": "Jean Is a 'Home Girl,' " Kansas   p. 50
City *Times*, December 8, 1931.

eastbound train: Kansas City *Times*, August 14, 1930.   p. 51

Harlow to Kansas City: Kansas City *Times*, November 21,   p. 51
1930.

local radio program: Interview by Landon Laird, WDAF,   p. 51
November 20, 1930.

Maude Carpenter: Mont C. Carpenter/Maude S. Price   p. 51
marriage certificate, September 18, 1928.

dentist . . . fixed Harlow's teeth: Robert Orth (friend of Mont p. 51
Carpenter) to DS.

"He should be ashamed": Kansas City *Star*, June 9, 1937.   p. 51

"a beautiful young girl": Caddo Company publicity release,   p. 51
June 1931.

"I know I'm the worst": Kansas City *Times*, June 9, 1937.   p. 51

"She was very unhappy": Arthur Landau notes.   p. 52

nominal figurehead: For the rest of Harlow's life, the   p. 52
Landau-Small Agency commissioned her income, though
Landau did little to earn it.

"She wasn't foolish": Richard Landau to DS.   p. 52

"business manager": "Never employed," noted Bello on his   p. 52
December 6, 1940, application for Social Security.

"persecuting": Telegram from Joseph P. Bickerton, Jr.   p. 52
(attorney for Jean Harlow), to Howard Hughes, October 20,
1930.

MISS HARLOW GENEROUSLY TREATED: Telegram from Neil S.   p. 52
McCarthy (attorney for Howard Hughes) to Joseph P.
Bickerton, Jr., October 20, 1930.

"I haven't seen him": "Redhead's Life Exciting Whirl," Los   p. 53
Angeles *Examiner*, June 26, 1932.

Chapter Seven

The Secret Six: Caddo Company and Metro-Goldwyn-Mayer   p. 54
contract, November 11, 1930.

"Neither of us knew": "What I Think About Jean Harlow, by   p. 54
Clark Gable," *Hollywood Magazine*, August 1935.

"She was quite an amateur": Joseph Newman to DS.   p. 54

forty-one-year-old: By now Mother Jean had subtracted two   p. 54
years from her actual birth date and admitted to age thirty-
nine.

"It is unfortunate": New York *Times*, April 18, 1931.   p. 54

"Woefully lacking": *Variety*, April 22, 1931.   p. 55

"You oughta go over": William Bakewell to DS; William   p. 55
Bakewell, *Hollywood Be Thy Name*; Lew Ayres to DS.

Warners was paying $1,000: Caddo Company and Warner   p. 56
Brothers Pictures contract, January 22, 1931.

she got $200: Letter from the Caddo Company to Jean   p. 56
Harlow, December 19, 1930.

"Her mother": Gabrielle Woods to DS.   p. 56

"She was an original": Mae Clarke to DS.   p. 56

"How . . . do you hold": John Kobal, *People Will Talk*.   p. 56

"I ice 'em": Ibid.   p. 56

"Come on, Baby": Virginia Cox (niece of Mary Williams) to   p. 56
DS.

"King of Broadway": Harry Richman and Richard Gehman,   p. 57
A Hell of a Life.

"Harry Richman would do anything": Lina Basquette to DS.   p. 57

Scarface: In the film, Harlow greets leading man Paul Muni   p. 57
in a nightclub. Her words are inaudible.

My dear Howard: Letter from Joseph Schenck to Howard   p. 58
Hughes, May 7, 1931.

SHE PROBABLY WORST ACTRESS: Telegram from Samuel   p. 59
Goldwyn to Joseph Schenck, May 22, 1931; A. Scott Berg,
Goldwyn.

"She dreaded personal appearances": "Is Jean Harlow   p. 59
Dead? Her Mother Says No!" *Modern Romances*, March and
April 1938.

"trembling like a leaf": Letter from Ethel Camens to Irving   p. 59
Shulman, August 9, 1964.

"That's all he had to do": Reginald Owen Oral History,   p. 59
Columbia University.

"Jean Harlow can't dance": *Variety*, May 27, 1931.   p. 59

Fisher Theater: *Variety*, June 2, 1931.   p. 59

"terrific drinker," "constant partyer": Lina Basquette to DS.   p. 60

died of liver disease: Ernest Torgler death certificate,   p. 60
February 14, 1967.

"She would borrow": Lina Basquette to DS.   p. 60

Abner Zwillman: FBI memorandum, April 13, 1954; Mark   p. 60
A. Stuart, *Gangster #2: Longy Zwillman, the Man Who
Invented Organized Crime.*

his father's death: Reuben Abram Zwillman death certificate,   p. 60
June 14, 1915.

"He was very charming": Barbara Brown to DS.   p. 61

"atrocious assault and battery": FBI memorandum, April 13,   p. 61
1954.

Al Capone: "I Cover Hollywood, by Lloyd Pantages," Los   p. 61
Angeles *Examiner*, April 23, 1935.

"He wanted to be": Vince Barbie to DS.   p. 61

"She *loved* to hang out": Lina Basquette to DS.   p. 61

securing a two-picture deal: John Steinbach (stepson of   p. 61
Longy Zwillman) to DS.

$5,000: Caddo Company and Columbia Pictures contract,   p. 61
May 23, 1931.

$250-a-week salary: Letter from the Caddo Company to Jean   p. 61
Harlow, July 27, 1931.

"obsessed": Christopher Finch & Linda Rosenkrantz, *Gone*   p. 62
Hollywood: The Movie Colony in the Golden Age.

charm bracelet . . . Cadillac: Blanche Williams to Kay   p. 62
Mulvey, October 16, 1964.

Chapter Eight

250,000 practicing Christian Scientists: The Christian   p. 64
Science Church released a membership figure of 269,000 in
1936.

"not to accept the God": "Is Jean Harlow Dead? Her Mother   p. 64
Says No!" *Modern Romances*, March–April 1938.

never joined the Mother Church: The First Church of Christ,   p. 64
Scientist to DS.

"human willpower is not Science": Mary Baker Eddy,   p. 64
Science and Health with Key to the Scriptures.

"Grandmother didn't like her": Leatrice Gilbert to DS.   p. 64

"To the Baby all churches": Jean Bello statement [c. 1955],   p. 64
AMPAS.

"Grandmother adored her": Leatrice Gilbert to DS.   p. 65

"I'll either be a good girl": "Platinum Reform Begins," Los   p. 65
Angeles *Herald*, September 5, 1931.

"The first day": Joseph Walker and Juanita Walker, *The*   p. 65
Light on Her Face.

"She didn't know": Frank Capra Oral History by Arthur B.   p. 65
Friedman, Columbia University.

"liberry": Joseph McBride, *Frank Capra: The Catastrophe of*   p. 65
Success.

"She wanted to learn": Frank Capra Oral History, Columbia   p. 65
University.

"spectacular rather than competent": New York *Times*,   p. 66
October 31, 1931.

"The Joy Girl," "The Passion Girl," etc.: Los Angeles   p. 66
Herald, December 28, 1930; *Motion Picture News*, December
27, 1930.

Gallagher to *Platinum Blonde*: At its final preview, on   p. 66
September 24, 1931, it was titled *The Gilded Cage*. (McBride,
Frank Capra.)

three would-be platinum blondes: "The Headline Career of   p. 66
Jean Harlow," *Motion Picture*, December 1932.

"I shampoo it": "Jean Harlow Answers Your Questions,"   p. 66
Motion Picture, July 1933.

"I used to bleach": Alfred Pagano to DS.   p. 67

Jim's Beauty Studio: Barbara Brown to DS; Jean Bello   p. 67
statement, AMPAS; Creditor's Claim of Jim's Beauty Studio,
Estate of Jean Harlow, Los Angeles County Superior Court,
September 28, 1937.

"bleach and dye specialist" Pearl Porterfield: Harold   p. 67
Porterfield (son) to DS; Dorothy Hesketh (niece) to DS.
Barbara Brown believes Harlow's hairdresser at Jim's Beauty
Studio was named "Jenny." (Barbara Brown to DS.)

"if it hadn't been for the color of my hair": Marcella Rabwin   p. 67
to DS.

"She wasn't too keen": Osmond Borradaile to DS.   p. 67

October 1: Letter from Columbia Pictures to the Caddo   p. 67
Company, October 6, 1931; letter from Jean Harlow (signed
by Mother Jean) to William Mortensen, October 10, 1931. In
both missives, *Three Wise Girls* is referred to by its original
title, *Blonde Baby*.

"wholesome part": "Platinum Reform Begins," Los Angeles   p. 67
Herald, September 5, 1931.

"She does her best": *Variety*, February 9, 1932.   p. 67

"She was embarrassing": Mae Clarke to DS.   p. 67

Freaks: Hollywood Reporter, October 31, 1931.   p. 67

"wretches": Gregory Mank, "Jean Harlow," *Films in Review*,   p. 68
December 1978.

The Beast of the City: Caddo Company and Metro-Goldwyn-   p. 68
Mayer contract, November 5, 1931. In a sign of Harlow's
diminished status, Caddo's fee for her services had fallen to
$1,000 per week.

$8,500: Letter from the Caddo Company to Jean Harlow,   p. 68
December 4, 1931. The exact sum was $8,358.33.

"Baby, I wish": Kansas City *Times*, December 8, 1931.   p. 68

"So do I": Ibid.   p. 68

"It can't be good": "Jean a Sleeping Beauty," Kansas City   p. 69
Star, December 8, 1931.

she collapsed: "Jean Harlow Is Stricken in East on Stage   p. 69
Tour," Los Angeles *Herald*, December 26, 1931.

"Her body just went to pieces": Ibid.   p. 69

"This tour . . . is too much": Ibid.   p. 69

"intestinal influenza": Ibid.   p. 69

Bello had to carry her: A photograph appears in *Photoplay*,   p. 69
March 1932.

"See if you can do anything," etc.: Nils Thor Granlund with   p. 69
Sid Feder and Ralph Hancock, *Blondes, Brunettes, and
Bullets*; letter from Nils Thor Granlund to Sam Bischoff, May
15, 1954.

"The curtains parted": Letter from Arthur Landau to Irving   p. 70
Shulman, August 15, 1962.

"Take my word": Granlund, *Blondes, Brunettes, and Bullets*.   p. 70

"The scene was pure corn": Ibid.   p. 70

Brooklyn's . . . Metropolitan Theater: *Variety*, January 12,   p. 70
1932; *Motion Picture News*, January 29, 1932.

police escort: Ibid.   p. 70

Ziegfeld offered Harlow: "The Headline Career of Jean   p. 70
Harlow," *Motion Picture*, December 1932.

Newark . . . State Theater . . . Riviera Hotel: John Steinbach   p. 70
to DS.

Cleveland's crowds . . . Jack Dempsey: Granlund, op. cit.   p. 70

"I don't remember her act," etc.: Harry Friedenberg to DS.   p. 71

"The platinum baby really acts": New York *Daily News*,   p. 71
March 12, 1932. *The Beast of the City* is the only film in
which Harlow's character dies.

"a shiny refinement of Clara Bow": *Time*, March 21, 1932.   p. 71

"On his way home," etc.: Irene Mayer Selznick to DS;   p. 71
Selznick, *A Private View*.

"I think": Irene Mayer Selznick to DS; Selznick, *A Private*   p. 72
View.

Crawford and Garbo . . . "gone platinum": The former in   p. 73
This Modern Age and *Laughing Sinners* (both 1931); the
latter in *As You Desire Me* (1932).

Bern called: "Is Jean Harlow Dead? . . ."   p. 74

sell her contract to M-G-M for $30,000: Caddo Company to   p. 74
Metro-Goldwyn-Mayer, assignment of contract, March 19,
1932; letter from the Caddo Company to Metro-Goldwyn-
Mayer, March 25, 1932.

"cooed and screwed": *Time*, August 5, 1991.   p. 74

Dear Mr. Thalberg: Letter from Lamar Trotti to Irving   pp. 74–75
Thalberg, April 27, 1932.

Offers to Clara Bow and Colleen Moore: "Clara said she   p. 75
could have returned in . . . *Red-Headed Woman*, which was
offered to her, 'But I didn't want to play a tart in my first
picture.' " (New York *Daily News*, November 30, 1932). Also,
Colleen Moore to Joe Yranski.

Nancy Carroll: Nancy Carroll to Douglas Whitney.   p. 75

second leads and starlets: Wynne Gibson screen-tested on   p. 75
December 8, 1931; Harriet [sic] Lake on December 21, 1931;
Dixie Lee on December 5, 1931; Margaret Perry on January
29, 1932; and Lillian Roth and Alice White on November 25,
1931.

GETTING TERRIBLY DESPERATE: Wire from Irving Thalberg to   p. 75
J. Robert Rubin [c. January 1932].

March 19: Wire from Ben Piazza to Irving Thalberg, March   p. 75
14, 1932.

"Well, you know": Bob Thomas, *Thalberg: Life and Legend*,   p. 76
Doubleday, 1969.

Harlow . . . disliked *Red-Headed Woman*: "The Baby didn't   p. 76
want to make that picture," Mother Jean remembered. "She
felt unhappy about it because she felt it to be another
unfavorable role . . ." ("Is Jean Harlow Dead? . . .")

JEAN'S SPEECHES: Telegram from Marino Bello to Irving   p. 76
Thalberg, March 30, 1932.

a test of Dorothy Mackaill: Telegram from Irving Thalberg to   p. 76
Charles J. Rubin, April 8, 1932.

REFERRING TO *RED-HEADED WOMAN*: Telegram from Marino   p. 76
Bello to Irving Thalberg, April 11, 1932.

"The public makes the stars": Thomas Schatz, *The Genius of*   p. 76
the System.

a seven-year contract: Metro-Goldwyn-Mayer and Jean   p. 76
Harlow agreement, April 12, 1932.

"I never quite believe": "Is Jean Harlow Dead? . . ."   p. 77

Chapter Nine

Jean Harlow . . . April 20, 1932: M-G-M payroll records.   p. 78

fifty-three-acre, etc.: Peter Hay, *M-G-M: When the Lion*   p. 78
Roars; "Metro-Goldwyn-Mayer," *Fortune*, December 1932.

"He refused": The Facts About My Romance and Marriage,   p. 78
by Jean Harlow," *New Movie Magazine*, December 1933.

"You can't understand": Ibid.   p. 78

"Scott tried to turn": Anita Loos, *Kiss Hollywood Good-by*.   p. 79

"make fun of its sex element": Ibid.   p. 79

"She looked about sixteen": Ibid.   p. 79

"Underlying Jean's raffish sense": Ibid.   p. 79

"We made it over": Anita Loos Oral History, Columbia   p. 80
University.

"She really didn't want to make": Virginia Conway to DS.   p. 80

"The problem": "The Facts About My Romance and   p. 80
Marriage, by Jean Harlow."

"It's the first chance": "Girl Tells Strange Hate for Jean   p. 80
Harlow," Los Angeles *Record*, May 11, 1932.

"Everybody loved her": Bill Edmondson to DS.   p. 80

Blanche Williams would serve: Ibid.; Barbara Brown to DS.   p. 80

"She had the most": Bill Edmondson to DS.   pp. 80–81

allergic reaction: "Jean broke out in a rash from makeup
after every picture. You could depend on it." (Statement by
Dr. Harold Barnard, August 1964, AMPAS.) Also, Kansas
City *Times*, June 9, 1937.   p. 81

Genevieve Smith: Jacqueline Smith (daughter) to DS;   p. 81
Leatrice Gilbert to DS; Barbara Brown to DS.

Dr. Harold Barnard: William Barnard (son) to DS.   p. 81

"Nudity was rarely seen": Loos, *Kiss Hollywood Good-by*.   p. 81

"I'm sorry": Ibid.   p. 81

"was rather like a boy": Anita Loos Oral History, Columbia   p. 81
University.

"a knockout": Barbara Brown to DS.   p. 82

Thalberg asked Loos: Loos, *Kiss Hollywood Good-by*.   p. 82

"For the first time": "Redhead's Life Exciting Whirl," Los   p. 83
Angeles *Examiner*, June 26, 1932.

premiere of *Grand Hotel*: April 29, 1932 (see Filmography, p. 83
Radio Appearances).

"Would you mind terribly": Irene Mayer Selznick to DS.   p. 83

"partly responsible": Ibid.; Irene Mayer Selznick, *A Private* p. 84
View.

"began playing very active 'footsie' ": Douglas Fairbanks, Jr., p. 84
The Salad Days.

"Paul was adamant": Selznick, *A Private View*.   p. 84

"Congratulations, Paul!": *Motion Picture*, September 1932. p. 85

"palace eunuch": Thomas Schatz, *The Genius of the System*. p. 85

"nothing more than a booby trap": Loos, *Kiss Hollywood*   p. 85
Good-by.

"a middle-aged mama's boy": Bill Edmondson to DS.   p. 85

"Everybody wondered": Ibid.   p. 85

"She worried about it": Marcella Rabwin to DS.   p. 86

BABY MINE: Signed photograph of Jean Bello, July 1, 1932.   p. 86
(Brian Bundy Collection.)

"She was pawed": Howard Hawks to Kevin Brownlow.   p. 86

"He explains things": Samuel Marx, *Mayer and Thalberg:*   p. 86
The Make-Believe Saints, Random House, 1975.

Virginia Conway insists: Virginia Conway to DS.   p. 86

"Bern was a pansy": Johnny Rosselli to Robert Slatzer.   p. 87

"Have you laid him?": Ibid.   p. 87

"No, I haven't": Ibid.   p. 87

"a neurotic, pretentious little man": Adela Rogers St. Johns   p. 87
Oral History, Columbia University.

Elaine St. Johns confirms: Elaine St. Johns to DS.   p. 87

"had no right to marry *any* woman": Adela Rogers St. Johns,   p. 87
Love, Laughter and Tears.

"Then it's true": Ibid.   p. 87

"Jean Harlow, hitherto": *Variety*, July 5, 1932.   p. 88

"This shapely beauty": New York *Daily Mirror*, July 1, 1932.   p. 88

"the sexiest performance": *Red-Headed Woman* preface by   p. 88
Leonard Maltin, M-G-M/UA Home Video.

King George kept a print: Loos, *Kiss Hollywood Good-by*.   p. 88

$761,000 . . . $401,000: Metro-Goldwyn-Mayer profit/loss   p. 88
ledger, Howard Strickling Collection, AMPAS.

"Dearest Pal": Letter from Jean Harlow to Lenore Heidorn   p. 88
[July 2, 1932]; Lenore Heidorn to DS.

8:30 P.M.: Paul Bern/Harlean Carpenter McGrew marriage   p. 88
certificate, July 2, 1932.

"admittedly with mixed feelings": Selznick, *A Private View*.   p. 88

toasting the couple: Barbara Brown to DS.   p. 89

9820 Easton Drive: Deed of Trust, September 7, 1929; Deed   p. 89
of Trust, August 27, 1930; "Jean Harlow, Paul Bern to
Remain Here," Hollywood *Citizen News*, July 2, 1932.

Chapter Ten

Paul Levy . . . immigrated to America: The Levy family   p. 90
arrived at Ellis Island on December 11, 1898, aboard the
Pennsylvania. (U.S. Immigration and Naturalization records,
August 24, 1910.)

East 114th Street: In the 1900 U.S. Census, Paul Levy lived   p. 90
at 56 East 114th Street.

"A brother and sister": Edward L. Bernays to DS.   p. 90

his father's death: Julius Levy death certificate, October 10,   p. 90
1908.

American Academy of Dramatic Arts: According to Paul   p. 91
Levy's audition report on September 13, 1909, the aspiring
actor recited Shylock's speech from *The Merchant of Venice*
with a German accent. By the time of his graduation in May
1911, he had lost his accent and become "Edward Paul
Bern." (AADA records.)

"Bernays" to "Bern": Edward L. Bernays to DS; Betsy Bern   p. 91
(niece) to DS.

acted on Broadway: Paul Bern played "Joe Cook" in a   p. 91
production of *Too Many Cooks*. (Theater program, March 30,
1914.)

Toronto film studio: Conness-Till Film Company. Bern   p. 91
worked there in 1914. (Toronto directory, 1914.)

managed a Manhattan theater: Yorkville Theatre. Bern   p. 91
worked there in 1915–16. (New York directory, 1915–16.)

family tragedy: Henrietta Levy death certificate, September   p. 91
15, 1920.

"accidental": Medical Examiner's report, September 15,   p. 91
1920.

"alienists": "Dr. S. P. Goodhart, a New York alienist and   p. 91
specialist in mental diseases, and I were recently discussing
. . . dreams," Bern told reporters in 1920. (New York *Times*,
November 21, 1920.)

"I heard Bern": Frances Marion, *Off with Their Heads!*   p. 91

"sadistic or masochistic": Ibid.   p. 91

"a German psycho": Anita Loos, *Kiss Hollywood Good-by.*   p. 92

"morbid, pessimistic side": Adela Rogers St. Johns, "The   p. 92
Private Life of Jean Harlow," *Liberty*, December 30, 1933.

"Mother said": Leatrice Gilbert to DS.   p. 92

"his courtly manner": Jim Tully, *A Dozen and One*, Murray   p. 92
and Gee, 1943.

"a student of the psychology": Marion, *Off with Their Heads!*   p. 92

"no right to marry *any* woman": Adela Rogers St. Johns,   p. 92
Love, Laughter and Tears.

"graphic, technical, and explicit": Ibid.   p. 93

"was the size of my pinkie": Leatrice Gilbert to DS.   p. 93

"The Baby's still a virgin": Blanche Williams to Barry   p. 93
Norman.

"Sex is not the most important": Sheilah Graham, "Jean   p. 93
Harlow Friends Unify in Crusade to Cleanse 'Sex Goddess'
from Stain," Hollywood *Citizen News*, January [day
unknown], 1965.

"There was no distress": Ibid.   p. 93

"As far as I could tell": Barbara Brown to DS.   p. 93

"if she was anything other": Colleen Moore, *Silent Star*.   p. 93

"Oh, Anita": Anita Page to DS.   p. 93

"everyone wondering why": Maureen O'Sullivan to DS.   p. 94

"genuine affection": Betsy Bern to DS.   p. 94

"a lovely person": Ibid.   p. 94

"Harlow was supposed to help": Pat McGilligan, *Backstory:*   p. 94
Interviews with Screenwriters of Hollywood's Golden Age.

"a seething pit of lust": *Red Dust* synopsis, May 15, 1930.   p. 94

"I saw Clark Gable": McGilligan, *Backstory*; Lyn Tornabene,   p. 94
Long Live the King: A Biography of Clark Gable.

"The prints showed": Clarence Sinclair Bull with Raymond   p. 95
Lee, *The Faces of Hollywood*.

"All I want": Moore, *Silent Star*.   p. 95

"A German stickler": Ibid.   p. 95

"His abuse was verbal": Elaine St. Johns to DS.   p. 96

"that she could least stand": Ibid.   p. 96

"a great issue": Loos, *Kiss Hollywood Good-by*.   p. 96

Dr. Herman Sugarman: Etta Sugarman (daughter) to DS;   p. 97
letter from Arthur Landau to Irving Shulman, April 11, 1962.

Dr. Edward B. Jones: J. Lorenz Jones (son) to DS; Philip C.   p. 97
Jones (son) to DS; Barbara E. Jones (daughter) to DS;
Creditor's Claim of Dr. Edward Brant Jones, November 14,
1932, *Estate of Paul Bern*, Los Angeles County Superior
Court.

August 4, 1932: Irene Mayer Selznick to DS.   p. 97

August 17: Letter from Paul Bern to Noel Sullivan, August   p. 97
22, 1932. "My wife went up [to San Francisco] on what we
hoped would be a three or four day vacation for her, but very
sudden changes at the studio compelled her to come back on
the same day that she arrived."

Mary Astor envied: Mary Astor, *A Life on Film*.   p. 97

"It was a difficult picture": Gene Raymond Oral History by   p. 97
Ronald L. Davis, Southern Methodist University (SMU).

"rising in waves": Astor, *A Life on Film*.   p. 98

Prop man Harry Edwards: Harry Edwards to DS.   p. 98

"Garbo and Shearer": Ibid.   p. 98

"If they don't get a break": Gil Perkins (M-G-M stunt man)   p. 98
to DS.

"Something for the boys": Bill Edmondson to DS.   p. 98

"Clark was *nuts*": Ibid.   p. 99

"She isn't full of shit": Ida Lupino to DS.   p. 99

"I've never seen two actors": Tornabene, *Long Live the King*.   p. 99

"will never get past": Sidney Skolsky, New York *Daily News*,   p. 99
August 30, 1932.

"shock": Ibid., September 8, 1932.   p. 99

"My first impression": Estelle Skolsky to DS.   p. 99

"Oh, that's a new gun": Sidney Skolsky, *Don't Get Me Wrong—I Love Hollywood*. p. 99

"too effeminate," "weird comment": Ibid. p. 99

Dr. Harry Brandel . . . $85,000: "Bern Policy Uncovered," Los Angeles *Times*, September 11, 1932. According to Dr. Brandel, Bern passed his examination "without trouble." p. 100

"Stoically he goes back": *China Seas* story by Paul Bern, September 2, 1932. Special Collections, USC. p. 100

"I won't go without my darling wife": Los Angeles County Coroner's Inquest transcript, September 8, 1932; "Police Quiz Actress," Los Angeles *Times*, September 7, 1932. p. 100

"We talked about the theater": Barbara Barondess to DS. p. 100

Discourse on the Worship of Priapus . . . The Glands Regulating Personality . . . The Biological Tragedy of Woman: Dora Ingram Book Shop invoice, November 15, 1932, *Estate of Paul Bern*. p. 101

"a big fight": Los Angeles County Grand Jury transcript, February 28, 1933. p. 101

"He wants me out": Blanche Williams to Herb Read. p. 101

Part Three: Who Killed Paul Bern?

photograph: Los Angeles Police Department file (Frank Hutchins Collection). Bern's corpse has been turned to the camera. p. 103

Chapter Eleven

Tetrick . . . Gable . . . Bello: Ted Tetrick to DS. p. 105

"It was quite pitiful": Los Angeles County Coroner's Inquest transcript, September 8, 1932. p. 105

"You know": Ibid.   p. 105

"Irving? My God!": Irene Mayer Selznick to DS; Irene Mayer   p. 106
Selznick, *A Private View*.

"It's Paul, he's killed himself": Selznick, *A Private View*.   p. 106

"Nobody was around": Virgil Apger to DS.   p. 106

morocco-bound guest book: "Death Message Finale in Gay   p. 107
Guest Book," Los Angeles *Herald*, September 6, 1932. That
same day another news report referred to it as an "ornate
private diary" ("Bern Death Mystifies," Los Angeles *Times*,
September 6, 1932), as did the coroner (Los Angeles County
Coroner's Register, September 8, 1932).

"I told him": Coroner's Inquest transcript.   p. 108

"He wasn't upset": Ted Tetrick to DS.   p. 109

"Isn't this too horrible": "Bern Death Mystifies," Los   p. 109
Angeles *Times*, September 6, 1932.

"under almost unbearable tension": "Brother Says Paul   p. 110
Lived Under Tension," Los Angeles *Herald*, September 7,
1932.

"I read the 'dearest dear' note": "Brother of Bern Flying to   p. 110
This City," Los Angeles *Times*, September 7, 1932.

"blissful": Coroner's Inquest transcript.   p. 110

"big limousine": Los Angeles County Grand Jury transcript,   p. 110
February 28, 1933.

"I saw a woman": Ibid.   p. 110

"a powerful car": "Police Quiz Actress," Los Angeles *Times*,   p. 110
September 7, 1932.

"You're talking too much": Grand Jury transcript.   p. 110

"vigorously denies": Los Angeles *Times*, September 7, 1932.   p. 110

"I have more money": Ibid.   p. 110

"ideally married": Ibid.   p. 110

"delirious": Ibid.   p. 111

"If Jean Harlow doesn't make Paul Bern happy": *Motion*   p. 111
Picture, September 1932.

"the press pilloried Jean": Selznick, *A Private View*.   p. 111

indict Harlow for murder: Samuel Marx, *Mayer and*   p. 111
Thalberg: The Make-Believe Saints, Random House, 1975.

"I can't understand": Los Angeles *Times*, September 7, 1932.   p. 111

"a terrific mental depression": "Doctor Terms Act   p. 112
'Personal,' " Los Angeles *Examiner*, September 8, 1932.

"domestic relations": Coroner's Inquest transcript.   p. 112

"My father told me": Irene Mayer Selznick to DS.   p. 112

"attempt to follow her husband": "Bern's Kin Arrives," Los   p. 112
Angeles *Times*, September 8, 1932.

"I had never seen him": "Police Quiz Actress," Los Angeles   p. 112
Times, September 7, 1932.

"acute melancholia": Los Angeles *Examiner*, September   p. 112
8, 1932; "Bern Last Will Gone from Box," Los Angeles
Times, September 14, 1932.

"a physical condition": "Nearest Kin, Widow Alone for Two   p. 112
Hours Discussing Motive for Paul's Suicide," Los Angeles
Examiner, September 8, 1932.

"unfit for matrimony": "Jean Harlow, Tired of Being a   p. 113
Vamp, Settles Down in a Cozy Apartment with a New
Husband," Kansas City *Star*, November 19, 1933.

"underdeveloped": Coroner's Inquest transcript.   p. 113

hermaphrodite: Harry Edwards to DS.   p. 113

Red Dust resumes: M-G-M files.   p. 113

"oily and patronizing": Tallulah Bankhead, *Tallulah*.   p. 113

"I want no secrecy": "Bern's Kin Arrives," Los Angeles   p. 113
Times, September 8, 1932.

"morally married": "Mystery Red-Haired Woman in Bern's   p. 113
Past," Los Angeles *Examiner*, September 8, 1932.

"She is alive": Ibid.   p. 113

"Certain complications": "New Complications Add to Bern   p. 114
Death Mystery," Los Angeles *Times*, September 9, 1932.

"Miss D. Millette": "Body of 'Other Wife' Sought Vainly in   p. 114
New Mystery as Paul Bern's Last Rites Held," Los Angeles
Examiner, September 10, 1932.

"Miss Jean Harlow [*sic*]": Coroner's Inquest transcript. All   p. 114
cited testimony is taken from here.

a letter from: Dr. Robert Kennicott only treated Harlow on   p. 114
this occasion.

"secret date": Los Angeles *Examiner*, September 10, 1932.   p. 116

"I needed this notoriety": Barbara Barondess to DS; Barbara   p. 116
Barondess MacLean, *One Life Is Not Enough*.

Desperate to disassociate herself: Sidney Skolsky, *Don't Get*   p. 116
Me Wrong—I Love Hollywood, does not mention Barondess
by name, but she confirms his account. (Barbara Barondess
to DS.)

$300 for an abortion: The father, wrote Barondess, was   p. 117
Broadway producer-director Jed Harris (1900–1979).
(MacLean, *One Life Is Not Enough*.)

"Howard Strickling was *amazed*": Barbara Barondess to DS.   p. 117

"mystery woman": "Bern Riddle Increases," Los Angeles   p. 117
Times, September 10, 1932.

"Mrs. Paul Bern": "New Complications Add to Bern Death   p. 117
Mystery," Los Angeles *Times*, September 9, 1932.

"phantom mate": "Body of 'Other Wife' Sought Vainly in   p. 117
New Mystery as Paul Bern's Last Rites Held," Los Angeles
Examiner, September 10, 1932.

"morally married": " 'Other Wife' of Paul Bern in S.F.   p. 117
When He Ended Life; Left Hotel Day After News," Los
Angeles *Examiner*, September 9, 1932.

"tragic affair": Ibid.   p. 117

March 15, 1884: Lowell Mellett/Dorothy Roddy marriage   p. 117
certificate, June 22, 1907.

Lowell Mellett: Ibid.   p. 117

"Registering as "Mrs. L. Mellett": American Academy of   p. 117
Dramatic Arts audition report, May 8, 1911. Millette did not
finish her first year.

Toronto . . . Woonsocket . . . Wilmington . . . Manhattan: p. 118
Estate of Dorothy Millette v. Jean Harlow, Los Angeles
County Superior Court, January 25, 1934.

"continual abandonment": *Lowell Mellett v. Dorothy Roddy*   p. 118
Mellett, King County [Washington] Superior Court, August
18, 1913.

"my wife": Irene Mayer Selznick to DS.   p. 118

"Our mother told Paul" . . . Friederike Bern Marcus: "Body   p. 118
of 'Other Wife' Sought Vainly in New Mystery as Paul Bern's
Last Rites Held," Los Angeles *Examiner*, September 10,
1932.

Henrietta Levy jumped: Henrietta Levy death certificate and   p. 118
Medical Examiner's report, September 15, 1920.

"a religious complex": "Bern Riddle Increases," Los Angeles   p. 118
Times, September 10, 1932.

"mental hygiene clinic": John Shillady, "Survey of Social   p. 118
Agencies and Programs of Greenwich, Connecticut,"
February 1933.

"Mrs. Paul Bern": Los Angeles *Examiner*, September 10,   p. 118
1932.

"husband": "The Headline Career of Jean Harlow," *Motion*   p. 119
Picture, December 1932.

"Paul talked about her": Irene Mayer Selznick to DS.   p. 119

"came away sick": "Bern Riddle Increases," Los Angeles   p. 119
Times, September 10, 1932.

"Miss D. Millette," etc.: " 'Other Wife' of Paul Bern in S.F.   p. 119
When He Ended Life; Left Hotel Day After News," Los
Angeles *Examiner*, September 9, 1932.

"other woman": " 'Other Woman' Letters from Bern   p. 119
Discovered," Los Angeles *Times*, September 12, 1932.

BERN RIDDLE INCREASES: Los Angeles *Times*, September 10,   p. 119
1932.

"the huge question mark": Ibid.   p. 119

"I wanted to tell her": Ibid.   p. 120

"I'm afraid poor Dorothy": "Body of 'Other Wife' Sought   p. 120
Vainly in New Mystery as Paul Bern's Last Rites Held," Los
Angeles *Examiner*, September 10, 1932.

"hoax suicide": " 'Other Woman' Letters from Bern   p. 120
Discovered," Los Angeles *Times*, September 12, 1932.

"The place was *swarming*": Dean Dorn to DS.   p. 120

"wan and haggard": "Bern Last Will Gone from Box," Los   p. 120
Angeles *Times*, September 14, 1932.

"leans heavily": "Rites Marked by Simplicity," Los Angeles   p. 120
Times, September 10, 1932.

"In shock": "Bern Riddle Increases," Los Angeles *Times*,   p. 120
September 10, 1932.

"simple and unpretentious": "Rites Marked by Simplicity,"   p. 121
Los Angeles *Times*, September 10, 1932.

"self-destruction": Ibid.   p. 121

"crying openly": Ibid.   p. 121

"When I left the chapel": "Hollywood Magic Revealed   p. 121
Again," New York *Times*, June 13, 1937.

"They asked other people": Harry Edwards to DS.   p. 121

"motive undetermined": Los Angeles County Coroner's   p. 121
Register, September 8, 1932.

suicide: Paul Bern death certificate, September 5, 1932.   p. 121

"Why did he do it?": "Bern Riddle Increases," Los Angeles   p. 121
Times, September 10, 1932.

"a secret meeting": "Jean Harlow Resumes Work to Forget   p. 122
Grief," Los Angeles *Times*, September 13, 1932.

"We knew nothing": Los Angeles *Herald*, September 7,   p. 122
1932.

"suicide hoax": " 'Other Woman' Letters from Bern   p. 122
Discovered," Los Angeles *Times*, September 12, 1932.

"If," etc.: "Is Jean Harlow Dead? Her Mother Says No!"   p. 122
Modern Romances, March and April 1938.

"Staying around here": "Jean Harlow Resumes Work to   p. 122
Forget Grief," Los Angeles *Times*, September 13, 1932.

"She was truly a heroine": Irene Mayer Selznick to DS;   p. 123
Selznick, *A Private View*.

"Jean is going on": *Photoplay*, November 1932.   p. 123

"The day she came back": Bill Edmondson to DS.   p. 123

"which wasn't his style": Ibid.   p. 123

"How": Mary Astor, *A Life on Film.*   p. 123

"There was a lot of deference": Bill Edmondson to DS.   p. 123

"I don't have to say that": John Lee Mahin to Barry Norman.   p. 124

"terribly decomposed": Sacramento County Coroner's   p. 124
Inquest transcript, September 21, 1932.

she had jumped: Dorothy Millette death certificate,   p. 124
September 7, 1932.

"asphyxiation by drowning": Sacramento County Coroner's   p. 124
record, September 14, 1932.

"suicide": Sacramento County Coroner's Inquest transcript.   p. 124

Millette's funeral: "$35 Funeral Seen for Bern Shadow   p. 124
Wife," San Francisco *Chronicle*, September 16, 1932.

Lowell Mellett: Washington *Daily News*, September 3, 1932.   p. 124

"a decent burial": "Harlow Saves Suicide from Potter's   p. 124
Field," San Francisco *Chronicle*, September 18, 1932.

A granite gravestone: "Dorothy Millette Bern" is buried in   p. 124
East Lawn Memorial Park, Sacramento.

Millette's two sisters: Mary Roddy Hartranft (1893–1933)   p. 124
and Violet Roddy Hessler (1889–1937).

sue Harlow for half: *Estate of Millette v. Harlow; Estate of*   p. 124
Dorothy Millette, Sacramento County Superior Court; "Jean
Harlow Sued for Half Bern's Estate," San Francisco
Chronicle, January 27, 1934.

Bern's estate: Last Will and Testament of Paul Bern, July 29,   p. 124
1932; *Estate of Paul Bern.*

"suicide clause": "Bern Policy Uncovered," Los Angeles   p. 125
Times, September 11, 1932.

Zwillman liked to take credit: Johnny Rosselli to Robert   p. 125
Slatzer.

Henry Bern blamed: Betsy Bern to DS.   p. 125

five months later: Los Angeles County Grand Jury transcript,   p. 125
February 28, 1933.

"Get out of my life!": Ibid.   p. 125

"This is the woman": Ibid.   p. 125

"scored with women": Henry Hathaway to Scott Eyman;   p. 126
Henry Hathaway Oral History by Ronald L. Davis, SMU;
Skip Hathaway (widow) to DS.

Paul had lived with a woman: Hathaway to Eyman; Henry   p. 126
Hathaway Oral History.

Bern's *other, unused* gun: A .38 Colt, serial #40739. The   p. 127
death weapon was also a .38 Colt, serial #572972. (Los
Angeles County Coroner's Inquest transcript; Los Angeles
County Coroner's Register, September 8, 1932.

"a suicide does not": Hedda Hopper, *From Under My Hat*,   p. 127
Doubleday, 1952.

"mistress" . . . Irene Harrison: Irving Shulman to DS; Kansas   p. 127
City *Star*, November 19, 1933, which exposes Bern's "secret
life with another woman" but does not divulge her name.

"I don't know anything," etc.: Irene Harrison to DS.   p. 128

"too gentle, too effeminate": Skolsky, *Don't Get Me Wrong—*   p. 128
I Love Hollywood.

"addressed to one of Bern's superiors": Ibid.   p. 128

"Bern was a homosexual": Ted Tetrick to DS.   p. 128

"attempted something along the homosexual line": Dr.   p. 129
Harold Barnard statement, AMPAS.

Charles Chaplin's teenage wife . . . fellatio: *Lita Grey Chaplin*   p. 129
v. Charles Chaplin, et al., Los Angeles County Superior
Court, November 10, 1927.

"There's something of Bern": Joseph L. Mankiewicz to DS.   p. 129

New York recognized common-law marriage: This statute   p. 130
was abolished in 1933.

"the very apotheosis of masochism": Anita Loos, *Kiss*   p. 130
Hollywood Good-by.

"She was in the house": Elaine St. Johns to DS.   p. 130

"the performance of her life": Johnny Rosselli to Robert   p. 131
Slatzer.

Sada's Flowers: Creditor's Claim of Sada's Flowers,   p. 131
November 15, 1932, *Estate of Paul Bern*.

I'd have liked to have gone to bed: Gary Herman, *The*   p. 131
Hollywood Book of Quotes, Omnibus Press, 1979.

"Hollywood is extremely proud of Jean Harlow": "What Has   p. 131
Happened to Jean Harlow?" *Hollywood Magazine*, March
1933.

"The best lines go to Harlow": *Time*, October 17, 1932.   p. 132

Comparison to a legendary stage star: Like Harlow in *Red*   p. 132
Dust, Jeanne Eagels (1894–1929) played a tropical prostitute
in *Rain*.

"clean up" in Kansas City: *Variety*, November 8, 1932.   p. 132

"get the dough" in Seattle: Ibid.   p. 132

"top the town" in New Haven: Ibid.   p. 132

"wow biz" in Detroit: *Variety*, November 1, 1932.   p. 132

"a winner" in Portland: Ibid.   p. 132

"a smash" in San Francisco: *Variety*, October 25, 1932.   p. 132

"the current box-office champ" in Cincinnati: *Variety*,   p. 132
November 1, 1932.

"b.o. dynamite" in Minneapolis: *Variety*, November 8, 1932.   p. 132

"*Red Dust* is gold dust": Ibid.   p. 132

"Harlow's draw is stronger": *Variety*, November 1, 1932.   p. 132

"platinum blondes on all sides": New York *Times*, November   p. 132
5, 1932.

$1.2 million . . . $408,000: M-G-M profit/loss ledger.   p. 132

season's number-one draw: Los Angeles *Herald*, December   p. 132
27, 1932.

"You don't have to": Irene Mayer Selznick to DS; Selznick, *A*   p. 133
Private View.

"a girl lying on the ground": Willard Sheldon to DS.   p. 134

"I just don't like the taste": Virginia Conway to DS.   p. 134

"After Paul's death": Jacqueline Smith to DS.   p. 134

"She *loved* craps": Barbara Brown to DS.   p. 134

I've got to have a drink: Jean Harlow, *Today Is Tonight*.   p. 134

Part Four: Bombshell

Chapter Twelve

"were waving like spaghetti": Ronald Haver, *David O.*   p. 140
Selznick's Hollywood.

"I was walking": "Jean Harlow Answers Your Questions,"   p. 140
Motion Picture, July 1933.

"she taught my wife": Richard Rodgers Oral History,   p. 140
Columbia University.

"Jean Harlow can't sing," etc.: *Hollywood Reporter*, July 5,   p. 140
1933.

"Blue Moon": At first "A Prayer" became "The Bad in Every   p. 140
Man," which Shirley Ross sang in *Manhattan Melodrama*
(1934). The following year it was recorded as "Blue Moon."

Anita Loos to write: Loos received sole story credit on *Hold*   p. 140
Your Man but shared screenplay credit with Howard Emmett
Rogers (see Filmography).

Black Orange Blossoms: M-G-M script files.   pp. 140–41

"They have me singing": "World's Fair Tires Jean," Kansas   p. 141
City *Star*, June 21, 1933.

"The popularity of the Harlow-Gable combination": New   p. 141
York *Times*, July 1, 1933. In *Red Dust*, Harlow had been
billed below Gable; in *Hold Your Man*, her name appeared
above his.

"the most promising money picture": *Variety*, July 4, 1933.   p. 141

$266,000 . . . $1.1 million: M-G-M profit/loss ledger.   p. 142

five Harlow films: Telegram from J. Robert Rubin to Louis B.   p. 142
Mayer, June 14, 1933.

"On the verge of ruin": Rudy Behlmer (editor), *Memo from*   p. 142
David O. Selznick.

"Joan was quite jealous": Dorothy Manners to DS.   p. 142

"one of Metro's real biggies": Roy Newquist, *Conversations*   p. 142
with Joan Crawford.

"controlled detestation": Fairbanks, Douglas, Jr., *The Salad*   p. 142
Days.

"The Baby and I became friends": Dorothy Manners to DS.   p. 142

"Joan, I don't know": Haver, *David O. Selznick's Hollywood*;   p. 143
Allen Rivkin to DS; Lee Server, *Screenwriter*.

"Look, Mr. Selznick": Allen Rivkin to DS.   p. 143

"She was so insecure": Marcella Rabwin to DS.   p. 143

"It's ironic": Ibid.   p. 144

"a big bottle": Ibid.   p. 144

"severe inferiority complex": Ibid.   p. 144

"Cukor gave her a lot of aid": Joseph Newman to DS.   p. 144

"When I first saw her": Statement by George Cukor,   p. 144
AMPAS; George Cukor Oral History, Director's Guild of
America.

"They said it couldn't be done": Thelma Hope to DS.   p. 145

"wiglet": Edith Hubner to Kay Mulvey, 1964. With the   p. 145
exception of *Red-Headed Woman*, Harlow had not worn a
wig prior to *Dinner at Eight*.

Selznick hired . . . Donald Ogden Stewart: M-G-M script   p. 145
files.

"The Baby and Dressler": Chester Schaeffer to DS.   p. 146

"Being in the same cast with Marie": Kansas City *Star*, June   p. 146
21, 1933.

"my best performance": "Jean Harlow Answers Your   p. 146
Questions."

Harlow . . . cried: Arthur Landau notes, AMPAS.   p. 146

"Carpentier": M-G-M publicity biography, January 14,   p. 146
1933.

"devoting her spare time": "What Has Happened to Jean   p. 146
Harlow?" *Hollywood Magazine*, March 1933.

a whitewashed account: Adela Rogers St. Johns, "Jean   p. 146
Harlow Tells the Inside Story," *Liberty*, November 26, 1932.

"I must relate to you Lady Oxford's latest": Letter from   p. 147
Lewis Einstein to Oliver Wendell Holmes, October 4, 1934.

"Who did you hear say that?": *Time*, August 19, 1935.   p. 147

"My God": Ibid.   p. 147

Norma Shearer's schizophrenic sister: Athole Shearer.   p. 147

"There she was": Howard Hawks to Kevin Brownlow. The   p. 147
conversation is recorded here.

Hawks slept with Harlow: John Lee Mahin to William   p. 148
MacAdams; John Lee Mahin to Scott Eyman.

his twentieth opponent: Frankie Campbell, whom Baer   p. 148
fought in San Francisco on August 25, 1930. Due to
Campbell's death, the California Boxing Commission
suspended Baer for a year.

"He was a tremendous showman": Max Baer, Jr., to DS.   p. 148

"a sweeping, brutal, berserk attack": Paul Gallico,   p. 148
"Prizefighter to Gentleman-En-Route," *The New Yorker*,
June 9, 1934.

"While Germany persecuted the Jews": Max Baer, Jr., to DS.   p. 148

"Jewish Adonis": "Hollywood's a Knock-Out!" *Screen Book*,   p. 149
December 1933.

"He has a satyrlike quality": Gallico, "Prizefighter to   p. 149
Gentleman-En-Route."

"Dad was like a big kid": Max Baer, Jr., to DS.   p. 149

"not to keep 'em warm": Ibid.   p. 149

"breach-of-promise" suit: Gallico, "Prizefighter to   p. 149
Gentleman-En-Route."

"She threw things at him": Max Baer, Jr., to DS.   p. 149

"I didn't care then": Dorothy Dunbar Baer to DS.   p. 149

$3,000 a week: M-G-M payroll records, August 7, 1933; p. 149
letter from J. Robert Rubin to Louis B. Mayer, July 6, 1933.

"This is pie": "Hollywood's a Knock-Out!"   p. 149

"Hello Baby!": "Motion Picture Career Awaits Champion p. 149
Baer," Los Angeles *Examiner*, June 14, 1934.

"Are you free tonight": Max Baer, Jr., to DS.   p. 149

Chapter Thirteen

"*Bombshell* was an unproduced play": Pat McGilligan, p. 150
Backstory.

"I said, 'Let's turn this . . .' ": Ibid.   p. 150

August 1933: M-G-M Company Shooting Schedule. p. 153

"She has a natural sense": Morris Abrams to DS. p. 153

"She never ran lines": Barbara Brown to DS.   p. 156

"I felt sorry for the Baby": Morris Abrams to DS. p. 156

"He was a loudmouth": Willard Sheldon to DS.   p. 156

"He hung around the studio": Marcella Rabwin to DS. p. 156

Men of the North: Metro-Goldwyn-Mayer and Marinello [*sic*] p. 156
Bello contract, April 15, 1930. Bello played "Sergeant
Mooney," portrayed in the film's English version by Robert
Elliott.

"He would strut": Willard Sheldon to DS.   p. 156

"Bello": Barbara Brown to DS.   p. 157

"the Sicilian pimp": Jean Bello to Herb Read. In truth, Marino Bello came from Trieste, a city far from Sicily. — p. 157

"more than a stepfather": Phyllis Cerf to DS. — p. 157

urged Harlow to marry Max Baer: Adela Rogers St. Johns, *The Jean Harlow Story* treatment, September 28, 1956. — p. 157

"Boy, was *she* a character": Dean Dorn to DS. — p. 157

"like a wild woman": Jean Bello statement, AMPAS. — p. 157

"Now why waste all that effort": Ibid. — p. 157

"Please don't make me ashamed": Ibid. — p. 157

214 South Beverly Glen Boulevard: Grant Deed of P.P. and Ethel Dabney to Jean Bello, May 16, 1932; Grant Deed of Jean Bello to Harlean Bern, July 11, 1933. — p. 157

"Whitest House in the World": *Motion Picture*, June 1934. — p. 157

"She told me": Anita Page to DS. — p. 158

"Get a load of this!": Judith Wood to DS. — p. 158

"Acting honors go to Harlow": *Variety*, August 29, 1933. — p. 158

$2.1 million: M-G-M profit/loss ledger. — p. 158

"Too much brain work": "Hollywood's a Knock-Out!" *Screen Book*, December 1933. — p. 158

"Dad liked her": Max Baer, Jr., to DS. — p. 158

"boring," "ducking": Ibid. — p. 159

"She'd sit in her car": Ibid. — p. 159

"the best work of her career": Louella O. Parsons, Los Angeles *Examiner*, August 30, 1933. — p. 159

"Jean Harlow parked inside": Louella O. Parsons, Los Angeles *Examiner*, August 24, 1933. — p. 159

"Max may be in love": Louella O. Parsons, Los Angeles   p. 159
Examiner, June 13, 1937.

"She seemed harassed": Morris Abrams to DS.   p. 159

"I remember sitting at dinner": Leatrice Gilbert to DS.   p. 159

"My father wasn't busy": Irene Mayer Selznick to DS.   pp. 159–60

Yuma: Harold Rosson/Harlean Carpenter Bern marriage   p. 160
certificate, September 18, 1933.

"Who is it": "Jean Harlow, Tired of Being a Vamp, Settles   p. 160
Down in a Cozy Apartment with a New Husband," Kansas
City *Star*, November 19, 1933.

Chapter Fourteen

"Putt-Putt": Bill Edmondson to DS; Morris Abrams to DS;   p. 161
Harry Edwards to DS.

"came as a total surprise": "The Truth About Jean Harlow's   p. 161
Marriage," *Screen Book*, December 1933; "Film Star Weds
L.A. Cameraman in Yuma at Sunrise Ceremony," Los
Angeles *Herald*, September 18, 1933.

"Hal Rosson . . . Paul Bern": "Jean Harlow, Tired of Being a   p. 161
Vamp, Settles Down in a Cozy Apartment with a New
Husband," Kansas City *Star*, November 19, 1933.

"a tremendous sense of humor": Robert Terry to DS.   p. 162

"Hal *loved* women": Ibid.   p. 162

Nina Betts: Harold Rosson/Nina Betts Dunay marriage   p. 162
certificate, July 30, 1925; *Harold Rosson v. Nina Rosson*, Los
Angeles County Superior Court, August 3, 1927.

"Long Dong": Bill Edmondson to DS.   p. 162

"I used to see them on the set": Dean Dorn to DS.   p. 162

"To me, love has always meant friendship": "Jean Tells Her Story," Kansas City *Times*, September 19, 1933.   p. 162

"a studio wedding": Virgil Apger to DS.   p. 162

"She only married him": Jacqueline Smith to DS.   p. 162

"fell for the gag": Ted Tetrick to DS.   p. 162

"Poor Hal": Ted Allan to DS.   p. 163

"It doesn't seem real": Louella O. Parsons, "Jean Harlow's Life Story" (memorial magazine), 1937.   p. 163

"Our decision to elope": *Screen Book*, December 1933.   p. 163

"Isn't he a precious?": Kansas City *Star*, November 19, 1933.   p. 163

"I'm not a handsome guy": Ibid.   p. 163

"I know it's trite": *Screen Book*, December 1933.   p. 163

"As long as I have been covering": Parsons, "Jean Harlow's Life Story."   p. 163

"How could you?": Dorothy Manners to DS.   p. 163

She did not speak to Manners: "After Jean died, I picked up the phone and this voice said, 'Oh, Dorothy, I just feel so sad and blue about Jean.' It was Joan! She said, 'How I loved that girl . . .' " (Ibid.)   p. 164

the Bellos . . . seized title: Grant Deed from Harlean Bern Rosson to Jean Bello, September 25, 1933.   p. 164

"community property": Harlean Rosson and Harold Rosson agreement, October 10, 1933.   p. 164

"*They* go or *we* go": Raymond Sarlot and Fred E. Basten, *Life at the Marmont*, Roundtable Publishing, 1987.   p. 164

Chateau Marmont: Ibid.   p. 164

Dorothy Baer filed for divorce: "Will Divorce Max Baer,"   p. 164
New York *Times*, September 28, 1933; "Mrs. Max Baer Gets
Divorce," New York *Times*, October 15, 1933.

September 29, 1933: "Jean Harlow to Place Prints in   p. 164
Chinese Cement," Los Angeles *Times*, September 23, 1933;
"Jean Harlow to Appear at Chinese Again," Los Angeles
Herald, September 28, 1933.

"When we took *Bombshell* out": Margaret Booth to DS.   p. 164

"snappy"; "as rapid as": *Variety*, September 29, 1933.   p. 164

"She is Clara Bow": New York *Daily News*, October 21,   p. 165
1933.

"*Bombshell* provides the first": New York *Herald Tribune*,   p. 165
October 21, 1933.

"completely ruins [a] scene": New York *Herald Tribune*,   p. 165
April 24, 1931.

"There can be no doubt now": New York *Herald Tribune*,   p. 165
October 21, 1933.

her favorite movie: Eleanor Packer, "Jean Harlow Confesses: p. 165
'Why I Can't Marry Bill Powell,' " [magazine/date
unknown].

Pops, darling: Letter from Jean Bello to Arthur Landau,   p. 165
September 30, 1933.

Dr. Sidney Burnap: Good Samaritan Hospital records.   p. 167

Platinum Blonde star: Robert Williams death certificate,   p. 167
November 3, 1931; "Williams Dies in L.A. as Film Career
Builds," *Variety*, November 10, 1931.

BABY PROGRESSING RAPIDLY: Telegram from Marino Bello to   p. 167
Arthur Landau, October 17, 1933.

Dr. Burnap detected: Good Samaritan Hospital records;   p. 167
Estelle Skolsky to DS.

"The Baby is weak and confused": Sarlot and Basten, *Life at the Marmont.* p. 167

"What are you doing?": Dorothy Manners to DS. p. 167

$761,000 . . . $344,000: M-G-M profit/loss ledger. p. 168

"A 'Jeanne Harlow' picture": "Paris Goes to the Cinema," New York *Times*, March 3, 1935. p. 168

"*la blonde platinée*": *Le Petit Parisien*, June 8, 1937. p. 168

Harlow placed third: Dorothy Manners, "Is Jean Harlow Hollywood's Most Underpaid Star?" *Motion Picture*, May 1934. p. 168

"I don't want to keep on": Kansas City *Star*, November 19, 1933. p. 168

"I think I've established myself": Dorothy Manners to DS. pp. 168–69

"I never in my life": Ibid. p. 169

"had nothing to sell": M-G-M memo, November 9, 1933. p. 169

The Age of Larceny: M-G-M script files. p. 169

"told him emphatically": M-G-M memo, November 9, 1933. p. 169

she was put on suspension: M-G-M payroll records, November 13, 1933. p. 169

"unappreciative of M-G-M": "Harlow After a 100% Tilt to $2,500 a Week," *Variety*, October 17, 1933. p. 169

"walking out on the job": "An Open Letter to Jean Harlow," *Picturegoer*, February 17, 1934. p. 169

"the dog house has a ladies' entrance": "Who's in the Dog House Now?" *Photoplay*, February 1934. p. 169

"Is Jean Harlow Hollywood's Most Underpaid Star?": *Motion Picture*, May 1934. p. 169

"You can't fight with your friends": "Jean Battles a Sea of   p. 169
Rumors," *Photoplay*, April 1934.

"never a complainer or agitator": Dorothy Manners to DS.   p. 170

Eadie Was a Lady: M-G-M script files.   p. 170

"We were on the same wavelength": George Hurrell (text by   p. 170
Whitney Stine), *50 Years of Photographing Hollywood: The
Hurrell Style*.

"She would drop her dress": George Hurrell to DS; Ibid.   p. 170

Today Is Tonight: Harlow, *Today Is Tonight*.   p. 171

"She's a girl with lots of love": "Jean Harlow Joins Ranks of   p. 171
Writers," San Francisco *Chronicle*, September 7, 1934.

$22,500: Chattel Mortgage between Jean Bello and Marino   p. 171
Bello and Investors Syndicate Corporation, November 23,
1933.

Bello paid . . . Tony Beacon: Jean Harlow and Tony Beacon   p. 172
agreement, September 7, 1934.

"The first time we met": Tony Beacon to DS.   p. 172

"Cut the comedy!": Harlow, *Today Is Tonight*.   p. 172

"rendering any services to any person": Metro-Goldwyn-   p. 173
Mayer and Jean Harlow agreement, April 12, 1932.

Carey Wilson polished its prose: Tony Beacon to DS. *Today   p. 173
Is Tonight* was finally published in 1964 (see Bibliography).

a new seven-year contract: Metro-Goldwyn Mayer and Jean   p. 173
Harlow agreement, May 11, 1934.

matron of honor at the wedding: Carey Wilson and   p. 173
Carmelita Geraghty marriage certificate, May 6, 1934.

"Did you guys know": Joseph L. Mankiewicz to DS; Betty   p. 174
Halsey (maid of honor) to DS.

"pandemonium": Ibid.   p. 174

"Our marriage is finished": Louella O. Parsons, "Jean   p. 174
Harlow and Hal Rosson Part; Divorce Planned," Los
Angeles *Examiner*, May 7, 1934.

"incompatibility": *Harlean Rosson v. Harold Rosson*, Los   p. 174
Angeles County Superior Court, November 28, 1934.

"I don't want to make a 'heavy' of Hal": "Why Jean Harlow's   p. 174
Last Marriage Collapsed," *Movie Classic*, July 1934.

"a captive daughter": Robert Terry to DS.   p. 174

"marriages of inconvenience": Loos, op. cit.   p. 174

"What's lacking in me?": John Lee Mahin to Barry Norman.   p. 174

Chapter Fifteen

Kansas City: William Powell graduated from Central High   p. 175
School in 1911, just months after Harlean Carpenter's birth.

American Academy of Dramatic Arts: Powell attended for   p. 175
the first half of 1912. Paul Bern had graduated the previous
May.

"washed up": Rudy Behlmer (editor), *Memo from David O.*   p. 175
Selznick.

"against everyone's protest": Ibid.   p. 176

ten-film, $500,000 contract: M-G-M memo, May 15, 1937.   p. 176

"a real gentleman": Anita Loos, *Kiss Hollywood Good-by*.   p. 176

"an attractive, interesting, darling": Irene Mayer Selznick to   p. 176
DS.

"the most impeccably groomed man": George Hurrell, *50*   p. 176
Years of Photographing Hollywood.

"the same person in life": Diana Lewis Powell to DS. p. 176

"He *was* Nick Charles": Judith Wood to DS. p. 176

photographs . . . on the *Manhattan Melodrama* set: M-G-M p. 176
photographs with dated negatives prove that Harlow and
Powell had met by March 26, 1934, when pictures of them
were taken.

"never had any dates": Statement by William Powell [August p. 176
1964], AMPAS.

"She worked Bill Powell": Joseph L. Mankiewicz to DS. p. 177

"She was looking for a father": Marcella Rabwin to DS. p. 177

"Poppy": "Is Jean Harlow Dead? Her Mother Says No!" p. 177
Modern Romances, March and April 1938.

"I've found him": "Did Jean Harlow Have a Premonition?" p. 177
Hollywood Magazine, August 1937.

Born to Be Kissed . . . Eadie Was a Lady: M-G-M script files. p. 177

Rosson . . . was stricken: "Jean Harlow's Husband Hit by p. 177
Paralysis," Los Angeles *Examiner*, June 19, 1934; "Jean
Harlow in Daily Calls As Mate Ill," Los Angeles *Herald*,
June 19, 1934.

M-G-M sent him to London: Rosson departed on July 16, p. 177
1934.

"read in their bedchamber": *Rosson v. Rosson*. p. 177

"one of the most ill-advised": Dentner Davies, *Jean Harlow:* p. 177
Hollywood Comet, Constable House, 1937.

"immoral pictures": "Film Boycott," *Newsweek*, July 7, 1934. p. 177

"indecent and un-Christian films": Ibid. p. 178

condemned . . . *The Public Enemy*: Letter from Joseph Breen p. 178
to Jack Warner, August 24, 1936.

"a two-woman campaign of sex-ridicule": New York *Times*,   p. 178
June 13, 1937.

"When women go wrong": Mae West in *She Done Him*   p. 178
Wrong (1933).

"I'm the girl": Mae West in *Sextette* (1978).   p. 178

"temporary hysteria": "Hollywood Cleans House," New York   p. 178
Times, July 15, 1934.

"morals director" Joseph Breen: Ibid.   p. 178

"one of the most torrid efforts": Ibid.   p. 178

100% Pure: M-G-M script files.   p. 178

"Miss Harlow": New York *Times*, August 9, 1934.   p. 179

"There is nothing": *Variety*, August 7, 1934.   p. 179

"I'm going to *The Girl from Missouri!*": Wayne Martin, "I   p. 179
Remember Harlow," *Hollywood Studio Magazine*, June
1987.

$1.1 million . . . $511,000: M-G-M profit/loss ledger.   p. 179

"We're just good friends": "Jean Harlow Seen Much with   p. 179
William Powell," Los Angeles *Times*, August 1, 1934.

A Woman Called Cheap: M-G-M script files.   p. 179

"I certainly never would have planned": Behlmer, *Memo*   p. 180
from David O. Selznick.

who threatened to sue: Jon Bradshaw, *Dreams That Money*   p. 180
Can Buy: The Tragic Life of Libby Holman, William Morrow,
1985.

dubbed her voice . . . doubled her dancing: Virginia Verrill to   p. 180
DS; Betty Halsey to DS.

"She was on the set": Loie Tilton to DS.   p. 180

"C'mon!": Movita to DS. p. 180

"I remember sitting": Rosalind Russell and Chris Chase, *Life* p. 181
Is a Banquet.

"very warm": Statement by Rosalind Russell, [August 1964], p. 181
AMPAS.

"It was awful": Marcel Machu to DS. p. 181

"Metro-Goldwyn-Mayer has taken": New York *Times*, April p. 182
20, 1935.

"*Reckless* is a good title": *Variety*, April 24, 1935. p. 182

$125,000 loss: M-G-M profit/loss ledger. p. 183

"super-special": *Time*, August 19, 1935. M-G-M assigned p. 183
the term to its big-budget productions.

uncredited work of John Lee Mahin: "I worked on *China* p. 183
Seas. Thalberg said, 'You fellas look this over. And Jim
[credited co-screenwriter James Keven McGuinness], you
help John.' " (Pat McGilligan, *Backstory*.)

"last scene is a pat on Harlow's fanny": *Red Dust* script notes p. 183
by Hunt Stromberg, September 14, 1932.

"the most important day of the year": Jean Bello statement, p. 184
AMPAS.

Dearest of all mothers: Note from Jean Harlow to Jean Bello, p. 184
May 12, 1935.

"the people who are responsible," etc.: Finch & Rosenkrantz, p. 184
op. cit.

"Few people were as badly used": William Powell statement, p. 184
AMPAS.

Powell refused to even eat: Herb Read to DS. p. 184

"Jean Harlow was crazy": Marion Davies, *The Times We Had*. p. 185

DARLING: Telegram from Jean Harlow to Jean Bello, May 29,   p. 185
1935.

Wyntoon: "Harlow and Powell Kiss," Los Angeles *Times*,   p. 185
July 23, 1935.

"Will you please tell Miss Harlow": Davies, *The Times We*   p. 185
Had.

"Would you get in bed with me?": Aileen Pringle to DS.   p. 185

"I found her absolutely adorable": Maureen O'Sullivan to   p. 186
DS.

Harlow . . . called Mont Carpenter: Barbara Brown to DS.   p. 186

"first-rate, lively, funny": *Time*, August 19, 1935.   p. 186

"Bello had a confederate": William Powell statement,   p. 187
AMPAS.

$250,000 . . . $22,000: Letter from Jetty Chadsey to Joe   p. 187
Boylan [c. January 1936].

$22,500: Property Settlement: Jean Bello and Marino Bello   p. 188
agreement, September 10, 1935.

Mayer obtained a bank loan: Letter from Metro-Goldwyn-   p. 188
Mayer to Jean Harlow, November 26, 1934; letter from the
Bank of America to Louis B. Mayer, November 26, 1934.

Mother Jean appeared in divorce court: *Jean Bello v. Marino*   p. 188
Bello, Los Angeles County Superior Court, September 27,
1935.

"The man truly acted": "Mrs. Bello Severs Ties," Los   p. 188
Angeles *Times*, September 27, 1935.

"He said he operated some mines": Ibid.   p. 188

buying annuities: *Estate of Jean Harlow* (see Chapter   p. 188
Twenty).

"Last Will and Testament": Last Will and Testament of Harlean Rosson, September 5, 1935.

p. 188

$2.9 million: M-G-M profit/loss ledger.

p. 188

"in defiance of the Legion of Decency": *Time*, August 19, 1935.

p. 188

Part Five: Brownette

Chapter Sixteen

"She's Not What You Think!": *Film Pictorial*, December 1936.

p. 191

"They tried everything": George Hurrell to DS.

p. 191

"The first requisite": Ted Allan to DS; John Kobal, *The Art of the Great Hollywood Portrait Photographers*.

p. 191

"I've always hated my hair": "The Real Reason Why Jean Harlow Hated Her Hair," *Picturegoer*, October 3, 1936.

p. 192

"No woman": Dentner Davies, *Jean Harlow: Hollywood Comet*, Constable House, 1937.

p. 192

latest bender delayed *Riffraff*: "They said he was 'sick,' so when we finally started, I told him I was sorry to hear he'd been sick. 'Sick, hell,' he said. 'I was *drunk!*' " (Judith Wood to DS.)

p. 192

a consummate professional: "To be late on a set is one of the most inconsiderate and costly things that can be done," Harlow told columnist Jess Krueger. ("Jean Harlow Describes Routine in Making of Film," Chicago *American*, June 16, 1934.)

p. 192

"What's wrong, Baby?": Layne Britton to DS.

p. 192

"When I shot them together": George Hurrell, *50 Years of Photographing Hollywood*.

p. 193

"grand girl": Spencer Tracy diary entry, June 7, 1937.   p. 193
Used by permission of Susan Tracy.

"a square shooter": Gary Herman, *The Hollywood Book of*   p. 193
Quotes, Omnibus Press, 1979.

"Not even a brunette rinse": New York *Times*, January 13,   p. 193
1936.

"Maybe it's the 'brownette' hair": Louella O. Parsons,   p. 193
"New Jean Harlow Makes Screen Bow in Riff Raff [*sic*],"
Los Angeles *Examiner*, February 7, 1936.

"Harlow has the rare opportunity": *Variety*, January 15,   p. 193
1936.

$1.05 million: M-G-M profit/loss ledger.   p. 194

"to try a different approach": Oscar A. Rimoldi, "Clarence   p. 194
Brown," *Films in Review*, October 1990.

"My God": James Kotsilibas-Davis and Myrna Loy, *Myrna*   p. 194
Loy: Being and Becoming.

"pink ivory": Gloria Holden to DS.   p. 195

"She was just wonderful": James Stewart to DS.   p. 195

$2.1 million: M-G-M profit/loss ledger.   p. 195

"Unquestionably": *Hollywood Reporter*, February 14, 1936.   p. 195

"but it is Harlow who profits": *Variety*, March 4, 1936.   p. 195

Harlow collapsed: "Illness Hits Jean Harlow," Los Angeles   p. 195
Examiner, December 13, 1935.

"They don't make doctors": Richard Chapman to DS.   p. 195

"fatigue caused by overwork": Los Angeles *Examiner*,   p. 196
December 13, 1935.

"She'd call from the studio": Richard Chapman to DS.   p. 196

"I'm *home*-conscious": "The One Star Who Has No Enemies," *Screen Book*, July 1934.　　p. 196

"She always played such sluts": Jeanette MacDonald Oral History, Columbia University.　　p. 196

"Having to be a sex symbol": Rosalind Russell statement, AMPAS.　　p. 196

"She was *meant* to be a housewife": Virginia Conway to DS.　　p. 196

"From a child's perspective": Juanita Quigley to DS.　　p. 196

"I loved her immediately": Edith Fellows to DS.　　p. 196

"because they stuck together better": Kay Mulvey to Barry Norman; Lois Williams (widow of Dick Mulvey) to DS; Gretchen Vernon (sister of Dick Mulvey) to DS.　　p. 196

"She was absolutely *mad*": Virginia Conway to DS.　　p. 197

"Kids have an instinct": Edith Fellows to DS.　　p. 197

George Raft took Siegel: Louella O. Parsons, Los Angeles *Examiner*, August 16, 1933.　　p. 197

"very blonde, very pretty": Millicent Siegel to DS.　　p. 198

MILLICENT DEAREST: Millicent Siegel Collection. Used by permission.　　p. 198

"She was just the opposite": Millicent Siegel to DS.　　p. 198

March 14, 1936: *Rosson v. Rosson*.　　p. 198

"a foregone conclusion": *Hollywood Reporter*, September 1935.　　p. 198

"I will never marry": Eleanor Packer, "Jean Harlow Confesses: 'Why I Can't Marry Bill Powell,' " [magazine/date unknown].　　p. 198

"Poppy feels," etc.: Louella O. Parsons, Los Angeles   p. 199
Examiner, June 14, 1937.

"She was in love with him": Virginia Conway to DS.   p. 199

"like a little puppet": Dorothy Manners to DS.   p. 199

she sold Beverly Glen: Grant Deed from Harlean Rosson to   p. 199
Frances J. Levine, May 11, 1936. Levine was the wife of
Nat Levine (1900–89), then-president of Republic
Pictures.

$125,000: Arthur Levine (son of Frances J. Levine) to DS.   p. 199

512 North Palm Drive: House lease from Harriett A.   p. 199
Breese to Jean Harlow, May 19, 1936.

"I never felt Bill loved the Baby": Louella O. Parsons,   p. 199
"Jean Harlow's Life Story" (memorial magazine), 1937.

"Harlean called last night": Letter from Jetty Chadsey to   p. 200
Joe Boylan, [c. January 1936].

Mother Jean barred Aunt Jetty: Hortense Williams to DS.   p. 200

"a pain in my side": Ibid.   p. 200

"They got along wonderfully": Virgil Apger to DS.   p. 200

Grant disliked: Pat McGilligan, *Backstory*; Lenore Coffee,   p. 200
Storyline.

dubbed by Eadie Adams: Miles Kreuger, "Dubbers to the   p. 200
Stars," *High Fidelity*, July 1972.

"a cold": *Hollywood Reporter*, May 1, 1936.   p. 200

"Once I delivered a script": Richard Landau to DS.   p. 200

"Mother was very emotional": Richard Chapman to DS.   p. 201

"went to Harlow's mother": Ibid.   p. 201

Dr. Chapman married Marcella Arthur: Leland Chapman/   p. 201
Marcella Arthur marriage certificate, May 2, 1936.

Chapter Seventeen

Mother: Note from Jean Harlow to Jean Bello, [May 10,   p. 202
1936].

"The grip she had": James Kotsilibas-Davis and Myrna   p. 202
Loy, *Myrna Loy: Being and Becoming*.

changed her legal name: *Order Changing Name of Harlean*   p. 202
Carpenter Rosson, Los Angeles County Superior Court, July
1, 1936; "Jean Legalizing Harlow," *Hollywood Reporter*,
May 28, 1936.

"Mrs. Jean Carpenter": Good Samaritan Hospital records.   p. 203

"Mrs. Graves calling": Donald Roberson to Herb Read.   p. 203

"weepy and nostalgic": Ibid.   p. 203

"a *different* brand": Ruth Brand (sister-in-law) to DS.   p. 203

"I was shocked": Sybil Brand to DS.   p. 203

"with padded horns of dialogue": New York *Times*, July   p. 204
25, 1936.

extended run: "Suzy Extended," *Hollywood Reporter*, July   p. 204
25, 1936.

$1.8 million . . . $614,000: M-G-M profit/loss ledger.   p. 204

$5,000 bonus: "In appreciation of the co-operation and   p. 204
excellent services rendered by you, we take great pleasure
in handing you herewith our check representing a bonus of
$5,000.00 . . ." (Letter from Metro-Goldwyn-Mayer to Jean
Harlow, July 11, 1936.)

"She was never supposed to": Virginia Conway to DS.   p. 204

"in agony": Barbara Brown to DS.   p. 204

Dr. Sidney Burnap: Naneen Burnap (daughter) to DS;   p. 204

"Beach Again Costly to Jean Harlow," Los Angeles *Examiner*, August 15, 1936.

"I've got pneumonia": *Elza Schallert Reviews*, August 28, 1936.   p. 204

"there were rumors": Carl Roup to DS.   p. 205

"one of the dearest moments": Vincent Canby, "How a 1936 Screwball Comedy Illuminates Movie History," New York *Times*, February 1, 1981.   p. 205

"We are pathetically grateful": New York *Times*, October 31, 1936.   p. 205

"Few actresses": *Variety*, October 5, 1936.   p. 205

$2.7 million: M-G-M profit/loss ledger.   p. 205

"I'm here to chaperone": "Harlow Gets New Role," San Francisco *Chronicle*, September 23, 1936.   p. 205

"Well, of course, it was hysterical": Kotsilibas-Davis and Loy, *Myrna Loy*.   p. 206

"The first time I went up": Jeanne Pope to DS.   p. 206

"tired easily": Kotsilibas-Davis and Loy, *Myrna Loy*.   p. 207

Pope's husband: Dr. Saxton Pope practiced psychiatry. Had she been willing, he would have sent Harlow to an internist.   p. 207

"Take a good look": Kotsilitas-Davis and Loy, *Myrna Loy*.   p. 207

"She used to take a glass": Jeanne Pope to DS.   p. 207

"She was pale": Ted Allan to DS.   p. 207

"It was big": John Gershgorn to DS.   p. 207

"really was *too* big": Kotsilitas-Davis and Loy, *Myrna Loy*.   p. 208

"proudly displayed": Ibid.   p. 208

"It is as far as I'm concerned!": Charles Francisco, *Gentleman: The William Powell Story*, St. Martin's, 1985.   p. 208

"I knew": Jeanne Pope to DS; Lillian Burns Sidney to DS.   p. 208

"It was almost like he was *trying*": Dorothy Manners to DS.   p. 208

"I liked Bill, but he put her down": Jeanne Pope to DS.   p. 208

"incredible glamour . . . reduced his ego": Anita Loos, *Kiss Hollywood Good-by*.   p. 208

"I learned my lesson": Elaine St. Johns to DS.   p. 208

"Lombard was an entirely different type": Harold Rosson Oral History, AFI.   p. 208

"Carole Lombard seems like a real movie star": Louella O. Parsons, Los Angeles *Examiner*, June 9, 1937.   p. 209

"Harlow wasn't Lombard": Lillian Burn Sidney to DS.   p. 209

"inside": Darcy O'Brien (son of George O'Brien) to DS.   p. 209

"she didn't stand a chance": Ibid.   p. 209

Harlow attended: Washington *Post*, January 30–31, 1937.   p. 209

J. Edgar Hoover: FBI records; *Time*, February 22, 1937.   p. 209

"We went up to his office": Marsha Hunt to DS.   p. 210

"seriously ill": "Jean Harlow Ill with Flu," Los Angeles *Examiner*, February 3, 1937.   p. 210

retakes of *Personal Property*: "M-G-M 'Property' Adds," *Hollywood Reporter*, March 3, 1937.   p. 210

"I could tell she wasn't well": George Hurrell to DS.   p. 210

The World's Our Oyster: *Hollywood Reporter*, March 4, 1937.   p. 210

"it was at a dead end": Dorothy Manners to DS.   p. 210

"She was a sad girl": Rosalind Russell and Chris Chase, *Life Is a Banquet*.   p. 211

"I never saw her get angry": Barbara Brown to DS.   p. 211

"The more she drank": Blanche Williams to Herb Read.   p. 211

"When she sobered up": Ibid.   p. 212

"when she thought I had been rude": Elaine St. Johns to DS.   p. 212

"were extremely frightening": Blanche Williams to Herb Read.   p. 212

"the Baby wasn't supposed to drink": Sybil Brand to DS.   p. 212

Pops darling: Letter from Jean Bello to Arthur Landau, [c. 1935].   pp. 212–13

"He was a good Mormon": Barbara Brown to DS.   p. 213

"She needed her wisdom teeth": Dr. Leroy Buckmiller to DS.   p. 213

March 23: Good Samaritan Hospital records.   p. 213

began what . . . routine surgery: Drs. Tholen, Dow, and Dunlop only treated Harlow on this occasion.   p. 214

"After three teeth": Dr. Leroy Buckmiller to DS.   p. 214

"It was very serious": Barbara Brown to DS.   p. 214

"Those four wisdom teeth": New York *American*, March 31, 1937.   p. 214

a last-minute substitution: Harlow was not set for *Saratoga* until March 24, the same day as her dental surgery. Afterward production was postponed until April 22. (M-G-M script files; " 'Saratoga' Ready," *Hollywood Reporter*, April 21, 1937.)   p. 214

April 10: Good Samaritan Hospital records.   p. 214

"After this experience": Letter from Jean Bello (as/for Jean Harlow) to Arthur Landau, April 13, 1937. p. 214

Dr. Harold Barnard: The Barnards lived at 610 North Palm Drive. p. 215

"she did it just to get away": Dr. Harold Barnard statement, AMPAS. p. 215

Chapter Eighteen

colorful past: Donald Friede, *The Mechanical Angel*. p. 216

hawking *Today Is Tonight*: New York *American*, May 1, 1937. Also, Harrison Carroll [newspaper unknown], May 8, 1937. p. 217

"He was in love with her": M. F. K. Fisher to DS. For the rest of his life, Friede cherished a card from Harlow on May 12, 1937, his thirty-sixth birthday. Her inscription: "love and no kidding." Her signature: "me." (Eleanor Friede Collection.) p. 217

"They planned to marry": Ibid. p. 217

"In the face of Hollywood's mounting suspicions": Harrison Carroll, May 8, 1937. p. 217

"we all knew": Phyllis Cerf to DS. p. 217

"coming and going": Ibid. p. 217

"I was in awe": Anne Shirley to DS. p. 217

"I've been worn out since that trip": Louella O. Parsons, "Jean Harlow's Life Story" (memorial magazine), 1937. p. 217

"her body looked bloated": Lillian Burns Sidney to DS. p. 218

Life magazine: Its photograph of Harlow was by Martin Munkacsi. p. 218

"Baby, you must take care": Dorothy Manners to DS.   p. 218

"Baby, why don't you tell us": Louella O. Parsons, Los   p. 218
Angeles *Examiner*, June 9, 1937.

"You're lucky I'm here": Ibid.   p. 218

DEAREST HEART: Telegram from Jean Bello to Jean   p. 218
Harlow, May 9, 1937.

"To my three-year-old": Louella O. Parsons, "Jean   pp. 218–19
Harlow's Life Story."

"I'm constantly trying": Louella O. Parsons, Los Angeles   p. 219
Examiner, June 9, 1937.

"escape . . .": Friede, *The Mechanical Angel*.   p. 219

"Do you mind": Barbara Brown to DS.   p. 219

"Toothache": George Sidney to DS.   p. 219

"shrugged apathetically": Ibid.   p. 219

"I've never seen her so beautiful": Clarence Sinclair Bull,   p. 219
The Faces of Hollywood.

"She looked pale and fragile": Maureen O'Sullivan to DS.   p. 220

"wasn't feeling well": Ibid.   p. 220

menstrual cramps: John Lee Mahin to Barry Norman.   p. 220

"shocked": Elois Andre (widow of Tom Andre) to DS.   p. 220

"We were in a tiny portable": Ted Tetrick to DS.   p. 220

"Please ask Walter": Carl Roup to DS.   p. 220

"Just before lunch": Lyn Tornabene, *Long Live the King*.   p. 220

she was on Catalina Island: Barbara Brown to DS; Blanche   p. 220
Williams to Kay Mulvey, October 16, 1964; Sheilah Graham,

"The Jean Harlow Story: Fact or Fiction?" New York *Journal-American*, January 11, 1965.

"He was sitting in a chair": Richard Thorpe to DS.   pp. 220–21

"He didn't seem particularly worried": Virgil Apger to DS.   p. 221

Part Six: "She Never Will"

Chapter Nineteen

Powell's mansion: Blanche Williams to Kay Mulvey,   p. 225
October 16, 1964.

Powell called Mother Jean: Sheilah Graham, "The Jean   p. 225
Harlow Story: Fact or Fiction?" New York *Journal-
American*, January 11, 1965.

"He waited": Ibid.   p. 225

Dr. Ernest Fishbaugh: Ernestine Fishbaugh (daughter) to   p. 225
DS: Richard Chapman to DS.

Ella Harlow: Good Samaritan Hospital records. Stricken   p. 225
with bronchopneumonia, she had been hospitalized from
April 18 to May 15.

"severe cold": "Beautiful Jean Harlow Dies," New York   p. 225
Daily News, June 8, 1937.

"stomach ailment": Ibid.   p. 225

Catherine Lemond: *Estate of Jean Harlow*, September 4,   p. 226
1937.

Grace Temple: Grace Temple to DS; *Estate of Jean   p. 226
Harlow*, April 26, 1938.

"Jack, I'm so sick": Virginia Conway to DS.   p. 226

in exchange for Tyrone Power: "Power for Harlow,"   p. 226
Hollywood Reporter, June 1, 1937; New York *Times*, June
2, 1937.

"box-office poison": The 1937 Brand Index, published by   p. 226
Harry Brand, president of the Independent Theater Owners
of America (and husband of Sybil Brand).

The Best Dressed Woman in Paris: "M-G-M Schedules 44   p. 226
New Pictures," New York *Times*, May 5, 1937.

The Shopworn Angel: *Hollywood Reporter*, June 22, 1937.   p. 226

Spring Tide: New York *Times*, May 5, 1937.   p. 226

Tell It to the Marines: *Hollywood Reporter*, May 15, 1937. p. 226

The World's Our Oyster: *Hollywood Reporter*, June 9, 1937. p. 226

"We knew she was sick": J. J. Cohn to DS.   p. 226

"delirious": "Jean Harlow Is Past Illness Crisis," Los   p. 227
Angeles *Herald*, June 3, 1937.

"too weak to be moved": Ibid.   p. 227

"special medical equipment": Ibid.   p. 227

"virtually a hospital": Ibid.   p. 227

Adah Wilson: Wilson Tait (son) to DS.   p. 227

cholecystitis: Louella O. Parsons, "Cinema Star Stricken   p. 227
on Studio Set," Los Angeles *Examiner*, June 3, 1937.

"critical condition": Ibid.   p. 227

"Miss Harlow": "Jean Harlow Improves as Crisis Passes,"   p. 227
Hollywood *Citizen News*, June 3, 1937.

JEAN HARLOW SERIOUSLY ILL: Los Angeles *Times*, June 3,   p. 227
1937.

CINEMA STAR STRICKEN: Los Angeles *Examiner*, June 3,   p. 227
1937.

"gallant fight against . . . cholecystitis": Ibid.   p. 227

HARLOW PAST ILLNESS CRISIS: Los Angeles *Herald*, June 3,   p. 227
1937.

"This baby of mine": Los Angeles *Examiner*, June 4, 1937.   p. 227

"bolster her strength": Ibid.   p. 228

dextrose injection: *Estate of Jean Harlow*, September 1,   p. 228
1937. Harlow received six such injections in the last days of
her life.

"expressed deep concern": "Jean Harlow Gains Slowly,"   p. 228
New York *Herald Tribune*, June 5, 1937.

"virtually recovered": "Jean Harlow Conquers Flu," Los   p. 228
Angeles *Times*, June 4, 1937.

"executives at Metro-Goldwyn-Mayer": Ibid.   p. 228

"I didn't presume": Barbara Brown to DS.   p. 228

"deeply hurt": Hortense Williams to DS.   p. 228

"bitterly angry": M. F. K. Fisher to DS.   p. 228

"She insisted": Patsy Ruth Miller to DS. At the time,   p. 228
Miller was married to John Lee Mahin.

"Mrs. Bello": Virginia Conway to DS.   p. 228

"We are Christian Scientists": Ibid.   p. 228

Here began the Hollywood myth: Because so many sources   p. 228
blame Harlow's death on her mother, there are too many to
mention here, and all are erroneous anyway.

blood and urine tests, etc.: Jean Harlow death certificate,   pp. 228–29
June 7, 1937.

Barbara Brown assumes: Barbara Brown to DS.   p. 229

"Probably drunk again": Anita Loos, *Kiss Hollywood*   p. 229
Good-by.

"a pretty stupid joke": Ibid.   p. 229

"shocking": John Lee Mahin to Barry Norman.   p. 229

"It was like kissing a dead person": Ibid.   p. 230

"The Baby is suffering": Louella O. Parsons, "Star's Brief   p. 230
Life an Unhappy One," Los Angeles *Examiner*, June 8,
1937.

"didn't want to have anything": Alfred Pagano to DS.   p. 230

"Mr. Mayer was furious": Gladys Searles to DS.   p. 230

"insanely jealous": Richard Chapman to DS.   p. 230

"You've got to help the Baby": Ibid.   p. 230

"Doctor, I hope I'm not overstepping": Ibid.; Wilson Tait   p. 231
to DS.

"It was too late": Richard Chapman to DS.   p. 231

acute nephritis: Good Samaritan Hospital records; Harlow   p. 231
death certificate.

"Fishbaugh had misdiagnosed": Richard Chapman to DS.   p. 231

"Fishbaugh was a good doctor": Ibid. Despite this   p. 231
statement, actress Fay Wray disagrees: two years before Dr.
Fishbaugh misdiagnosed Harlow's nephritis, Wray (who
was referred by fellow film star Dolores Del Rio, whom Dr.
Fishbaugh had hospitalized for "a kidney problem")
watched him inject her alcoholic husband, screenwriter
John Monk Saunders, with an unknown substance.
"Beyond the syringe," recalled Wray later, "the only
suggestion Dr. Fishbaugh had to make was that we should
go on a vacation together." Saunders committed suicide in
1940. (Fay Wray, *On the Other Hand: A Life Story*, St.
Martin's Press, 1989.)

misdiagnosis: Unaware of Dr. Fishbaugh's error, the press assumed Harlow's cholecystitis caused her nephritis. There is no truth to this. — p. 231

Harlow was back at M-G-M: *Variety*, June 9, 1937; *Film Daily*, June 8, 1937; New York *Herald Tribune*, June 8, 1937. — p. 231

uremia: Good Samaritan Hospital records; Harlow death certificate. — p. 231

"in intense, horrible pain": Barbara Brown to DS. — p. 231

"There wasn't anything I could do": Richard Chapman to DS. — p. 232

"She didn't *want* to be saved": Ibid. — p. 232

"Poor little soul": Grace Temple to DS. — p. 232

"polio as a child": Sybil Brand to DS. — p. 232

"a very faithful": Los Angeles *Examiner*, June 4, 1937. — p. 233

Bernadine Hayes: Madrine Molen (daughter) to DS. The morning of Harlow's death, Louella Parsons linked Powell and Hayes in her column. A day later she ran an uncharacteristic retraction: "[Powell] did not go there [the Tropics restaurant] or anywhere else with Miss Hayes. He was constantly at Jean Harlow's bedside and had not been out with any other woman since he and Jean made up their quarrel a few weeks ago." (Louella O. Parsons, Los Angeles *Examiner*, June 7 and 8, 1937.) — p. 233

"I thought she looked wan": New York *Journal-American*, January 11, 1965. — p. 233

"You look fuzzy": Ibid. — p. 233

"Her kidneys were completely gone": Virginia Cox to DS. — p. 233

"before I get back": Blanche Williams to Kay Mulvey, October 16, 1964. — p. 233

SHE NEVER WILL: Ibid.; Wilson Tait to DS. — p. 233

"Miss Jean Harlow": Good Samaritan Hospital records.   p. 234

"very much a shock": Dr. Harold Barnard statement,   p. 234
AMPAS.

two blood transfusions: New York *Sun*, June 7, 1937.   p. 234

Mona Campbell: Creditor's Claim, *Estate of Jean Harlow*,   p. 234
October 13, 1937.

Miriam Godshall: Ibid., September 27, 1937.   p. 234

Nora Uren: Ibid., September 16, 1937.   p. 234

"cerebral edema": "Star Will Not Lie in State," Los   p. 234
Angeles *Times*, June 8, 1937.

JEAN HARLOW DYING: New York *Sun*, June 7, 1937.   p. 234

"an old friend of the family": Los Angeles *Times*, June 8,   p. 234
1937.

"When Bill came out": Virginia Conway to DS.   p. 234

"You'd better come now": Ibid.   p. 234

"I wouldn't have been allowed": Letter from Jetty Chadsey   p. 235
to Joe Boylan, August 2, 1937. The conversation is
recorded here.

"inhalator squad": see Prologue.   p. 235

"shaking her lightly": "Battle for Life Told by Fireman,"   p. 235
Los Angeles *Examiner*, June 8, 1937.

"I talked to her for two hours": "Is Jean Harlow Dead? Her   p. 235
Mother Says No!" *Modern Romances*, March and April
1938.

11:38 that morning: Harlow death certificate.   p. 235

Chapter Twenty

"the Valhalla of the cinema business": *Time*, June 21, 1937.   p. 236

the tightest security: "Absolutely no one to see Miss Harlow." (Pierce Brothers Mortuary records, June 8, 1937.)   p. 236

"It was the first big Hollywood funeral": J. J. Cohn to DS.   p. 236

"my gang": Barbara Brown, Blanche Williams, Violet Denoyer, and Edith Hubner. Peggy McDonald assisted Hubner on *Saratoga*.   p. 236

Pierce Brothers morticians: Pierce Brothers Mortuary records, June 8, 1937.   p. 237

"She looked beautiful": Barbara Brown to DS.   p. 237

"hysterical": Hollywood *Citizen News*, June 9, 1937.   p. 237

"He was crying and shaking": Teet Carle to DS.   p. 237

"The day the Baby died": Gregory Mank, "Jean Harlow," *Films in Review*, December 1978.   p. 237

"The whole studio": Mickey Rooney in *M-G-M: When the Lion Roars* (Turner Entertainment).   p. 237

roses . . . larkspur . . . bouquets: "Film Favorites Crowd Harlow Funeral Rites," Los Angeles *Evening News*, June 9, 1937.   p. 237

"Her outstanding attributes": "Jean Harlow Laid to Rest," New York *Sun*, June 10, 1937.   p. 237

"I've been to every big Hollywood funeral": Virginia Conway to DS.   p. 238

"seeped into her brain": Maureen Donaldson and William Royce, *An Affair to Remember: My Life With Cary Grant*, G. P. Putnam's Sons, 1989.   p. 238

"I hold that woman responsible": James Kotsilibas-Davis and Myrna Loy, *Myrna Loy: Being and Becoming*.   p. 238

"She killed the one": Marcella Rabwin to DS.   p. 238

"I believe it is only fair": Kansas City *Times*, June 12, 1937;   p. 238

"Bill Powell Buys Crypt for Harlow," San Francisco
Chronicle, June 12, 1937.

$30,000: Richard Chapman to DS. p. 239

"dumbstruck": Ibid. p. 239

"The poor slob," etc.: Ibid. p. 239

$1 million: Los Angeles *Examiner*, June 8, 1937. p. 239

records reveal otherwise: *Estate of Jean Harlow*. p. 239

retirement annuities . . . $105,000: "On or subsequent to p. 239
September 30, 1935," Harlow purchased twenty-five
policies from the Mutual Life Insurance Company of New
York (see Chapter Fifteen). (Report of Inheritance Tax
Appraiser, *Estate of Jean Harlow*, January 7, 1939.)

"reader," "talent scout": Metro-Goldwyn-Mayer and Jean p. 239
Bello agreement, December 8, 1937.

GREAT DEMAND FOR HARLOW FILMS: *Hollywood Reporter*, p. 239
June 9, 1937.

"Exhibitors are anxious": Ibid. p. 240

$1.8 million . . . $299,000: M-G-M profit/loss ledger. p. 240

Hell's Angels . . . The Iron Man . . . Platinum Blonde: p. 240
Hollywood Reporter, June 9, 1937.

The Public Enemy: see Chapter Fifteen. p. 240

"In accordance with our policy": "Death of Jean Harlow p. 240
Scraps Many Pic Plans," *Hollywood Reporter*, June 8,
1937.

Carole Lombard: Larry Swindell, *Screwball: The Life of* p. 240
Carole Lombard, William Morrow, 1975.

Jean Arthur, Virginia Bruce: "Arthur, Bruce Eyed for p. 240
Harlow Spot in 'Saratoga,' " *Hollywood Reporter*, June 9,
1937.

Gladys George: Louella O. Parsons, Los Angeles   p. 240
Examiner, June 15, 1937.

"The public went wild": Virginia Conway to DS.   p. 240

"the gruesome task": George Sidney to DS.   p. 240

Virginia Grey: Lillian Burns Sidney to DS.   p. 240

Rita Johnson: *Time*, June 21, 1937.   p. 240

Peggy McDonald: Michael Desosa (son) to DS; Bill Tuttle   p. 240
to DS.

Jean Phillips: Layne Britton to DS.   p. 240

"It was awful": Bill Edmondson to DS.   p. 240

"a grim thrill": "Alabama Girl Has Perfect Accent," New   p. 241
York *Daily Mirror*, November 23, 1937.

she refuses to discuss *Saratoga*: Mary Dees to Scott   p. 241
Eyman.

"You saw her": Paula Winslowe to DS.   p. 241

"laughably obvious": David Shipman, *The Great Movie*   p. 241
Stars: The Golden Years, Hill and Wang, 1979.

"It wasn't hard to edit": Margaret Booth to DS.   p. 241

"peculiarly delicate problem": *Variety*, July 14, 1937.   p. 241

"was patently not her tempestuous self": New York   pp. 241–42
Times, July 23, 1937.

"looking ill much of the time": New York *Herald Tribune*,   p. 242
July 23, 1937.

"tough and conscienceless": *Night and Day*, August 26,   p. 242
1937.

"all-time house records": *Variety*, July 28, 1937.   p. 242

$3.3 million: M-G-M profit/loss ledger.   p. 242

"He was so devastated": Virgil Apger to DS.   p. 242

"poor Powell": Ted Allan to DS.   p. 242

"I hardly recognized his voice": George Hurrell, *50 Years of* p. 242
Photographing Hollywood.

"sobbing his heart out": Hortense Williams to DS.   p. 242

contemplated suicide: Kotsilibas-Davis and Loy, *Myrna*   p. 242
Loy.

"She was a sad little girl": Mank, *Films in Review.*   p. 242

"He blamed himself": Kotsilibas-Davis and Loy, *Myrna Loy.*   p. 242

"adhesions" . . . rectal cancer: Charles Francisco, *Gentleman:* p. 242
The William Powell Story, St. Martin's, 1985.

"He was a different man": Virginia Conway to DS.   p. 243

"Her nickname was 'Mousie' ": Elaine St. Johns to DS.   p. 243

"Bill never discussed her": Diana Lewis Powell to DS.   p. 243

"Poor soul, I pity her": Letter from Jetty Chadsey to Joe   p. 243
Boylan, [July] 7, [1937].

"There were photographs all over": Sheilah Graham, "The   p. 243
Jean Harlow Story: Fact or Fiction?" New York *Journal-*
American, January 11, 1965.

"went away": "Is Jean Harlow Dead? Her Mother Says No!"   p. 243
Modern Romances, March and April 1938.

consulted psychics: Elaine St. Johns to DS.   p. 243

Mother Jean married: H. Vincent Brand and Jean Poe   p. 243
Harlow marriage certificate, March 16, 1944.

Divorced two years later: *Jean Bello Brand v. H. Vincent*   p. 243
Brand, Los Angeles County Superior Court, August 16,
1946; "H. V. Brand to Ask for Annulment," Los Angeles

Times, August 23, 1946. Mother Jean did not keep Brand's name.

the same street: 2257½ South Beverly Glen Boulevard. Her   p. 243
former mansion was at 214 South Beverly Glen Boulevard.

Aunt Jetty . . . Ella Harlow . . . Skip Harlow: Jetta B. Chadsey   p. 243
death certificate, June 2, 1941; Ella Harlow death certificate,
September 17, 1942; Skip D. Harlow death certificate,
February 22, 1947.

"She wouldn't go out": Herb Read to DS.   p. 243

"Dad never charged her": Richard Chapman to DS.   p. 244

"If there isn't a dress": Handwritten will by Jean Harlow   p. 244
Bello, June 4, 1958; *Estate of Jean Harlow Bello*, Los Angeles
County Superior Court, February 3, 1959.

she died: Jean Harlow Bello death certificate, June 11, 1958.   p. 244

"To the world we were two": "Is Jean Harlow Dead? . . ."   p. 244

"I get a cold chill": Maurice Zolotow, *Marilyn Monroe*,   p. 244
Harcourt Brace, 1960.

"I used to look": Sandra Shevey, *The Marilyn Scandal*,   p. 244
Sidgwick & Jackson, 1987.

Pearl Porterfield: Harold Porterfield to DS: Dorothy Hesketh   p. 245
to DS.

"She and Marilyn were quite different": George Cukor   p. 245
statement, AMPAS.

"Monroe was smart": Joseph Newman to DS.   p. 245

"in the old days of Jean Harlow": Fred Lawrence Guiles,   p. 245
Norma Jean: The Life of Marilyn Monroe, McGraw-Hill,
1969.

Monroe portray Harlow: "Fox to Make Harlow Story with   p. 245
Monroe," *Hollywood Reporter*, June 4, 1956.

"She should be done humanly": Earl Wilson (syndicated   p. 245
newspaper columnist), October 6, 1955.

Ben Hecht: *The Jean Harlow Story* treatment, August 24,   p. 245
1959.

Adela Rogers St. Johns: *The Jean Harlow Story* treatment,   p. 245
September 28, 1956.

Sidney Skolsky: *Platinum Blonde* treatment, October 27,   p. 245
1964.

Life: December 22, 1958.   p. 245

"I hope they don't do that": Guiles, *Norma Jean.*   p. 245

agreed to see Skolsky: "On the Sunday they found Marilyn   p. 245
dead, I had an appointment with her for that afternoon at
four to work on *The Jean Harlow Story.*" (Randall Riese &
Neal Hitchens, *The Unabridged Marilyn*, Corgi Books, 1988.)

"Sonofabitching": Irving Shulman, *Harlow: An Intimate*   p. 246
Biography, Bernard Geis Associates, 1964.

"A standard by which to measure": *Newsweek*, June 22,   p. 246
1964.

"Sordidly vivisective": New York *Times*, May 15, 1965.   p. 246

"I've never read": Maureen O'Sullivan on *The Today Show*   p. 246
(NBC), June 30, 1964.

"a blatant lie": Richard Chapman to DS.   p. 246

"I meant to kill him": Elaine St. Johns to DS.   p. 246

"The line between biographical fiction": Irving Shulman on   p. 246
The Today Show (NBC), June 30, 1964.

presumed dead: While writing *Harlow*, Shulman asked about   p. 246
her father. "Dead," Landau assured him. (Arthur Landau
notes, AMPAS.)

Mont Carpenter sued: *Mont Clair Carpenter v. Random*   p. 246
House, Bernard Geis and Associates, Dell Publishing, Irving
Shulman, and Ward Parkway Book Shop, Jackson County

Circuit Court, November 20, 1964. In a separate libel lawsuit, Marino Bello's widow demanded $1 million. The Missouri Supreme Court dismissed her case. (*Violette H. Bello v. Random House, Bernard Geis, Dell Publishing,Irving Shulman, and Ward Parkway Book Shop*, Jackson County Circuit Court.)

"That book broke his heart": Herb Read to DS.   p. 246

"Electronovision": *Harlow* was photographed by multiple   p. 247
electronic cameras, then recorded onto 35mm film. Shot in
eight days, the result looked as low-budget as it sounds.

replacement for Judy Garland: *Variety*, March 23, 1965.   p. 247

Landau died: *Variety*, February 14, 1966.   p. 247

John Wayne's private collection: "Hughes' 'Hell's Angels'   p. 247
Color Restored by UCLA," *Variety*, January 20, 1989.

"Jean was a figment": Virginia Conway to DS.   p. 248

"I wasn't born an actress": "My Advice to Myself—Jean   p. 248
Harlow," *Motion Picture*, March 1937.

"I'm lucky, and I know it": New York *Times*, June 13, 1937.   p. 248

"she would be dumbfounded": Barbara Brown to DS.   p. 248

Postscript

David "Thor" Arnold: David Peter Arnold (son) to DS; David   p. 249
Thornton Arnold death certificate, December 4, 1984.

Marino Bello accompanied *Benjamin "Bugsy" Siegel*: FBI   p. 249
memorandum, October 31, 1938.

"Siegel let him bring his nurse": Richard Gully to DS.   p. 249

"married her": Their wedding took place at sea on   p. 249
September 23, 1938. (*Evelyn Bello v. Marino Bello*, Los
Angeles County Superior Court, August 15, 1941.)

Violette Hartman: Death certificate, November 21, 1982.   p. 249

"oil conversion prospects": Letter from Arthur Landau to   p. 249
Marino Bello, April 7, 1942. (Marvin Paige Collection.)

died: Marino Bello death certificate, August 15, 1953.   p. 249

Jay Sebring rented: "He was renting the house from me   p. 249
when he was murdered. I spoke to him the day before . . ."
(Milo Frank to DS.)

Henry Bern: Death certificate, December 5, 1971.   p. 249

Heinie Brand: Death certificate, May 25, 1971.   p. 249

Mont Carpenter: Death certificate, May 1, 1974.   p. 250

Maude Carpenter: Death certificate, June 17, 1985.   p. 250

Dr. Leland Chapman: Death certificate, July 12, 1977.   p. 250

Marcella Chapman: Death certificate, November 29, 1959;   p. 250
autopsy report, Los Angeles County Coroner, November 29,
1959.

Donald Friede: New York *Times*, May 31, 1965.   p. 250

Chuck McGrew: Death certificate, January 2, 1971.   p. 251

Lowell Mellett: Death certificate, April 6, 1960.   p. 251

Lincoln Quarberg: Death certificate, April 24, 1979.   p. 251

Don Roberson: Dianne Roberson (daughter) to DS; Donald   p. 251
Roberson death certificate, August 8, 1982.

Hal Rosson: Death certificate, September 6, 1988.   p. 251

Genevieve Smith: Death certificate, June 13, 1956.   p. 251

Blanche Williams: Death certificate, June 12, 1984.   p. 251

Rosalind Russell: Rosalind Russell statement, AMPAS.   p. 251

Hedy Lamarr: Hedy Lamarr to George Cowap.   p. 251

Zsa Zsa Gabor: Barbara Brown to DS.   p. 251

Longy Zwillman: FBI bulletin, February 26, 1959.   p. 252

Index

About the Author

DAVID STENN is a Yale graduate whose writer-producer credits for television include *Hill Street Blues, 21 Jump Street,* and *Beverly Hills, 90210. Film Comment* called his previous biography, *Clara Bow: Runnin' Wild,* "another worthy addition to the few brilliant reappraisals of Hollywood in its Golden Age." He lives in Los Angeles and New York.